Literature and the Relational Self

Literature and Psychoanalysis

General Editor: Jeffrey Berman

1. *The Beginning of Terror: A Psychological Study of Rainer Maria Rilke's Life and Work*
   by David Kleinbard

2. *Loathsome Jews and Engulfing Women: Metaphors of Projection in the Works of Wyndham Lewis, Charles Williams, and Graham Green*
   by Andrea Freud Loewenstein

3. *Literature and the Relational Self*
   by Barbara Ann Schapiro

Literature and the Relational Self

Barbara Ann Schapiro

New York University Press
New York and London

NEW YORK UNIVERSITY PRESS
New York and London

Library of Congress Cataloging-in-Publication Data
Schapiro, Barbara A.
Literature and the relational self / Barbara Ann Schapiro.
p.   cm. — (Literature and psychoanalysis ; 3)
Includes bibliographical references and index.
ISBN 0-8147-7969-7 (alk. paper)
1. Psychoanalysis and literature.   2. Self in Literature.
3. Object relations (Psychoanalysis) in literature.
4. Interpersonal relations in literature.   I. Title.   II. Series.
PN56.P92S33   1993
809'.93353—dc20   93-12879
                                        CIP

New York University Press books are printed on acid-free paper,
and their binding materials are chosen for strength and durability.

Manufactured in the United States of America

10   9   8   7   6   5   4   3   2   1

To Ed, Nancy, Ellen, and Jane.
And to Scotty, Owen, and Mira.

Contents

Foreword by Jeffrey Berman   ix

Acknowledgments   xv

1. Introduction   1

    The Relational Paradigm   1
    Psychoanalytic Relational Concepts: An Overview   5
    The Relational Model and Feminist Theory   14
    Transitional Phenomena, Creativity, and Culture   20
    Applications to Literary Criticism   22

2. Wordsworth and the Relational Model of Mind   29

3. The Rebirth of Catherine Earnshaw: Splitting and
   Reintegration of Self in *Wuthering Heights*   46

4. Gender, Self, and the Relational Matrix: D. H. Lawrence
   and Virginia Woolf   62

5. Boundaries and Betrayal in Jean Rhys's *Wide Sargasso Sea*   84

6. Updike, God, and Women: The Drama of the Gifted Child   105

7. Internal World and the Social Environment: Toni Morrison's
   Beloved   127

8. Ann Beattie and the Culture of Narcissism   144

9. Desire and Uses of Illusion: Alice Hoffman's
    Seventh Heaven 160

10. Afterword 180

    Notes 183

    Works Cited 189

    Index 197

Foreword

As New York University Press inaugurates a new series of books on literature and psychoanalysis, it seems appropriate to pause and reflect briefly upon the history of psychoanalytic literary criticism. For a century now it has struggled to define its relationship to its two contentious progenitors and come of age. After glancing at its origins, we may be in a better position to speculate on its future.

Psychoanalytic literary criticism was conceived at the precise moment in which Freud, reflecting upon his self-analysis, made a connection to two plays and thus gave us a radically new approach to reading literature. Writing to his friend Wilhelm Fliess in 1897, Freud breathlessly advanced the idea that "love of the mother and jealousy of the father" are universal phenomena of early childhood (*Origins*, 223–24). He referred immediately to the gripping power of *Oedipus Rex* and *Hamlet* for confirmation of, and perhaps inspiration for, his compelling perception of family drama, naming his theory the "Oedipus complex" after Sophocles' legendary fictional hero.

Freud acknowledged repeatedly his indebtedness to literature, mythology, and philosophy. There is no doubt that he was a great humanist, steeped in world literature, able to read several languages and range across disciplinary boundaries. He regarded creative writers as allies, investigating the same psychic terrain and intuiting similar human truths. "[P]sycho-analytic observation must concede priority of imaginative writers," he declared in 1901 in *The Psychopathology of Everyday Life* (*SE* 6:213), a concession he was generally happy to make. The only exceptions were writers like Schopenhauer, Nietzsche, and Schnitzler, whom he avoided reading because of the anxiety of influence. He quoted effortlessly from Sophocles, Shakespeare, Goethe, and Dostoevsky, and was himself a master prose stylist, the recipient of the coveted Goethe Prize in 1930. When he was considered for the Nobel Prize, it was not for medicine but for literature. Upon being greeted as the discoverer of the unconscious, he disclaimed the title and instead paid generous tribute to the poets and philosophers who preceded him.

And yet Freud's forays into literary criticism have not been welcomed uniformly by creative writers, largely because of his allegiance to science rather than art. Despite his admiration for art, he viewed the artist as an introvert, not far removed from neurosis. The artist, he wrote in a well-known passage in the *Introductory Lectures on Psycho-Analysis* (1916–17), "is oppressed by excessively powerful instinctual needs. He desires to win honour, power, wealth, fame and the love of women; but he lacks the means for achieving these satisfactions" (*SE* 16:376). Consequently, Freud argued, artists retreat from reality into the world of fantasy, where they attempt to make their dreams come true. While conceding that true artists manage to shape their daydreams in such a way as to find a path back to reality, thus fulfilling their wishes, Freud nevertheless theorized art as a substitute gratification. Little wonder, then, that few artists have been pleased with Freud's pronouncements.

Nor have many artists been sympathetic to Freud's preoccupation with sexuality and aggression; his deterministic vision of human life; his combative, polemical temperament; his self-fulfilling belief that psychoanalysis brings out the worst in people; and his imperialistic claim that psychoanalysis, which he regarded as his personal creation, would explore and conquer vast new territories. He chose as the epigraph for *The Interpretation of Dreams* (1900) a quotation from *The Aeneid*: "Flectere si nequeo superos, Acheronta movebo" ("If I cannot bend the Higher Powers, I will move the Infernal Regions"). Although he denied that there was anything Promethean about his work, he regarded himself as one of the disturbers of the world's sleep. The man who asserted that "psychoanalysis is in a position to speak the decisive word in all questions that touch upon the imaginative life of man" (*SE* 19:208) could hardly expect to win many converts among creative writers, who were no less familiar with the imaginative life of humankind and who resented his intrusion into their domain.

Freud viewed psychoanalysts as scientists, committed to the reality principle and to heroic self-renunciation. He perceived artists, by contrast—and women—as neurotic and highly narcissistic, devoted to the pleasure principle, intuiting mysterious truths which they could not rationally understand. "Kindly nature has given the artist the ability to express his most secret mental impulses, which are hidden even from himself," he stated in *Leonardo da Vinci and a Memory of His Childhood* in 1910 (*SE* 11:107). The artist, in Freud's judgment, creates beauty, but the psychoanalyst analyzes its meaning and "penetrates" it, with all the phallic implications thereof. As much as he admired artists, Freud did not want to give them credit for knowing what they are doing. Moreover, although he always referred to artists as male, he assumed that art itself was essentially female; and he was drawn to the "seductive" nature of art even as he resisted its embrace, lest he lose his masculine analytical power. He wanted to be called a scientist, not an artist.

From the beginning of his career, then, the marriage Freud envisioned between the artist and the analyst was distinctly unequal and patriarchal. For their part, most creative writers have remained wary of psychoanalysis. Franz Kafka, James Joyce, and D. H. Lawrence were fascinated by psychoanalytic theory and appropriated it, in varying degrees, in their stories, but they all remained skeptical of Freud's therapeutic claims and declined to be analyzed.

Most artists do not want to be "cured," fearing that their creativity will be imperiled, and they certainly do not want psychoanalysts to probe their work; they agree with Wordsworth that to dissect is to murder. Vladimir Nabokov's sardonic reference to Freud as the "Viennese witch doctor" and his contemptuous dismissal of psychoanalysis as black magic are extreme examples of creative writers' mistrust of psychoanalytic interpretations of literature. "[A]ll my books should be stamped Freudians Keep Out," Nabokov writes in *Bend Sinister* (xii). Humbert Humbert speaks for his creator when he observes in *Lolita* that the difference between the rapist and therapist is but a matter of spacing (147).

Freud never lost faith that psychoanalysis could cast light upon a wide variety of academic subjects. In the short essay "On the Teaching of Psycho-Analysis in Universities" (1919), he maintained that his new science has a role not only in medical schools but also in the "solutions of problems" in art, philosophy, religion, literature, mythology, and history. "The fertilizing effects of psycho-analytic thought on these other disciplines," Freud wrote enthusiastically, "would certainly contribute greatly towards forging a closer link, in the sense of a *universitas literarum*, between medical science and the branches of learning which lie within the sphere of philosophy and the arts" (*SE* 17:173). Regrettably, he did not envision in the same essay a cross-fertilization, a desire, that is, for other disciplines to pollinate psychoanalysis.

Elsewhere, though, Freud was willing to acknowledge a more reciprocal relationship between the analyst and the creative writer. He opened his first published essay on literary criticism, "Delusions and Dreams in Jensen's *Gradiva*" (1907), with the egalitarian statement that "creative writers are valued allies and their evidence is to be highly prized, for they are apt to know a whole host of things between heaven and earth of which our philosophy has not yet let us dream" (*SE* 9:8), an allusion to his beloved Hamlet's affirmation of the mystery of all things. Conceding that literary artists have been, from time immemorial, precursors to scientists, Freud concluded that the "creative writer cannot evade the psychiatrist nor the psychiatrist the creative writer, and the poetic treatment of a psychiatric theme can turn out to be correct without any sacrifice of its beauty" (*SE* 9:44).

It is in the spirit of this equal partnership between literature and psychoanalysis that New York University Press launches the present series. We intend to publish books that are genuinely interdisciplinary, theoretically sophisticated, and clinically informed. The literary critic's insights into psychoanalysis are no less valuable than the psychoanalyst's insights into literature. Gone are the days when psychoanalytic critics assumed that Freud had a master key to unlock the secrets of literature. Instead of reading literature to confirm psychoanalytic theory, many critics are now reading Freud to discover how his understanding of literature shaped the evolution of his theory. In short, the master-slave relationship traditionally implicit in the marriage between the literary critic and the psychoanalyst has given way to a healthier dialogic relationship, in which each learns from and contributes to the other's discipline.

Indeed, the prevailing ideas of the late twentieth century are strikingly different from those of the late nineteenth century, when literature and psychoanalysis were first allied. In contrast to Freud, who assumed he was discovering absolute truth, we now believe that knowledge, particularly in the humanities and social sciences, is relative and dependent upon cultural contexts. Freud's classical drive theory, with its mechanistic implications of cathectic energy, has given way to newer relational models such as object relations, self psychology, and interpersonal psychoanalysis, affirming the importance of human interaction. Many early psychoanalytic ideas, such as the death instinct and the phylogenetic transmission of memories, have fallen by the wayside, and Freud's theorizing on female psychology has been recognized as a reflection of his cultural bias.

Significant developments have also taken place in psychoanalytic literary theory. An extraordinary variety and synthesis of competing approaches have emerged, including post-Freudian, Jungian, Lacanian, Horneyan, feminist, deconstructive, psycholinguistic, and reader response. Interest in psychoanalytic literary criticism is at an all-time high, not just in the handful of journals devoted to psychological criticism, but in dozens of mainstream journals that have traditionally avoided psychological approaches to literature. Scholars are working on identity theory, narcissism, gender theory, mourning and loss, and creativity. Additionally, they are investigating new areas, such as composition theory and pedagogy, and exploring the roles of resistance, transference, and countertransference in the classroom.

"In the end we depend / On the creatures we made," Freud observed at the close of his life (*Letters*, 425), quoting from Goethe's *Faust*; and in the end psychoanalytic literary criticism depends on the scholars who continue to shape it. All serious scholarship is an act of love and devotion, and for many of the authors in this series, including myself, psychoanalytic literary criticism has become a consuming passion, in some cases a lifelong one. Like other passions, there is an element of idealization here. For despite our criticisms of Freud, we stand in awe of his achievements; and even as we recognize the limitations of any single approach to literature, we find that psychoanalysis has profoundly illuminated the human condition and inspired countless artists. In the words of the fictional "Freud" in D. M. Thomas's extraordinary novel *The White Hotel*

(1981), "Long may poetry and psychoanalysis continue to highlight, from their different perspectives, the human face in all its nobility and sorrow" (143n.).

JEFFREY BERMAN
Professor of English
State University of New York at Albany

Works Cited

Freud, Sigmund. *The Letters of Sigmund Freud*. Ed. Ernst Freud. Trans. Tania and James Stern. New York: Basic Books, 1975.

———. *The Origins of Psychoanalysis*. Ed. Marie Bonaparte, Anna Freud, and Ernst Kris. Trans. Eric Mosbacher and James Strachey. New York: Basic Books, 1954; rpt. 1977.

———. *The Standard Edition of the Complete Psychological Works of Sigmund Freud*. Ed. James Strachey. 24 vols. London: Hogarth Press, 1953–74.

Nabokov, Vladimir. Introduction to *Bend Sinister*. New York: McGraw Hill, 1974.

———. *Lolita*. London: Weidenfeld and Nicolson, 1959.

Thomas, D. M. *The White Hotel*. New York: Viking, 1981.

Acknowledgments

Many relationships, both professional and personal, have facilitated my writing of this book. I would especially like to thank Lynne Layton, who read and offered many helpful comments on the introduction and on several of the essays. Her critical insights and her friendship have been invaluable to me. I would also like to thank my Rhode Island College colleague Maureen Reddy for her enthusiastic reading of the *Beloved* chapter, and Claudia Springer, another friend and colleague, for her unfailing support and advice. I am grateful as well to my chair, Joan Dagle, for giving me released time to work on this project, and to Jeffrey Berman for his encouragement and editorial suggestions. My thanks also to Evelyn Hinz, editor of *Mosaic*, for the particular care she took in editing the Wordsworth essay.

I would like to thank the following journals in which earlier versions of five of the essays originally appeared: *Contemporary Literature* published by the University of Wisconsin Press, *Mosaic, Nineteenth Century Studies, Soundings*, and *The Webster Review*.

Finally, I would like to thank the following for giving me permission to reprint from copyrighted material: Toni Morrison and Alfred A. Knopf, Inc., for permission to quote from *Beloved* by Toni Morrison. Copyright © 1987 by Toni Morrison; W. W. Norton & Co., Inc., and Andre Deutsch, Ltd., for permission to quote from *Wide Sargasso Sea* by Jean Rhys. Copyright © 1966 by Jean Rhys; Alice Hoffman, the Putnam Publishing Group, and the Elaine Markson Agency for permission to quote from *Seventh Heaven* by Alice Hoffman. Copyright © 1990 by Alice Hoffman.

Literature and the Relational Self

Chapter 1

Introduction

The Relational Paradigm

The scientific theories of any age, as Thomas Kuhn has argued, are dependent on the presuppositions, the underlying belief systems and models of reality that determine the experiments, the observations, and the consequent "facts" on which the theories are built. Freud's psychoanalytic model of the mind was highly determined by a Newtonian and Cartesian-based scientific paradigm. His concept of mind as a closed-energy, hydraulics-type system reflects the Newtonian mechanical model of nature; and the conflict and division he assumes between the subjective inner world and an objective external reality is premised on a Cartesian duality. Drive theory, as Stephen Mitchell argues, was not only "perfectly congruent with the philosophy of science of its day," but was also consistent "with what was known of brain physiology and neuroanatomy. This is no longer the case. The principles of tension reduction, the reflex arc model, the closed energy system—these have all been superseded in our understanding of how the brain operates. Consequently, even zealous defenders of the drive concept have struggled to update it," and Mitchell concludes that "for most contemporary theorists and clinicians, drive theory (at least as Freud conceived and developed it) is no longer by itself a serviceable metapsychological system" (*Relational Concepts in Psychoanalysis* 135; hereafter referred to as RCP).

Mitchell's thesis is that the drive model in psychoanalysis is currently being supplanted by what he calls "relational-model theories." The relational model encompasses a wide range of Anglo-American psychoanalytic theories that, while heterogeneous, nevertheless share a common view of the self

not as a conglomeration of physically based urges, but as being shaped by and inevitably embedded within a matrix of relationships with other people, struggling both to maintain our ties to others and to differentiate ourselves from them. In this vision the basic unit of study is not the individual as a separate entity whose desires clash with an external reality, but an interactional field within which the individual arises and struggles to make contact and to articulate himself. *Desire is experienced always in the context of relatedness*, and it is that context which defines its meaning. Mind is composed of relational configurations. (RCP 3)

According to this model, the psyche cannot be understood as a discrete, autonomous structure; in the analysis of psychic reality, nothing is more fundamental than relational patterns and interactions. This view gives us a holistic conception of self in which, as Mitchell states, "The person is comprehensible only within the tapestry of relationships, past and present. . . . the figure is always *in* the tapestry, and the threads of the tapestry (via identifications and introjections) are always in the figure" (RCP 3).

The psychoanalytic relational model corresponds with current models in the natural sciences, with quantum mechanics and systems and field theories. At the deepest, subatomic level of the physical universe, quantum theory tells us, identity is observer dependent; so too in the psychological universe, theorists are increasingly suggesting, identity at the core level of the self is other dependent, and inextricably bound up with human recognition. Like the relational model of the mind, quantum theory presents a model of reality in which nothing is more fundamental than dynamic, interactive patterns and relationships. According to physicist Henry Stapp, "an elementary particle is not an independently existing unanalyzable entity. It is, in essence, a set of relationships that reach outward to other things" (Zukov 71). Similarly, Werner Heisenberg describes the world from the perspective of contemporary theoretical physics as divided "not into different groups of objects but into different groups of connections. . . . What can be distinguished is the kind of connection which is primarily important in a certain phenomenon. . . . The world thus appears as a complicated tissue of events, in which connections of different kinds alternate or overlap or combine and thereby determine the texture of the whole" (107).

Chaos and systems theories also present nature as an intricate web or process structure in which complex, seemingly chaotic systems generate pattern and order in terms of the whole. The well-known Butterfly Effect in chaos theory, "the notion that a butterfly stirring the air today in Peking can transform storm systems next month in New York" (Gleick 8), captures the holistic, weblike nature of this perspective. Contemporary physics, wrote Alfred North Whitehead, "has swept away space and matter, and has substituted the study of internal relations within a complex state of activity" (15). The model of the universe is no longer one of separate working parts; the lens of the new sciences delineates a view of the universe as a dynamic patterning of interactions, connections, and interrelationships.

Mitchell's description of relational-model theories in psychoanalysis reveals the same underlying paradigm. The psyche too is now viewed essentially as a matter of relational patterns rather than of anatomy and inherent energy forces or drives. As Mitchell states, "Mind has been redefined from a set of predetermined structures emerging from inside an individual organism to transactional patterns and internal structures derived from an interactive, interpersonal field" (RCP 17). Psychological reality is thus both intrapsychic and interpersonal. According to Mitchell, the relational model does not negate the importance of conflict nor of bodily, sexual experience so fundamental to the classical model. Rather, it argues the significance of conflict and sexuality as both implicit in and shaped by the larger relational matrix.

Mitchell proposes a specific "relational-conflict model" in which "the antagonists in the central psychodynamic conflicts are relational configurations" (RCP 10). Conflict is always implied in relatedness. Ambivalence and conflictual passions revolving around issues of autonomy and dependence are inevitable in any single significant relationship; and conflict is equally unavoidable among the competing claims of different significant relationships in one's life. Sexuality is the "medium par excellence for the experience of self in interaction with others" (RCP 11). It provides the prime arena for the playing out of relational issues because, as Mitchell explains, bodily sensations and processes dominate the child's early experience, and "sexuality entails an interpenetration of bodies and needs" that makes "its endless variations ideally suited to represent longings, conflicts, and negotiations in the relations between self and others" (RCP 103). Oedipal wishes and oedipal guilt, too, may still be considered as universal, as Hans Loewald has argued, but not because they express or are derivative of inherent drives. Rather, they can be understood as out-growths of our earliest primary relationship in which we wish to remain tied to our source of origin but also fear engulfment. The incest taboo thus serves to protect against a regressive dedifferentiation. Oedipal con-flict, Mitchell believes, is part "of the unavoidably conflictual struggle for self-definition within a relational matrix" (RCP 87), and he concludes that "the problem of sexuality is located not in its a priori nature, but in an interactive relational field—the vicissitudes of object relations—from which it takes its meanings" (RCP 88).

Psychoanalytic relational-model theories also imply a breakdown of absolute norms or categories for evaluating health or pathology since, as Mitchell explains, "if each person is a specifically self-designed creation, styled to fit within a particular interpersonal context, there is no generic standard against which deviations can be measured" (RCP 277). Never-theless, evaluations can still be made in terms of the relative rigidity and constrictedness of one's relational patterns (particularly in regard to the earliest attachments), and the degree to which internalized conflictual patterns limit and restrict one's present experiences and relationships.

Despite the absence of universal absolutes, relational-model theories find meaning in the specific nature of the connections and in the patterning of the relationships that construct the individual and that the individual also constructs. The notion of a patterned, structured self, forged in the relational matrix, is still a fundamental assumption of relational-model psychoanalytic theories—the achievement of a cohesive self is indeed a goal of most psychoanalytic therapies. Unlike Lacanian and postmodern critical theories, psychoanalytic relational-model theories affirm the meaning of self as subject. As Mitchell makes clear, the self is both creation and creator, designer and design; the self both shapes and is shaped by the relational matrix.

In postmodern critical theory, the self is considered only as cultural construct, only as designed; that design, furthermore, can always be unraveled since it lacks even the potential for authentic coherence.[1] As such, poststructuralist theory collapses the boundaries between subject and context. Relational-model theories, on the other hand, maintain boundaries and a necessary tension between the self and the social surround, *while at the same time* stressing a dynamic flexibility and inter-penetration of the two: again, "the figure is always *in* the tapestry, and the threads of the tapestry are always in the figure." From Mitchell's view, too, psychoanalytic emphasis should be as much on the present as on the past; his relational-conflict model represents the self not merely as a passive victim of experience but as an active creator and perpetuator of conflictual relational patterns as well. The emphasis gives a less deterministic cast to the psychoanalytic view of the self, revitalizing existentialist notions of freedom and choice.

The relational model in the social and natural sciences has implications for the critical models and frameworks that we bring to the study of literature and the arts. With its focus on dynamic, interactive patterns and relationships, the relational paradigm can redirect our attention to the interconnections, and not just the disruptions, in our cultural and literary analyses. While dismissing essentialist structures and absolute categories or truths, the relational model nevertheless highlights significant orders of connection and relationship; it expands the possibilities for meaning in our understanding of human experience, and in the creative reconstruction of that experience in art and literature.

Psychoanalytic Relational Concepts: An Overview

In the language of psychoanalysis, the term "object" refers to something in the external environment—usually a person—significant to the subject's inner psychic life. While "objects" and the relationships with them are not primary determinants in Freud's dual-drive model of psychic development, the evolution of his theory does reflect their increasing importance. This is apparent in the move from his early topographic—unconscious-preconscious-conscious—model of the mind to his later structural model of id-ego-superego. The ego and superego are psychic structures defined by their functional relationship with the external environment; furthermore, they are deeply affected by a specific relational history and development—the Oedipus complex. As Greenberg and Mitchell explain, however, Freud downplays "interpersonal observations in favor of constitutional factors" (*Object Relations in Psychoanalytic Theory* 73; hereafter referred to as ORPT) in his theoretical exposition of the Oedipus complex, emphasizing heredity and preordained developmental phases in the oedipal drama's establishment and unfolding.

Freud makes his strongest statement on the importance of object relations to intrapsychic structure in his 1917 paper analyzing depression, "Mourning and Melancholia." In it, he postulates that the loss of an object in reality can be experienced as a loss in the ego: there is "an *identification* of the ego with the abandoned object. Thus the shadow of the object fell upon the ego. . . . In this way an object-loss was transformed into an ego-loss and the conflict between the ego and the loved person into a cleavage between the critical activity of the ego and the ego as altered by identification" (249). Conflict and ambivalence originally experienced in relation to the object are transformed into a cleavage within the ego itself; in intense love and suicide, Freud believed, the ego is overwhelmed by the internalized object. The concepts expressed here—particularly the process of identification and its structural effect on the ego—provide the groundwork for later object relations theories.

It is not surprising that several of the most influential object relational theorists—Melanie Klein, D. W. Winnicott, and Margaret Mahler, for instance—began by working with children. As Greenberg and Mitchell point out, with children, "instinctual aims are difficult to discern," but what is most conspicuous "is the child's vulnerability"—his or her need for security and other people. This forces attention on "the exquisite interaction between the child and his caretakers" (ORPT 74–75). Klein's work—generally considered the foundation of the British school of object-relations theory—grew out of her observations and interpretations of children's play. While she saw her theory as largely consistent with Freud's drive development model, her work nevertheless represents some significant revisions, particularly in its emphasis on an elaborate, preoedipal, unconscious fantasy life highly involved with the mother's body. Her theory also presents an important elaboration of Freud's concept of identification and the processes of internalization, splitting, and projection.[2]

Klein postulates two "positions" in the infant's developing relations, both internal and external, with the primary object. In the first six months of life, the "paranoid-schizoid position" dominates: the object is experienced as both "good" (a source of libidinal gratification) and "bad" (frustrating and withholding), and in an attempt to protect the good object and the self, the object is split—the good and bad are kept separate and isolated. In the "depressive position" of the latter half of the first year, the ego has developed enough to integrate the split and perceive the mother as a single whole, both good and bad. The key developmental task here is the toleration of ambivalence. The paranoid anxiety is that the self will be destroyed by the bad external object or world, while the more developed depressive anxiety concerns fear for the object due to one's own aggression and destructive fantasies. The depressive anxiety and accompanying guilt lead to the desire for "reparation"—an attempt to repair the damage and restore the mother (Klein and Riviere 65–69).

Klein extended the depressive position, as Greenberg and Mitchell explain, "to subsume the Oedipus complex itself, which is redefined and now portrayed largely as a vehicle for depressive anxiety and attempts at reparation" (ORPT 126). In summarizing Klein's contribution to the development of the psychoanalytic relational model, Greenberg and Mitchell stress her subtle but important reformulation of the Freudian concept of the drives. For Freud, drives are physical forces or bodily tensions that seek release and gratification, and the object "remains temporally secondary and always functionally subordinate to the aims of drive gratification" (ORPT 136). For Klein, on the other hand, drives "are not discrete quantities of energy arising from specific body tensions but passionate feelings of love and hate directed toward others and utilizing the body as a vehicle of expression. *Drives, for Klein, are relationships*" (ORPT 146; italics theirs).

Klein's work was transitional for later theorists in the British school, such as Harry Guntrip and W. R. D. Fairbairn, who abandoned the dual-instinct concept altogether. "Libidinal aims are of secondary importance in comparison with object-relations. . . . a relationship with an object and not the gratification of an impulse is the ultimate aim of libidinal striving," claims Fairbairn (50). Even the term "libidinal" can be misleading here, since Fairbairn did not conceive of libido in the Freudian sense of an entity or form of energy separate from the person. Furthermore, although aggression plays an important role in Fairbairn's theory, he did not see it as a primary drive, or even in Klein's sense, as a primary motivator. As Greenberg and Mitchell explain, "Fairbairn felt that aggression is not a primary *motivational* factor. Rather than arising spontaneously, it is a reaction to the frustration of the primary motivational aim—the striving for contact with objects" (ORPT 159). Fairbairn's theory concentrates on the internalization of frustrating, bad objects. Fairbairn saw internalization as a defense: internalizing objects is an attempt to control or master them. His work explores the consequences of these internalized and then repressed bad objects on the emotional life and intrapsychic structure of the individual's inner world. Psychopathology, he believed, resolves itself into "a study of the relationships of ego to its internalized objects" (Fairbairn 60).

As an analysand of Fairbairn, Guntrip devoted much of his work to elucidating and promoting Fairbairn's theory as an alternative to Freud's. The most lucid and synthetic writer of the British object relations theorists, Guntrip, as Greenberg and Mitchell note, often depicts psychodynamic issues within a specifically moral context. Guntrip objected to what he saw as the dangerously depersonalized, biologistic foundation of the Freudian model: "Science has to discover whether and how it can deal with the 'person,' the 'unique individual,' we will dare to say the 'spiritual self' with all the motives, values, hopes, fears and purposes that constitute the real life of man, and make a purely 'organic' approach to man inadequate" (*Personality Structure* 15). He argues, furthermore, that "love-object relationships . . . and the conflicts over them are an intense and devastating drama of need, fear, anger and hopelessness. To attempt to account for this by a hedonistic theory of motivation, namely that the person is seeking the satisfactions of oral, anal and genital pleasure, is so impersonal and inadequate that it takes on the aspect of being itself a product of schizoid thinking" (287).

Guntrip's work focuses on the schizoid personality, on the "regressed ego" that due to severe deprivation of a nurturing relationship has totally withdrawn from objects, both internal and external. The regressed ego seeks to return to the security of the womb, to a deathlike, objectless state free from the intense fear and rage that its conflictual object relations have produced. Whereas for Fairbairn, psychopathology arises out of sustained attachment to bad objects, for Guntrip, psychopathology is rooted in an abandonment of objects and a retreat from object relations altogether. Both theorists, however, see psychic life as originating in a state of infantile dependency that must be negotiated.[3] Winnicott's work probes even more specifically into the various needs of the infant in that earliest dependent state, and the maternal provisions necessary to its successful negotiation.

Winnicott introduces the concept of the "good-enough-mother," the mother who provides a "facilitating environment" for the infant's emerging self (*Maturational Processes*). The facilitating tasks include providing a "holding environment" for the infant—"an infant who has no one person to gather his bits together starts with a handicap in his own self-integrating task" (*Through Paediatrics* 150); empathically anticipating the baby's needs and participating in its "moment of illusion" or hallucinatory omnipotence (i.e., presenting the breast when the infant is excited and ready to "hallucinate" it); and functioning as a mirror so as to reflect the infant's own experience and being—"When I look I am seen, so I exist" (*Playing and Reality* 134). The mother's early, intense empathic participation in the infant's life, however, naturally and gradually diminishes, and as Greenberg and Mitchell summarize Winnicott's position, "The mother's 'graduated failure of adaptation' is essential to the development of separation, differentiation, and realization" (ORPT 194).

Excessive or prolonged impingement of the maternal environment can lead to an atrophy of the infant's own expression of spontaneous needs and responses—a loss of what Winnicott characterizes as the "true self"—and the cultivation of a compliant "false self," constructed out of the mother's expectations and serving "to hide the true Self" (*Maturational Processes* 147).[4] In Winnicott's later writings, he stresses the importance of the mother's increasing separateness and her capacity to sustain the child's "use" and even "destruction" of her in fantasy:

The subject says to the object: "I destroyed you," and the object is there to receive the communication. From now on the subject says: "Hullo object!" "I destroyed you." "I love you." "You have value for me because of your survival of my destruction of you." "While I am loving you I am all the time destroying you in (unconscious) *fantasy*." Here fantasy begins for the individual. The subject can now *use* the object that has survived. (*Playing and Reality* 90; hereafter referred to as PR)

Thus the child's "destruction" of the object paradoxically enhances its reality. As Greenberg and Mitchell explain, "The survival of the object is crucial. The mother's nonretaliatory durability allows the infant the experience of unconcerned 'usage,' which in turn aids him in establishing a belief in resilient others outside his omnipotent control" (ORPT 196).

For Winnicott, unlike Freud, the recognition of external reality is not only or even predominantly painful, but can indeed be a deeply joyful discovery. Infantile narcissism and the destructive fantasies bound up with the illusion of omnipotence can be terrifying, and thus the acknowledgment of limits and boundaries—of a real world outside the self—can be profoundly liberating. Finally, one other important phase in Winnicott's formulation of the infant's ongoing negotiations with mother and the external world involves the creation of "transitional objects," a concept that will be discussed more fully in a later section of this introduction.

In contrast to the British school, with its almost exclusive focus on the mother-child dyad, the development of relationally based psychoanalytic theories in America has involved a stronger emphasis on the social and cultural context. A movement known as interpersonal psychoanalysis emerged in the late 1930s with the work of Harry Stack Sullivan, and includes the work of such other prominent theorists as Erich Fromm and Karen Horney. Their theories stress the concrete circumstances and social reality of their patients' lives, and is informed by a characteristically American "pragmatic sensibility" (ORPT 82). In a clear break with Freud, Sullivan asserts, "The field of Psychiatry is the field of interpersonal relations—a personality can never be isolated from the complex of interpersonal relations in which the person lives and has his being" (10).

As Greenberg and Mitchell explain, Sullivan drew explicitly on modern physics, as well as the metaphysics of Whitehead, in his conceptualization of personality as "an interpersonal field" and not a concrete structure that can be known or measured in any objective sense. "For Sullivan, as for Whitehead, the mind is a temporal phenomenon, energy transforming itself through time. The only meaningful referent for the term 'structure' is a pattern of activity; the only meaningful referrent for the concept of a psychic 'energy' is the entire stuff of mental life, not separable quantities that propel mental life" (ORPT 91). Sullivan has been enormously influential on contemporary psychoanalytic thinking, but Greenberg and Mitchell argue that because he never formally systematized or unified his concepts, his writings are rarely studied in the original nor is he credited with having been the first to formulate so many current psychoanalytic ideas and approaches.

The other dominant strain in American psychoanalytic relational theories draws on the ego psychology of Heinz Hartmann, and includes the work of Edith Jacobson, Margaret Mahler, and Otto Kernberg. Greenberg and Mitchell classify their work as "theories of accommodation" because their relational concepts are elaborated within the classical drive model; unlike the work of Sullivan or the British school, their ideas do not significantly modify the drive concept or present an alternative to it. These theories nevertheless highlight relational issues by stressing the adaptive strategies of the ego in its developing relationship with the external environment, and unlike Freud, they assign a crucial role to the preoedipal infant-mother dyad. They focus on a process of increasing individuation and internal integration as the infant separates out from the original relational matrix. Mahler, Pine, and Bergman posit a continuum of "psychological birth" that begins with an undifferentiated autistic and symbiotic phase and gradually moves toward a fully differentiated and autonomously functioning ego. Erik Erikson's influential theory of personality development, though it works within a broader psychosocial framework than Mahler's, similarly focuses on a developmental continuum that stresses increasing separation-individuation. This emphasis has recently come under attack by some feminist psychoanalytic theorists who, as I will discuss more fully later, see this perspective as reflecting a particularly gendered, male concern that is especially inappropriate to female psychological development.

Another current approach to infant development that challenges Mahler's perspective is that of Daniel Stern. Basing his views on the most recent empirical findings in infant research, Stern maintains that the baby possesses a basic core sense of self from the beginning, and he rejects the developmental continuum that begins with symbiotic fusion and progresses to a state of separateness and autonomy. According to Stern, the infant is interpersonal from the start, capable of recognizing and responding to its caretakers and evoking responses from them. Rather than seeing the infant-mother dyad in terms of self and object, Stern stresses an "intersubjective relatedness" (*Interpersonal World of the Infant* 124–38; hereafter referred to as IWOI). The self develops by building on initial sets or units of interpersonal interaction, a development that does not involve separation or movement out of the relational matrix; human beings remain fundamentally interpersonal to the end.

Stern's perspective also places more emphasis on the "fit" between the particular infant and the particular mother or caretaker, viewing the interaction as a mutual engagement in which the baby brings his or her own constitutional and temperamental qualities to bear on the relationship. This view offers an important corrective to a tendency in object relations theory to see the baby only as a passive recipient of the mother's failures or successes at nurturance. The most important element of early interpersonal experience, according to Stern, is the sharing of affect, or "interaffectivity"—"interaffectivity may be the first, most pervasive, and most immediately important form of sharing subjective experiences" (IWOI 132). For Stern, the "affective attunement" between caretaker and child is the determining factor in the development of a strong sense of self.

Finally, Heinz Kohut's "self psychology" represents another significant model in American psychoanalytic theory that has relational aspects. A key feature of Kohut's theory is the concept of "selfobjects"—"objects . . . which are either used in the service of the self and of the maintenance of its instinctual investment, or objects which are themselves experienced as part of the self" (*Analysis of the Self* xiv; hereafter referred to as AOS). The emergence of a cohesive self depends on particular self-selfobject relations: the primary selfobjects must provide an empathic mirroring response to the self's early grandiosity and exhibitionism (a function Kohut generally associates with the mother), and they must sustain the self's idealized projections (a role the father usually assumes) as the self gives over its own previous sense of perfection and omnipotence. These two "bipolar" selfobject relationships are "transmuted" into "psychic structures" of the self (AOS 49). Kohut sees psychopathology as arising not out of conflict, as in the classical model, but out of deficient selfobject relations and a resultant "deficit" in self-structure. Kohut also divides libidinal energy into two realms—narcissistic libido and object libido—with each representing a separate, independent line of development. Narcissistic libido cathects selfobjects and leads to the development of self-esteem or healthy narcissism, while object libido cathects "true" objects (objects experienced as separate from the self) and leads to the development of object love.

Kohut's work shares with other relational-model theories an emphasis on mirroring and empathic resonance as crucial factors in healthy self-development. His theory is also founded on the conviction that the self is conceived out of its relationships with early objects (as well as the belief that the need for these relationships is never outgrown). Nevertheless, his dual lines of development suggest that his theory may not be as relational as it might appear. Lynne Layton indeed argues convincingly "that despite appearances, and to the detriment of the theory, Kohut's formulations ignore relationship" (420). Kohut's self may be born from relationship, but as Layton points out, "not from relationships with others experienced as separate and distinct centers of initiative. Rather, these relationships are with others experienced as coexistent with the subject and under the subject's control" (421). She argues, furthermore, that "it is absurd to assign empathy to a realm of selfobject relations that is sharply differentiated from the realm of object love. . . . relationships with others undoubtedly include both what Kohut describes as selfobject functions and what Freud describes as object functions, but the two mix in ways that make them inseparable," and I agree with her that "they are falsely and incompletely understood if looked at separately" (426).

One of the accusations sometimes leveled against object relations and relationally based theories is that they assume that conflict-free perfection—a state of complete happiness and integration—is possible if only parents respond appropriately and provide a properly relational, nurturing environment for their children. While the implications of some particular theories—Guntrip's, for instance, or Kohut's, as it ignores conflict—might make this a valid charge, it is not true of the relational view in general. Mitchell, in his synthetic "relational-conflict model," insists that conflict is always involved in relatedness: "In the relational-conflict model, the antagonists in the central psychodynamic conflicts are relational configurations; the inevitable conflictual passions within any single relationship, and the competing claims, necessarily incompatible, among different significant relationships and identifications" (RCP 10). From this perspective, the elimination of conflict would not even be a therapeutic goal; rather, as Marion Milner has suggested, the key to healthy living would be the ability to *tolerate* conflict—"the capacity to bear the tensions of doubt and of unsatisfied need and the willingness to hold judgment in suspense until finer and finer solutions can be discovered which integrate more and more the claims of both sides" (10).

Object relations theories are also commonly charged with devoting attention too exclusively to the infant-mother dyad and ignoring larger cultural and social influences. While, again, this may be a fair charge in some cases, it is not a weakness necessarily intrinsic to the relational-model perspective. While the focus may be interpersonal and intrapsychic, most relational-model theorists would not deny that interpersonal relationships and intrapsychic dynamics are deeply affected by historical and cultural circumstances. Object relations theorist Arnold Modell, for instance, argues that the current increase in narcissistic personality disorders reflects "the impact of historical processes upon the ego" and is "secondary to cultural change" (*Psychoanalysis* 267–68). He believes that culture influences development primarily in adolescence, when a "certain

selective reinforcing or reorganization of the personality" can occur:
"Our contemporary world confronts the adolescent with failures in the
protective environment analogous to those experienced earlier in relationship to the parental environment. This second disillusionment will
involve similar coping strategies" (270). Modell's view is much the same
as Christopher Lasch's in *The Culture of Narcissism*, where he argues
that the general "warlike conditions that pervade American society" (64)
foster narcissistic anxieties and encourage the sorts of defenses—such as
lack of emotional depth and commitment—characteristic of pathological
narcissism.

From a relational perspective, culture can also influence psychic development in an earlier phase as it is transmitted through the person of
the caretaker and affects his or her interactions with the child. As Jane
Flax explains, "The caretaker brings to the relationship a complex series
of experiences including not only personal history and feelings about
being a particular gender, but also the whole range of social experience—
work, friends, interaction with political and economic institutions, and
so on" (122). While I agree with Flax that more work needs to be done
in this area, the psychoanalytic relational model does not inherently exclude acknowledgment of cultural and historical forces in its conception
of self-formation and development.

The Relational Model and Feminist Theory

Because object relations theories have shifted the emphasis away from
the oedipal, father-based model to a preoedipal, mother-based view of
psychological development, they have been of particular interest to feminist theorists. Nancy Chodorow, in her influential book *The Reproduction of Mothering*, applies object relations theory to a study of the
social construction of gender in Western culture. If mothers so profoundly
affect emotional and psychic growth, what are the implications, Chodorow asks, of the fact that women, and not men, mother in our culture?
One consequence is that women are forever tied to the intense experience
of infantile dependency—to the frightening feelings of helplessness and
ambivalence in relation to the all-powerful mother. Children also "expect
and assume women's unique capacities for sacrifice, caring, and mothering," Chodorow explains, "and associate women with their own fears
of regression and powerlessness. They fantasize more about men, and

associate them with idealized virtues and growth" (83). Males and females, furthermore, "experience different interpersonal environments as they grow up" and thus "feminine and masculine personality will develop differently and be preoccupied with different issues. The structure of the family and family practices create certain differential relational needs and capacities in men and women that contribute to the reproduction of women as mothers" (51).

Chodorow argues that the mother's unconscious attitudes and relations with her children are deeply influenced by their gender: she will experience a girl as an extension of herself, often discouraging her from forming a separate identity, while she will experience the boy as "other," encouraging him to differentiate and move out into the external world. Girls, then, will develop less firm ego boundaries, and due to the prolonged preoedipal bond, will remain throughout their lives preoccupied with relational and affective issues. Boys, on the other hand, will be more occupied with issues of separation and differentiation—with establishing their masculine identity in opposition to the mother and her femininity. "Masculine personality, then, comes to be defined more in terms of denial of relation and connection (and denial of femininity), whereas feminine personality comes to include a fundamental definition of self in relationship" (169). Chodorow thus argues for a restructuring of the typical nuclear household so that men would participate equally with women in primary child care: "Children could be dependent from the outset on people of both genders and establish an individuated sense of self in relation to both. In this way, masculinity would not become tied to denial of dependence and devaluation of women" (218).

Chodorow's account is open to some questions and possible objections. Stephen Frosh, for instance, complains that the feminist object relations view "suffers from a subtle form of determinism, suggesting that the systematic similarities between women is due to the similarity in the *actual* behavior of all their mothers. Although such similarities exist, so too do substantial differences" (Frosh 184). Jane Flax makes a similar point, arguing that each woman brings her own particular social history— her class and race, for instance—to her mothering, and this is not adequately recognized in Chodorow's uniform depiction of the mother-child dyad (Flax 122–24). From Flax's view, Chodorow is universalizing a particular white, middle-class family and mothering dynamic. Madelon Sprengnether believes that the "essentialist bias" of object relations theory undermines Chodorow's argument for the cultural construction of gender and femininity: "The object relations concept of mother-infant fusion, by focusing on the physical as well as the emotional bond between mother and child, introduces an instability into Chodorow's argument for the predominance of social factors in the psychological construction of gender. The result is a drift towards essentialism, which threatens to reinscribe (albeit in a more positive way) the existing stereotypes of masculinity and femininity" (194).

One might also ask if the child's gender really determines the degree of separateness or connection in the mother-child relationship to the extent that Chodorow suggests, or if other specific aspects of the mother's relational history—her relationship with her parents, her husband, her community, for instance—might not be the more powerful factors in determining how the mother bonds and separates from her child, regardless of the child's sex. Chodorow's characterization of the mother-daughter connection, furthermore, is particularly questionable since at times it seems to normalize a pathological relationship in which the mother experiences her child *only* as a narcissistic extension or projection of herself. It is indeed possible for a mother to experience her female child as both same *and* separate from herself. There is a tendency among some feminist theorists to glorify the preoedipal mother-daughter relationship, but a prolonged, undifferentiated preoedipal bond, far from producing a healthy or flexible relational capacity in the daughter, would severely problematize boundary issues and relationships for her.

The work of Dorothy Dinnerstein and Carol Gilligan shares several of Chodorow's assumptions. In *The Mermaid and the Minotaur*, Dinnerstein argues that the sexual division of labor in child care has not only adversely affected the relations between men and women but also is responsible for our current ecological crisis and our general state of malaise. The need to master and dominate nature is an extension of the need to dominate women, the source of which, again, is that intensely ambivalent, infantile experience of the mother's early omnipotence. Dinnerstein sees the original division of labor as rooted in biology: because of pregnancy and lactation, women have been tied to the domestic realm while men have had a more "wide ranging mobility" (20) that privileges them in the "making" of history. Our masculine-determined history is thus characterized by a denial of the irrational, bodily, and relational realm—the realm of the threatening infantile experience of the mother.

While Dinnerstein's theory is illuminating and suggestive, in its broadly based depiction of a universal mother-child experience it presents a deterministic perspective that lacks historical specificity. As Flax comments, "Although we are all born helpless and dependent, grow up, and die, how we experience these processes is socially mediated," and she suggests that a general theory of mothering and social psychology needs to be more concretely grounded, placing "childbearing and rearing into a political, economic, and social context" (165).

Gilligan's work is less abstract and wide ranging than Dinnerstein's. Her 1982 study *In a Different Voice* draws explicitly on Chodorow's work and focuses on differing modes of thought in male and female moral development. Boys, she says, tend to abstract a moral problem from its interpersonal situation while girls will see it as inextricable from a complex network or "web" of relationships. Because of differing preoedipal relations, boys will conceive of self in relation to world in terms of separation, autonomy, and control, and will feel most threatened by intimacy; girls, on the other hand, will have a more seamless, interrelational view, and will feel more danger in situations of separation or isolation than closeness. Women's development, she concludes, "points towards a different history of human attachment, stressing continuity and change in configuration, rather than replacement and separation, elucidating a different response to loss, and changing the metaphor of growth" (48).

This is the same view held by the Stone Center theorists, whose writings are compiled in the recent volume *Women's Growth in Connection* (Jordan, et al.; hereafter referred to as WGC). Jean Baker Miller argues that the earliest internal representation of self is that of a " 'being-in-relationship' "—a sense of self "that reflects what is happening *between* people" (WGC 13). The core of the self, she explains, is emotional, and the earliest mental representation of that core self is one that

is attended to by the other(s) and in turn, begins to attend to the emotions of the other(s). Part of this internal image of oneself includes feeling the other's emotions and *acting on* them as they are in interplay with one's own emotions. This means that the beginnings of the concept of self are not those of a static and lone self being ministered to by another (incidentally, this construct has a strong male flavor), but rather of a self inseparable from dynamic interaction. And the central character of that interaction involves attending to each other's mental states and emotions. (WGC 14)

While this early "interacting sense of self" pertains to infants of both sexes, Miller argues that cultural attitudes toward such emotionally attuned interaction or "caretaking" affects the development of this basic sense of self differently in girls and boys. Girls are encouraged to cultivate their empathic and caretaking ability, while boys "are systematically diverted from it" (WGC 14). Thus a girl's self-esteem, unlike a boy's, is bound up with her sense of herself as in relationship and as "taking care" of relationships. As Miller argues in an earlier study, "women's sense of self becomes very much organized around being able to make and then to maintain affiliation and relationships" (*Towards a New Psychology of Women* 83). Girls are thus seeking a different *kind* of identity, she concludes, than that which has been defined and prescribed for boys.

The Stone Center theorists' expression "self-in-relation" implies, as Janet Surrey explains, "an evolutionary process of development through relationship. Such language is used to differentiate this notion from a static self construct and to describe an experiential process implying openness, flexibility, and change" (WGC 59). These theorists argue that relationship and connection are vitally important to psychic life throughout the life span, and they posit a model of "relationship-differentiation" as opposed to the Erikson and Mahler concept of "separation-individuation." This "new model emphasizes," Miller explains, "that the direction of growth is not toward greater degrees of autonomy or individuation and the breaking of early emotional ties, but toward a process of growth within relationship" (WGC 60). As with Chodorow's argument, some of the Stone Center's sweeping generalizations about differences in the mothering of boys and girls are highly questionable. Surrey's statement, for instance, that "the mother's easier emotional openness with the daughter than with the son, along with her sense of identification with this style of personal learning and exploration, probably leave the daughter feeling more emotionally connected, understood, and recognized" (WGC 56) is a dubious assertion indeed.

Nevertheless, the Stone Center theorists make some valuable arguments. They discuss empathy, for instance, as a significant, and particularly female, mode of relation that is distinctly different from merger, fusion, or symbiosis. Judith Jordan maintains that empathy involves, as Kohut has stated, " 'a recognition of the self in the other' " that implies a simultaneous connection and separateness. The "paradox of empathy," she says, is that "in the joining process one develops a more articulated and differentiated image of the other and hence responds in a more accurate and specific way, quite the opposite of what regressive merging would lead to" (WGC 73). Stone Center theorists also prefer Stern's notion of intersubjectivity, or what they term "subject relations theory," as opposed to an "object relations theory" where the object "may not be experienced fully as a subject with his or her own comprehensive personal construction of continuous reality" (WGC 61). The failure to conceive of the mother as a subject in her own right, with her own desires and bodily reality outside of the child's experience of her, is a problem, as Jane Flax has noted, that many feminist critics find with object relations theory. "Within object relations theory," Flax says, "the story of human development is told from the child's viewpoint. . . . Mother and child are presented as misleadingly isomorphic" (123).[5]

Finally, Jessica Benjamin has also addressed this issue, and her study *The Bonds of Love* presents an "intersubjective" view that argues that the child has a fundamental need to see the mother "as an independent subject, not simply as the 'external world' or an adjunct of [the baby's] ego" (23). It is precisely the failure of "mutual recognition" between infant and m/other as separate, independent subjects, Benjamin believes, that lies at the root of various forms of domination in our culture. Drawing on Stern's work, she argues that the central issue in psychological development is not "how we separate from oneness, but also how we connect to and recognize others; the issue is not how we become free of the other, but how we actively engage and make ourselves known in relationship to the other" (18). The essential interaction between self and other involves a combination of resonance and difference, and a delicate tension between self-assertion and mutual recognition "that allows self and other to meet as sovereign equals" (12). When that necessary tension breaks down, the dynamics of domination and submission result. The search for recognition can become a struggle for power, and assertion a form of aggressive control. If the need for attunement has not been satisfied, patterns of submission can result as the self seeks to remain attuned by surrendering completely to the other's power and will. Benjamin analyzes the manifestation of these dynamics both in sexual relations and in our contemporary social institutions. Her work demonstrates the usefulness of psychoanalytic intersubjective theory to feminist and cultural analyses.

Transitional Phenomena, Creativity, and Culture

Just as contemporary physics has broken down the strict Cartesian division between mind and matter, so relational-model theories in psychoanalysis have loosened rigid distinctions between the subjective internal world and the external object world. Psychological meaning, in fact, resides in the interactive space between the two. Winnicott's influential concepts of the "transitional object" and "potential space" highlight this intermediate, transactional realm. Transitional objects are those objects—such as teddy bears, dolls, or blankets—that infants use to master the anxiety of individuation and separation from the mother. These objects "are not part of the infant's body yet are not fully recognized as belonging to external reality"; they occupy a transitional realm between inside and outside, an "intermediate area of *experiencing* to which inner reality and external life both contribute. It is an area that is not challenged, because no claim is made on its behalf except that it shall exist as a resting-place for the individual engaged in the perpetual human task of keeping inner and outer reality separate yet interrelated" (PR 2).

Winnicott calls this area or transitional realm between baby and mother "potential space" because it occupies a dimension that is neither internal nor external. Potential space is the area of play, and it forms the ground for creativity, symbolization, and for culture as a whole. In his essay on "Playing," Winnicott repeatedly stresses its intermediary status:

This area of playing is not inner psychic reality. It is outside the individual, but it is not the external world. . . . Without hallucinating the child puts out a sample of dream potential and lives with this sample in a chosen setting of fragments from external reality. . . . In playing, the child manipulates external phenomena in the service of the dream and invests chosen external phenomena with dream meaning and feeling. (PR 51)

In this potential space where absolute categories are suspended, connection coexists with division. Susan Deri argues that transitional or potential space "is the space for creative symbol-formation, because it is the function of symbols to connect and unite opposites. This transitional space, a space for connectedness, accounts for an order in the world based on an *inner relatedness* instead of a Cartesian principle of dividedness. The processes taking place within this intermediate space eliminate the disruption of the life space between the person and his environment" (50). Winnicott's concept of potential space is also compatible with intersubjective theory, for even if one rejects an initial state of symbiosis that eventually gives way to autonomy and separation, the baby still needs to discover and negotiate boundaries. The Stone Center theorists, for instance, acknowledge the infant's process of increasing "differentiation" from the m/other that occurs within the larger context of ongoing connection and relationship.

Winnicott believes that transitional phenomena or play forms the foundation for the construction of all human meaning—for understanding the contours of one's own subjectivity and one's relationship with the external object world: "The transitional phenomena represent the early stages of the use of illusion, without which there is no meaning for the human being in the idea of a relationship with an object that is perceived by others as external to that being" (PR 11). The child's individual play, furthermore, leads to "shared playing, and from this to cultural experience" (PR 51). Thus the creation of "illusion" in Winnicott's sense—the investing of external reality with the meanings and fantasies of the internal world—is an essentially constructive phenomenon that is different from deception or delusion.[6]

This perspective on illusion allows us to regard the products of human culture—particularly art, literature, and religion—not merely as the products of instinctual sublimation and defense, as they are in the classical Freudian view, but as various forms, in Gilbert Rose's terms, of "reality construction." From this point of view, Rose argues, "the function of myth, religion, art, language, and science is not, for example, escape through wishful distortion of the world, but orientation to it—a system of ideas to envisage one's relationship to society, the world, life and death—all in the service of the reality principle" ("Creativity of Everyday Life" 349). The arts, and creative symbol-formation in general, exemplify the human construction of meaning that always occurs in that intermediary realm of internal and external, of subjective and objective. Winnicott's perspective on play and illusion supports Suzanne Langer's contention that symbolizing activity is the definitive human activity; only through the act of symbolizing do we give meaning to ourselves and our experience.[7]

Recent psychoanalytic theorists of religion (see, for instance, Ana-Maria Rizzuto, William Meissner, John McDargh, and James Jones) have found Winnicott's notions of illusion and transitional phenomena particularly valuable. Religion may indeed be an "illusion," but not, they believe, in the way Freud held it to be. William Meissner, for instance, argues that "in a healthy resolution to crises of development, there emerges a residual capacity for illusion that is among the most significant dimensions of man's existence. . . . Man cannot do without illusion, since it gives meaning and sustenance to his experience of himself" (16–17). From a relational-model view, in other words, religious faith can be seen as creative and adaptive. James Jones points out that faith is fundamentally "a *relationship* (with God, the sacred, the cosmos, or some reality beyond the phenomenal world of space and time)" (63). While it may have infantile and regressive features, such a relational experience can also reflect mature and integrated psychic growth. Meissner believes that we "can characterize levels of religious experience as reflecting various phases of development from very primitive infantile stages to the most mature, integrated, and adaptive levels of psychic functioning" (14).

Jones prefers to see religious experience in less developmental terms and more as a repetition of the child's most primal and intense experience of the mother as a "transformational object."[8] Religious experience permits a reentry into a "timeless and transforming psychological space from which renewal and creativity emerge" (134), and that space represents neither a defensive retreat nor a "neurotic response to the threat of instinctual forces but rather a continuation of the primary experience that constitutes and reconstitutes the self" (122). The relational-model perspective prompts Jones to conclude his study with the following speculative remark: "If selves necessarily stand in relation, it is not necessarily irrational to ask if this complex of selves in relation does not itself stand in relation" (135).

Applications to Literary Criticism

The linguistic emphasis of Lacanian psychoanalysis has contributed to that theory's popularity with literary critics and scholars. Much of the current clinical research, however—particularly empirical work such as Stern's on the early interactions and responses of infants—would seem to belie Lacan's view of the primacy of language in the construction of subjectivity. Affective attunement precedes linguistic development and creates its own idiom. In Christopher Bollas's words, "we learn the grammar of our being before we grasp the rules of our language" (36). Arnold Modell has argued a similar point: "The capacity of a child to know the affective state of its mother and conversely the capacity of the mother to 'know' the affective state of the child . . . antedates the acquisition of language and persists after the acquisition of language. So affects and symbolization are inseparable" (*Psychoanalysis* 234). Feeling and cognition, Modell maintains, are inextricably connected—a fact that is not adequately recognized in either Freudian or Lacanian theory. In Lacan's system, furthermore, language acts as an alienating force; in the relational model, contrarily, language can be seen as playing a binding and unifying role. Stern argues that "every word learned is the by-product of uniting two mentalities in a common symbol system, a forging of shared meaning. With each word, children solidify their mental commonality with the parent and later with the other members of the language culture, when they discover that their personal experiential knowledge is part of a larger experience of knowledge, that they are unified with others in a common culture base" (IWOI 172).

Stern also talks about language as a form of transitional phenomena. "The word is given to the infant from the outside, by mother, but there exists a thought for it to be given to. . . . It occupies a midway position between the infant's subjectivity and the mother's objectivity. . . . It is in this deeper sense that language is a union experience, permitting a new level of mental relatedness through shared meaning" (IWOI 172). Loewald, too, has discussed language as a unifying principle that both bridges primary and secondary processes and also joins together self and object world: "Language . . . in its most genuine and autonomous function is a binding power. It ties together human beings and self and object world," and it also reconciles the bodily concreteness of primary process with the rational and abstract thought of secondary process (*Papers* 204).

Relational-model theories, in other words, offer an alternative view of language that is also applicable to the psychoanalysis of a literary text. Robert Rogers has applied object relations theory to a psychoanalytic study of metaphor. He discusses metaphor and figures of speech in terms of relational dynamics involving the restitution of lost objects. Metaphor has a "paradoxical potential," he believes, for "representing a present absence" (*Metaphor* 112).[9] Reading and aesthetic experience involve a *relationship* with the text or work of art and thus relational-model concepts are especially relevant. Murray Schwartz has argued that we experience a literary text much as a transitional object: as we read, the text feels both inside and outside, part of our own inner world as well as part of the external material and cultural world ("Where Is Literature?"). For Christopher Bollas, aesthetic experience is a reenactment of the infant's primal experience of "fitting" with the mother: the aesthetic moment acts as "a spell which holds self and other in symmetry and solitude. Time seems suspended. As the aesthetic moment constitutes a deep rapport between subject and object, it provides the person with a generative illusion of fitting with an object" (32).

Because relational-model theories locate psychological meaning in the intermediate, interactive space between self and other, they are also particularly applicable to reader-response criticism. Meanings, as Norman Holland has argued, are constructed out of the interaction of reader and author relating through the text.[10] That same assumption underlies the essays in this volume, even though they are focused on the text rather than the reader. While recognizing the inevitable limitations of my own psychological defenses and resistances, it is possible, I believe, to read empathically—to enter into the subjective world of the text and to experience, both emotionally and intellectually, its organizing patterns.[11] Robert Rogers, drawing on Holland's model of the introjecting reader (*Dynamics of Literary Response*), speaks of the "elaborate matching" that takes place between the internal worlds of reader and author. The author's projections of his or her internal world, as they are represented in the text, are introjected by me as reader; these introjects I then "match with internalizations of my own, and then respond to—or not, as the case may be—cognitively and affectively, at both conscious and unconscious levels" (*Self and Other* 33). George Atwood and Robert Stolorow have described psychoanalytic understanding as "an intersubjective process involving a dialogue between two personal universes," the "goal" of which, they argue, "is the illumination of the inner pattern of a life, that distinctive structure of meanings that connects the different parts of an individual's world into an intelligible whole" (5). This is a goal that the psychoanalytic readings in this collection also pursue.

The one feature that emerges most prominently in all of the essays in this volume is the dominant role of loss and rage in the creation of the text's subjective world. At first this may seem to contradict Winnicott's argument about creativity, with its emphasis on the healthy and facilitating environment necessary for symbolic play. Nevertheless, his model also shows creative, transitional play as triggered by the onset of anxieties over separation and loss. Loss and trauma can spur a creative response, but perhaps the issue is a matter of degree: if traumatic experience is too severe—if deprivation or abuse, for instance, overwhelm the personality—then trauma will have the opposite effect, blocking the ability, as Winnicott has described, to play at all. Gilbert Rose has written about the creative artist's particular sensitivity to loss: "One might say that the unconscious reminiscence of lost unity before the birth of self and otherness is probably universal, but the creative artist is loss-sensitive and separation-prone. Therefore, his wound may be deeper; the split in the ego is such that it is set on an endless course of repeating the loss in order to repair it.... The novelist, then, would be one who refinds his lost world by creating one of his own, peopled with products of self" (*Trauma and Mastery* 127).[12]

The essays in this book bring relational-model perspectives to bear on specific works of nineteenth-and twentieth-century literature. While these psychoanalytic theories are certainly applicable to the literature of any period, the heightened and self-conscious exploration of subjectivity in literary works of the past two centuries makes them particularly suitable for this sort of inquiry. Four of the essays, furthermore, focus explicitly on contemporary American literature. The cultural influences that have led to the development of the relational paradigm in the social and natural sciences at this particular historical moment have also affected the art and literature of our time, making these relational issues and dynamics, I believe, exceptionally pertinent.

The essay on Wordsworth applies Winnicott's concept of transitional phenomena to the poet's writing on the imagination. Like Winnicott, Wordsworth depicts the creative imagination as an essentially interactive faculty that functions in a paradoxical state of separateness and union, originating in the child's earliest negotiations of separateness and union with the mother. A relational-model framework illuminates Wordsworth's preeminent theme about the connection of moral development to imaginative growth, and it offers a view of Wordsworth's "mystical" or visionary imagination as a form of reality construction rather than (as it is often seen from a classical psychoanalytic perspective) a regressive defense against reality. The essay also examines the connection in *The*

Prelude between the growth of the poet's imagination and his religious faith; both can be understood as examples of transitional phenomena involving trust and developing along a relational continuum.

The essay on *Wuthering Heights* analyzes the novel's structure and character development in terms of the psychodynamics of narcissistic rage and splitting. The Catherine-Heathcliff relationship reflects the interior relational world of a single but divided self—a self that is split between idealized all-good and contemptuous all-bad self and object images. Split-off rage, along with other components of Klein's "schizoid position"—such as extreme envy and hunger—inform all of the characterizations, as well as the imagery and narrative perspective of the novel. The essay argues, however, that the second half of the novel demonstrates a gradual acknowledgment and tolerance of internal rage, and an empathy with one's own lost and angry self, that reflects a movement towards reintegration and wholeness.

The essay on Woolf and Lawrence compares identity issues in their fiction from the perspective of current feminist object relations and relational-model theories. The works of both writers are fueled by conflicts surrounding infantile dependence, merging, and separation; both reveal deep ambivalence toward the mother, along with attendant problems in self-cohesion and ego boundaries. The essay studies how gender and relational issues affect and complicate each other. The threat to masculine identity that feminist theorists believe always lurks in the maternal bond becomes intensified for Lawrence by an intrusive and dominating mother, and thus the predominant metaphor of self-in-relation in his fiction is one that follows the pattern Gilligan has described of hierarchy and stratified levels of power. As much as female identity is particularly involved with the need to feel *in* relationship and affectively attuned to others, identity becomes problematized for Woolf by a seemingly distant and inaccessible mother. The web metaphor that feminist theorists associate with the female perspective indeed dominates Woolf's work, the threat to identity residing not in intimacy, as it does for Lawrence, but in severed connection and psychic isolation.

Jean Rhys's *Wide Sargasso Sea* shares the modernist view of self and universe in which "normal" or conventional structures are collapsing and the only certainty is an ultimate and inescapable isolation. My essay examines the psychological sources of this condition in the novel, tracing relational patterns of self and other that repeatedly enact an original dynamic of betrayal and loss. The psychic consequences of this primal experience of betrayal are figured thematically and stylistically throughout the novel. As Winnicott has discussed, lack of trust in a good or stable other can impede the process of differentiation in which boundaries are established and a reality is recognized that is external to the self. Without those boundaries, the self is trapped in a state of infantile omnipotence that is far more terrifying than pleasurable. Rhys's novel powerfully demonstrates the enraged and destructive fantasies bound up with that infantile, solipsistic state.

Many critics have commented on the intertwining of the erotic and the religious in Updike's fiction. My study of his work focuses on his representations of God and women, revealing how they are both psychologically determined by the same conflictual relational narrative involving dependency, power, and the need for recognition. Drawing on current psychoanalytic studies of religion that locate the formation of the God representation in the child's earliest mirroring experience, the essay looks at problems of mirroring in the fiction and its roots in a narcissistic relationship with the mother. The drama Alice Miller describes of the "gifted" child's acute sensitivity to the emotional needs of a narcissistic parent, the resultant loss of the "true self" along with alternating depression and grandiosity, is also particularly applicable to the dynamics of Updike's fictional world. The essay examines how this drama is manifested not only in plotting, imagery, and characterizations, but also in Updike's prose style itself—in his use of language and in the relationship he sets up with the reader.

The essay on Toni Morrison's *Beloved* concentrates on the interrelationship of social and intrapsychic reality. Morrison's characters suffer the psychic consequences of living in a culture in which domination and objectification of the self have been institutionalized. The novel reveals how the condition of enslavement in the external world, particularly the denial of one's status as a human subject, has deep repercussions in the individual's internal world. If from the earliest years on, one's fundamental need to be recognized and affirmed as a human subject is denied, that need can take on fantastic and destructive proportions in the inner world: intense hunger, fantasized fears of either being swallowed or exploding can tyrannize one's life even when one is freed from the external bonds of oppression. The novel wrestles with the central problem of recognizing and claiming one's own subjectivity, and it shows how this cannot be achieved independently of the social environment. The essay analyzes *Beloved* in light of Jessica Benjamin's thesis that a free, autonomous self is an inherently social self, rooted in relationship and dependent on the recognizing response of an other.

Ann Beattie's fiction has been celebrated for its incisive and witty portrayal of the lives and relationships of the baby boom generation in the post-Woodstock era. My study of her work examines the world she depicts from the perspective of Christopher Lasch's argument about the cultural narcissism of contemporary America. Her characters are unable to break out of a general condition of emptiness, boredom, and paralyzing passivity. Relationships are desired, but ultimately feared and shunned; her fiction depicts above all else the profound insularity of contemporary life, a disconnection and discontinuity that the culture enforces and perpetuates. We see in her work, for instance, the nostalgia for the past and the cult of celebrity so typical of our social world. A psychoanalytic inquiry into these aspects of her fiction reveals their source in a projected, idealized image of self. Such idealization, as usual, is split off from an intolerable rage and hostility. Beneath the surface of the characters' enervated lives, as well as beneath the surface of Beattie's icy, polished prose style, is the threat of impending disintegration and a terror of the raging destructiveness in both self and others.

Finally, Alice Hoffman's *Seventh Heaven* offers a more positive, encouraging view of contemporary life. The novel depicts both the pain and the joys of dismantling a false-self defense and surrendering to desire, to the full ambivalence of passionate existence. Narcissistic illusions are a vital part of Hoffman's world but they are of a benign rather than malignant nature; they are the illusions of creative, transitional play that lead to the discovery of limits. Hoffman sets her novel in the fifties, within the particularly rigid confines of suburbia's conformity and its ideal of the good life. The relationship between the central character, Nora Silk, and the suburban community struggles toward that mutual recognition that feminist theorists advocate. Nora is a loving but imperfect mother; she is also a fully sexual being, and a distinctly individual subject. The community first reacts to her presence with dismay and alarm, but ultimately it is her integrity as a unique subject that liberates the community and makes genuine relationships possible. The essay explores the relational grounds of the novel's redemptive faith in self and other and in the potential it assumes for authentic living.

Chapter 2

Wordsworth and the Relational Model of Mind

A long-standing debate in Wordsworth criticism concerns the relative weight or dominance of the visionary mind: one view stresses the perception of nature in the poetry as mind dependent, while the opposing view emphasizes nature as concrete and solidly "other" than the mind. Some critics, such as C. C. Clarke and Eugene Stelzig, have focused on the tension between these two perspectives as the source of Wordsworth's creative genius. Stelzig takes issue with Geoffrey Hartman, who has argued that Wordsworth fails to achieve the visionary or apocalyptic imaginative power of Blake or Milton because of his blind allegiance to nature. On the contrary, Stelzig contends, "the so-called tension between nature and imagination does not prevent Wordsworth from becoming a visionary poet; it is in fact the fruitful tension out of which his best work grew" (173).

The debate rests on a Cartesian opposition or dualism that Wordsworth's poetry in fact undercuts: imagination and nature, or the subjective mind and the external object world, are less antithetical than vitally interdependent and interconnected. The poetry indeed demonstrates how it is the very solidity and otherness of nature that promotes the full development of subjectivity, allowing for symbolic thinking and imaginative growth. This is precisely the premise of the current relational

29

model in psychoanalytic theory: the mind, in order to develop and grow, requires a separate, external other with which to interact and interrelate.

From the relational perspective, the mind or psyche is fundamentally social, and its basic constituents are not inherent energy forces, but relational configurations: "Mind has been redefined from a set of predetermined structures emerging from inside an individual organism to transactional patterns and internal structures derived from an interactive, interpersonal field" (Mitchell 17). Wordsworth is the poet par excellence of this relational paradigm of the mind: his work traces the intricate relational patterns and interactive dynamics that constitute his developing poetic and moral consciousness. His poetry effectively shows how the creative imagination and the moral consciousness together are derived from socially negotiated states.

John Turner, in a rich and suggestive essay on Wordsworth and D. W. Winnicott, maintains that the cultural origins of several of Winnicott's influential psychoanalytic ideas can be found in the concept of the Romantic, and particularly the Wordsworthian, imagination. He points out both Wordsworth's and Winnicott's "hostility to the post-Cartesian division of experience into the categories of subjective and objective" (495), and he emphasizes the importance of paradox in the work of both writers. Turner's essay culminates in a historical and political critique of Winnicott's ideas, and his literary analysis concentrates on the paradoxes of Wordsworth's ode "Intimations of Immortality." The following essay further pursues the implications of these important parallels Turner notes, in regard both to Wordsworth's writing on the imagination and to the psychoanalytic relational model in general.

Certain passages in Wordsworth's poetry strikingly anticipate the relational paradigm in their depiction of the mind as an interactional construct. In book 12 of *The Prelude* (1805 edition), for instance, Wordsworth claims that the imagination has

>   for its base
> That whence our dignity originates,
> That which both gives it being and maintains
> A balance, an ennobling interchange
> Of action from within and from without,

The excellence, pure spirit, and best power
Both of the object seen, and eye that sees. (373–79)

Similarly, in the language of psychoanalytic relational-model theories, the mind is "fundamentally dyadic and *interactive;* above all else, mind seeks contact with other minds. Psychic organization and structures are built from the patterns which shape those interactions" (Mitchell 3). Or again, Wordsworth describes the "infant Babe" in book 2 as

An inmate of this *active* universe;
From nature largely he receives; nor so
Is satisfied, but largely gives again,
For feeling has to him imparted strength,
And powerful in all sentiments of grief,
Of exultation, fear, and joy, his mind,
Even as an agent of the one great mind,
Creates, creator and receiver both,
Working but in alliance with the works
Which it beholds. (266–75)

According to Daniel Stern, "the infant's states of consciousness and activity are ultimately socially negotiated states" (104), and "the infant's life is so thoroughly social that most of the things the infant does, feels and perceives occur in differing kinds of relationships" (118).

Wordsworth's poetry reflects this intersubjective, profoundly social view of mental development in its depiction of the relational dynamics with nature (as a manifestation of the mother or maternal mind) and, even more generally, in the fundamentally social orientation of the poetic style and form. Wordsworth's insistence on using "the real language of men" and "incidents and situations from common life," as he says in the "Preface to the Second Edition of the Lyrical Ballads," stresses the priority that poetry has for him as a vehicle for interpersonal communication of inner affective states or feelings. "Humble and rustic life was generally chosen," he explains, "because in that condition of life our elementary feelings co-exist in a state of greater simplicity, and, consequently, may be more accurately contemplated, and more forcibly communicated." The essentially interpersonal or intersubjective thrust of Wordsworth's poetic style is manifest in the dialogue form that many of his lyrics assume, and also in his continual reference to a personal other, be it Dorothy or Coleridge, in his most deeply introspective poems.

In a psychoanalytic study of metaphor, Robert Rogers reminds us that "everyone's first motive for using language is to communicate with a nurturing, protecting Other" (*Metaphor* 140). The crucial role of such an other is everywhere apparent in Wordsworth's poetry. *The Prelude*, for instance, is addressed to Coleridge, and references abound to this Friend "so prompt in sympathy" (1:645–46), who allows the poet to speak "unapprehensive of contempt" (2:470) and "Who in my thoughts art ever at my side" (3:200). "Tintern Abbey," too, ends with an address to his "dearest Friend" and sister Dorothy, in whom he sees a version of his former childhood self: "in thy voice I catch / The language of my former heart, and read / My former pleasures in the shooting lights / Of thy wild eyes" (116–19). In this case Wordsworth himself plays the role of the empathic, nurturing, and protecting other; after imagining that Dorothy will inevitably experience her own share of "solitude, or fear, or pain, or grief," he exclaims, "with what healing thoughts / Of tender joy wilt thou remember me, / And these my exhortations!" (143–47). "Tintern Abbey" concludes with an expression of deep gratitude, with a feeling "Of holier love" for the landscapes of his youth that are now "More dear, both for themselves and for thy sake!" The abiding presence of the other, of both Dorothy, who will carry his consoling thoughts in her memory after he is gone, and the concrete forms—the woods and cliffs—of nature that have remained throughout the poet's absences and changes, allow Wordsworth to experience a love, and a sense of self, that is indeed "holier" or more *whole* than he had previously known.

Having suffered profound feelings of loss, absence, and betrayal in relation to the maternal other, Wordsworth nevertheless reveals a perpetual struggle in his work to maintain faith in the mother's reliability and goodness—"Nature never did betray / The heart that loved her" (122–23)—that also implies a reaffirmation, a re-cognition, of the solid "thereness" and separateness of the mother. In an earlier study (*The Romantic Mother*) I have argued that Wordsworth's struggle to maintain faith in the mother's goodness reflects his struggle to resolve an internal split stemming from deep ambivalence toward her. My argument here extends that thesis: Wordsworth's ability to tolerate ambivalence is integrally related to his ability to recognize the mother (and an external reality) that is separate, solid, and other than the self. As Winnicott has argued, the baby must first be able to "destroy" the object in fantasy before the baby can perceive the object as real and independent of the self. The baby "destroys" the object, but the object *survives*. Thus "destruction becomes the unconscious backcloth for love of a real object; that is, an object outside the area of the subject's omnipotent control" (PR 94). This notion is, typically for Winnicott, deeply paradoxical: only by relinquishing one's concern for the object—by ceasing to overprotect the object from one's own ruthlessness—can one develop real concern for a real object. The paradox is crucial to an understanding of Wordsworth's poetry: only by tolerating his own aggression and "destroying" his mother, in other words, is Wordsworth assured of her reality and her love.

Other psychoanalytic studies of Wordsworth, such as those by Richard Onorato and Michael Friedman, have also highlighted the importance of relations with the mother, particularly the feelings of abandonment and grief over the mother's death (she died when Wordsworth was eight years old) and the oedipal desires and conflicts. Those studies, however, do not look specifically at the relational *interplay* of oneness and separateness that is the particular focus of my discussion here. The poetry demonstrates how the play of relational dynamics between self and m/other—particularly in regard to issues of separateness and union, of absence, trust, and presence—is crucial not only to the psychic construction of the self but also to the growth of the creative imagination, of moral consciousness, and of religious faith as well.

Psychoanalytic relational-model theories position psychological meaning in the interactive space between self and other. The space between the subjective internal world and the external object world is the "potential space" of Winnicott's "transitional" realm. The transitional objects, such as teddy bears or blankets, that infants use to master the anxiety of differentiation and separation from the mother "are not part of the infant's body yet are not fully recognized as belonging to external reality"; they occupy a transitional realm between inside and outside, an "intermediate area of *experiencing* to which inner reality and external life both contribute" (PR 2). In this potential space where absolute categories are suspended, connection coexists with division. Winnicott indeed emphasizes the opposition or paradox of union and separateness implicit in the use of the transitional object: "The use of an object symbolizes the union of two now separate things, baby and mother, *at the point in time and space of the initiation of their state of separateness.* . . . This is the place that I have set out to examine, the separation that is not a separation but a form of union" (PR 96–98). Separateness in the transitional realm is thus the sine qua non of union.

This key paradox of separateness and union is central to Wordsworth's poetry, and particularly to his concept of the imagination as expressed in *The Prelude*. In two of the most visionary passages, the Simplon Pass of book 6, and the climb up Snowdon in book 13, the essential creative activity—"The Soul, the Imagination of the whole" (65)—is located in a "chasm." In the Simplon Pass, the violent paradoxical action "Of woods decaying, never to be decay'd / The stationary blasts of water-falls" (557–58) occurs along a "hollow rent" (559), and the oppositions—"Tumult and peace, the darkness and the light"—all reflect to Wordsworth's mind the "workings of one mind, the features / Of the same face, blossoms upon one tree, / Characters of the great Apocalypse" (567–70). In the Snowdon passage, it is a "fracture" (56), a "breach / Through which the homeless voice of waters rose" (62–63). The Wordsworthian imagination is an energy or voice that unites, combines, and makes one, and it arises precisely out of a fractured state of separateness. In all of Wordsworth's visionary or mystical passages, separateness and union coexist in a single paradoxical state that is the transitional domain.

The eulogy to the "blest Babe" in book 2 offers perhaps the most explicit view of the imagination as a form of transitional phenomenon arising out of the child's negotiation of separateness and union with the mother:

> Nurs'd in his Mother's arms, the Babe who sleeps
> Upon his Mother's breast, who, when his soul
> Claims manifest kindred with an earthly soul,
> Doth gather passion from his Mother's eye!
> Such feelings pass into his torpid life
> Like an awakening breeze, and hence his mind
> Even in the first trial of its powers
> Is prompt and watchful, eager to combine
> In one appearance, all the elements

And parts of the same object, else detach'd
And loth to coalesce. (239–50)

These lines then lead into the passage about the child being "creator and receiver both" and "Such, verily," Wordsworth concludes, "is the first / Poetic spirit of our human life" (275–76). In transitional play, the child is indeed both receiving and creating; the unifying creative illusion depends on the forms given from the external world. Throughout his poetry, Wordsworth expresses an awareness of the intermediary status of the imagination. In book 2 he speaks of an abiding "plastic power" within him that was at times rebellious, "but for the most / Subservient strictly to the external things / With which it commun'd. An auxiliar light / Came from my mind which on the setting sun / Bestow'd new splendor" (381–89). In "Tintern Abbey" he refers to "all the mighty world / Of eye, and ear,—both what they half create / And what perceive" (55–57), and again in book 7 of *The Prelude* he recalls "the things which I had shaped / And yet not shaped, had seen, and scarcely seen" (514–15).

Turner maintains that both Wordsworth and Winnicott were able to "find *substantial* hope in the future of an *illusion*" (493); both were expanding the whole concept of illusion in positive and nonpositivistic terms. Hans Loewald has pointed out that the word "illusion" derives from the Latin *ludere*, to play (*Papers* 354), and for Winnicott (and Wordsworth), illusion is indeed a form of play that is quite different from "delusion." Alfred Flarsheim has argued that Winnicott's use of the term "illusion" involves a "greater respect for and acknowledgment of the actual characteristics of the external object than is implied by the term *delusion*" (508). Winnicott, he explains, allows us to understand that the perception of external reality is enriched by its integration with internal reality. "This can be contrasted with hallucination on the one hand and with a totally unimaginative perception of the external world on the other" (508). The area of illusion, Flarsheim concludes, is an intermediate area involving a "simultaneous awareness of two kinds of reality" (509).

Understanding Wordsworth's visionary imagination as "illusion" in this sense—as a form of relational play involving a "simultaneous awareness of two kinds of reality"—makes possible an analytic framework that is far less reductive than the classical Freudian perspective. From the traditional psychoanalytic view, Wordsworth's visionary passages are generally regarded as defensive and sublimatory, as forms of regressive illusions. In a Freudian study of the spots of time, for instance, David Ellis sees the Wordsworthian imagination as pitted in a perpetual battle against death, and thus "imaginative power" becomes an "antidote to the threat of extinction" (95), providing an illusion that the mind dominates or absorbs the external world. Ellis points to the final lines of the Winander Boy passage in *The Prelude,* for instance, in which Wordsworth describes how

> the visible scene
> Would enter unawares into his mind
> With all its solemn imagery, its rocks,
> Its woods, and that uncertain Heaven, receiv'd
> Into the bosom of the steady Lake. (5:409–13)

Ellis argues that the lake that receives the "uncertain Heaven" is an analogy for the boy's mind incorporating the uncertain, transitory material world, and he concludes that the "enclosure of the world within the self makes death an impossibility" (121).

In another psychoanalytic study, however, James Heffernan argues that the context for the Winander Boy passage in *The Prelude*—the ensuing scene of the boy's death, followed by the incident of the drowned man—shows that "the boy's quest for reunion with his mother can lead only to his death" (270). Heffernan argues for an awareness of the crucial role of separation, and not just idealized union, in the development of Wordsworth's imaginative power. He makes the further point that "returning to the past in memory and re-enacting it in words are not the same as regressing to infancy or returning to the womb. In killing off the boy of Winander, Wordsworth repudiates his own regressive wish and yet recovers the power to blow—not the infantile instinct to suck but the creative power to make the prophetic music we hear in his poem" (270). This is a crucial point, for words and language indeed become a form of transitional object for Wordsworth. Arising out of the cavern of separateness, poetic language becomes a vehicle for union; the poetic images occupy an intermediary realm between the internal world of the poet's mind and the external world of reference.

At the end of book 5, Wordsworth writes,

        Visionary Power
Attends upon the motions of the winds
Embodied in the mystery of words.
There darkness makes abode, and all the host
Of shadowy things do work their changes there,
As in a mansion like their proper home;
Even forms and substances are circumfus'd
By that transparent veil with light divine;
And through the turnings intricate of Verse,
Present themselves as objects recognis'd,
In flashes, and with a glory scarce their own. (620–29)

The visionary power of poetic language not only transforms objects, bestowing "light divine" and "a glory scarce their own," but just as importantly, it allows those forms to "Present themselves as objects recognis'd." Recognition implies the separate preexistence of those forms; the mind does not create the objects, the objects themselves are re-presented and re-cognized by the mind. The imagination again reveals its intermediary function for Wordsworth, operating within a simultaneous awareness of two kinds of reality.

This same type of awareness is manifest in other aspects of Wordsworth's poetic style as well. Turner focuses on the importance of paradox in the ode "Intimations of Immortality," arguing that paradox allows the poet to play across categorical boundary lines: "The ordinary categories of our language . . . are inadequate to the complex relational structures that make up the self and its multiple ways of perceiving both the world and itself. Wordsworth's use of paradox and myth, therefore, is designed to disturb those old familiar categories and facilitate the release of new mental power" (484). The coexistence of opposing or paradoxical realities throughout Wordsworth's poetry is enforced further by the poet's ubiquitous use of negatives in his affirmative statements. His assertion, for instance, that "Nature never did betray / The heart that loved her" introduces the idea of betrayal at the same time that it denies it. "A Slumber Did My Spirit Seal" employs such negatives most effectively:

A slumber did my spirit seal;
    I had no human fears;
She seemed a thing that could not feel
    The touch of earthly years.

No motion has she now, no force;
  She neither hears nor sees;
Rolled round in earth's diurnal course,
  With rocks, and stones, and trees.

The negatives again serve to make us more acutely aware of the very human and earthly things—the feelings, motion, force, sights, and sounds—that are being negated or denied. Here again Wordsworth entertains a paradox—the notion of Lucy's death being both a sad and a joyous occasion. Equally paradoxical and significant, however, is the fact that Lucy has entered into an eternal union with nature that also maintains separateness. The union described here is not one of merged fusion, but of distinct forms—the "rocks, and stones, and trees"—with which Lucy's form too orbits in balanced harmony. This same separateness in union also holds true for that visionary passage in "Tintern Abbey" in which the poet celebrates the "sense sublime"

Whose dwelling is the light of setting suns,
And the round ocean and the living air,
And the blue sky, and in the mind of man:
A motion and a spirit, that impels
All thinking things, all objects of all thought,
And rolls through all things. (97–102)

These so-called mystical passages in Wordsworth's poetry do not express regressive refusion or the merged oneness of a grandiose absorption of the world into the mind. As in the "Lucy" lyric, the distinctness, and therefore separateness, of the forms and images—"setting suns," "round ocean," "blue sky"—are celebrated, and "the mind of man" too participates in this union in which boundaries are maintained while also crossed.

Otto Kernberg has written about this type of nonregressive union with the other:

In contrast to regressive merger phenomena which blur self-nonself differentiation, concurring with the crossing of boundaries of the self—a step in the direction of identification with structures beyond the self—is the persistent experience of a discrete self. In this process, there is a basic creation of meaning, of a subjective ordering of the world outside the self, which actualizes the potential structuring of human experience in terms of biological, interpersonal, and value systems. Crossing the boundaries of self, thus defined, is the basis for the subjective experience of transcendence. Psychotic identifications with their dissolution of self-object boundaries interfere with the capacity for passion thus defined. (*Internal World* 289–90)

While Kernberg is talking here about crossing the boundaries of the self in the context of sexual passion, the analogy can be made to the mystical state. As William Meissner has observed, the "capacity to reach beyond the boundaries of self, to empty out the self, as it were, in the loving embrace of the object, is a transcendent capacity of the psyche to immerse itself in a loving object relationship. This need not in itself be regarded as regressive" (152). This type of loving embrace—a simultaneous separateness and union—is the hallmark of the most aspiring and visionary passages in Wordsworth's poetry. As opposed to the indistinct formlessness of regressive merger, these passages always highlight the distinctness of image and form. The profound joy bound up with these experiences is indeed a product of the very solidity of the forms and images, of the ability of nature to maintain her separate boundaries while the poet simultaneously experiences union with her. In book 8 of *The Prelude*, Wordsworth describes how his imagination was sometimes subject to fits of "wilful fancy" (584), but that growing up in nature, "I had forms distinct / To steady me" (598–99), and "I still / At all times had a real solid world / Of images about me" (603–5). Similarly, in the "Fenwick Notes," Wordsworth describes how as a boy, to recall himself from slipping into an "abyss of idealism," he "grasped at a wall or tree" (*Prose* 194).

The consoling quality that resides in the distinctness of image and form, in the solidity of the external world, can also contribute to our understanding of the spots of time, and the "pleasure" and "radiance" that those ultradistinct images possessed for Wordsworth. His description of the images in the second "spot," for instance, highlights the singleness, the separateness and "indisputable" nature of the "shapes":

The single sheep, and the one blasted tree,
And the bleak music of that old stone wall,
The noise of wood and water, and the mist
Which on the line of each of those two Roads
Advanced in such indisputable shapes,
All these were spectacles and sounds to which

I often would repair and thence would drink,
As at a fountain. (*Prelude* 11:378–85)

Ellis concentrates solely on the separateness of the images in the spots as signals of the poet's anxiety about his own separateness and mortality. This is only one side, however, to a larger psychoanalytic picture in which the separateness of the image embraces both anxiety *and* consolation. Other psychoanalytic studies of the spots have concentrated on oedipal anxiety—on sexual transgression and guilt—which are indeed significant components in the total psychological composition of the spots. Contemporary relational-model theories do not deny the importance of oedipal conflict or sexuality in psychic development; rather, they see conflict and sexuality as both implicit in and shaped by the larger relational matrix (Mitchell 67–122).

The separateness of self and m/other is a source of both sorrow and joy, and Wordsworth's art, as usual, expresses the paradox. The spots of time also reflect the paradoxical nature of transitional objects in that they reside in an intermediary realm between internal and external; the images are "given" from the outer world but are equally endowed with projections from the poet's inner world. They occupy that potential space in which the question " 'Did you conceive of this or was it presented to you from without?' " (Winnicott, PR 12) is not to be asked. The "spots" reflect that interactive faculty of the imagination that is "creator and receiver both, / Working but in alliance with the works / Which it beholds."

Not only does symbolic thinking and the creative imagination grow out of these negotiations of separateness and union in the relational play of self and other, but so too does moral consciousness. One of Wordsworth's dominant themes, as he states in *The Prelude*, is "to retrace the way that led me on / Through nature to the love of human Kind" (8:587–88). The recognition of the separate subjectivity of nature/mother—"Earth fills her lap with pleasures of her own; / Yearnings she hath in her own natural kind" ("Ode: Intimations of Immortality" 77–78)—is the seed of moral awareness. As Jessica Benjamin has argued, the child needs to experience the mother or most significant other as an independent subject, not just as the external world or as a mirror or extension of the self. The m/other must embody something of the "not-me"; her recognition of the child "will be meaningful only to the extent that it reflects her own equally separate subjectivity" (24). In such intersubjective experience lie the roots of empathy and compassion; the mutual recognition of true intersubjectivity prevents the enraged need for aggressive domination and possession of the other. The re-cognition of the mother's separateness is also a reaffirmation of her solid "thereness," of her durability and stability, and therefore lays the foundation for trust, for faith in an abiding strength and goodness in the world as well.

The psychoanalytic relational model of mental development thus throws into clearer relief the correlation in Wordsworth's poetry between the growth of imagination and that of religious faith, or what the poet calls "intellectual love." In the "Conclusion" of *The Prelude*, Wordsworth claims that from charting the progress of his imagination, he has also

> drawn
> The feeling of life endless, the great thought
> By which we live, Infinity and God.
> Imagination having been our theme,
> So also hath that intellectual love,
> For they are each in each, and cannot stand
> Dividually. (175–81)

The symbolic play of imagination, as Winnicott has argued, goes hand in hand with faith in a good and stable "thereness" of the other or external world. Artistic creativity and religious faith both belong to that transitional realm of illusion that is not simply, as Freud would have it, a defensive delusion. Rather, illusion in Winnicott's and Wordsworth's sense represents an intermediate area in which subjective and objective reality interact; illusion as such is the means by which human beings give meaning and a sense of continuity to their experience of themselves and their world. In other words, illusion is the means by which we construct the reality of ourselves and our universe.

Arguing from a relational-model perspective, Meissner indeed maintains that religious faith can be understood as developing along a continuum similar to that of identity formation: "the element of trust . . . as an inherent constituent of the experience of faith, cannot be envisioned simply as an infantile, narcissistic investment in and dependence on a need-satisfying object; it should be envisioned as spanning a continuum of developmental states in which the elements of trust are progressively modified to represent increasingly mature levels of integration and expression" (150).

Wordsworth's chronicle of his own imaginative growth is, finally, also a chronicle of trust in a course of developing relational dynamics between self and other. The mind's subjective world, the poetry reveals, is constituted of complex interactions with the objective or outer world. The development of Wordsworth's visionary mind is thus not thwarted by allegiance to nature or the external world, but on the contrary, is facilitated by it. Rosemary Dinnage makes a similar point in a discussion of Winnicott's ideas in relation to artistic creativity:

A history of imagination in each individual life would start... from the first demarcation of self against object, and continue through the increasingly complex perceptual transactions that end in the average man's taking his existence for granted in a world of objects, but which in the artist are never finished. Spanning the self/other boundary line is the intermediate area that permits objective and personal truth to interact, as the artist interacts with his material; and the richness or impoverishment of this area, where objects are recreated and recombined symbolically, depends on the way the outer world coincides with imaginative expectation in early life: on the *fit* between inner constructions and the behavior of things outside. (370)

The "fit" between mind and the external world or nature is indeed one of Wordsworth's frequent themes: "How exquisitely the individual Mind / . . . to the external World / Is fitted:—and how exquisitely, too / . . . The external world is fitted to the Mind" (63–68), he proclaims in the preface to *The Excursion*. Dinnage goes one to conclude that "if objects are unpredictable, too much absent or present, the experience of solid identity and of traffic with them fluctuates. If ideas and expectations in the mind coincide frequently and comfortably with things outside, the growing human being knows and retains the experience of *making* his world—of exercising the curious human trick of meeting fact halfway and recreating it into a different kind of time" (370). Similarly, in the "Conclusion" of *The Prelude*, Wordsworth maintains that in "higher" artistic or creative human minds we find a "genuine Counterpart" to the creative power of nature:

They from their native selves can send abroad
Like transformations, for themselves create
A like existence, and whene'er it is
Created for them, catch it by an instinct;
Them the enduring and the transient both
Serve to exalt; they build up greatest things
From least suggestions, ever on the watch,
Willing to work and to be wrought upon. (93–100)

From such interactive creative power comes, Wordsworth believes, "the highest bliss / That can be known." That bliss is the joy of experiencing a deep sense of reality. The "illusions" of the creative imagination promote the subjective experience of cohesiveness and continuity—the self's experience of its own reality—as well as the sense of cohesiveness and "thereness"—the glorious reality—of all the world outside the self:

hence the highest bliss
That can be known is theirs, the consciousness
Of whom they are habitually infused
Through every image, and through every thought,
And all impressions; hence religion, faith,
And endless occupation for the soul
Whether discursive or intuitive
Hence chearfulness in every act of life
Hence truth in moral judgements and delight
That fails not in the external universe. (*Prelude* "Conclusion": 107–16)

The characteristic use here of a negative in the affirmation—"delight / That fails not in the external universe"—consciously confirms a dependable experience of pleasure in the external object world while at the same time inserting the thought, or reminding us of the possibility, of failure. Tension and conflict are always present in Wordsworth's poetry, but this passage above all celebrates the finding of reality—the reality of the self as a coherent being "infused" through every thought and perception, and the reality of a good and enduring "external universe." Marion Milner has referred to transitional phenomena such as creative symbolization and play as "a two-way journey: both to the finding of the objective reality of the object and to the finding of the objective reality of the subject—

the I AM" (251). In summarizing the work of Marjorie Brierly, Milner also remarks that "blissful experience is not the element most emphasized by Christian mystics, rather it is their overwhelming conviction of the reality of God: and she speaks of the mystics' conviction that religion is the only true realism" (266).

John McDargh makes a similar point in his object-relational study of religious faith. He claims that "the lure of the transcendent derives from the human yearning for communion with more and more reality" (108), and he quotes from theologian Louis Dupre: " 'More primary than the sense of the holiness or power of transcendent reality is the sense of its ontological richness—God is eminently *real.*' " The "motivating hunger for the real," the "creative inquiry into the more-that-is-possible," McDargh argues, is rooted in "the child's first efforts at configuring a lasting and reliable sense of the enduring reality of the parent" through the use of transitional objects and "the creation of a symbolic sphere" (113).

Thus the discovery of reality, as both Wordsworth's poetry and relational-model theories emphasize, is relationally determined, founded on the tension of oneness and separateness and constructed out of the creative negotiations of self and other. Both the poetry and the theories suggest that oneness and separateness, subjectivity and objectivity, are dualities that nevertheless do not form a rigid dualism. These dualities are paradoxically interdependent and mutually necessary. The experience of fusion and the illusion of oneness may indeed be a prerequisite, as Winnicott has argued, to separation and the ability to perceive the reality of the external world at all; the illusion must first be had in order to be surrendered. Conversely, some experience of separation, of rupture or absence, is necessary in order to enter the creative transitional realm and joyfully partake again in the illusion of oneness.

Wordsworth's poetry makes abundantly clear that the work of the creative imagination is at once, as Loewald has suggested about all acts of symbolic play, a form of mourning and of celebration: "both a mourning of lost original oneness and a celebration of oneness regained" (*Sublimation* 81). By describing the complex paradoxes of the human mind, relational-model theories can help us understand the paradoxical nature of Wordsworth's poetry and free us from the dualistic trap in our critical interpretations. The theories can illuminate the visionary and religious dimensions of the Wordsworthian imagination in a less reductive light than they have formerly been seen. The poetry, in turn, by engaging our whole mind—the mind that dreams as well as thinks—permits us actually to experience those creative paradoxes that psychoanalysis can only describe.

Chapter 3

The Rebirth of Catherine Earnshaw: Splitting and Reintegration of Self in *Wuthering Heights*

Perhaps no line from *Wuthering Heights* has been quoted more often than Catherine's exclamation, " 'Nelly, I *am* Heathcliff...' " (E. Brontë 74). The fused identity of these two characters—Catherine's assertion that "he's more myself than I am" (72) and Heathcliff's furious lament over Catherine's dead body, " 'I *cannot* live without my life! I *cannot* live without my soul!' " (139)—sparks the central psychological current of the novel. One's interpretation of this fused relationship will indeed affect one's reading of the novel as a whole. Gilbert and Gubar, for instance, argue from a feminist sociohistorical viewpoint that Heathcliff's original arrival on the scene forces a "shift in family dynamics" that empowers Catherine, the "dispossessed younger sister" (265). They thus see the two as forming an androgynous, initially vital and joyous "undivided self." Such wholeness, however, is ultimately disallowed, "conquered by the concerted forces of patriarchy" (276).

Psychoanalytic readings of the Catherine-Heathcliff relationship have typically focused on its incestuous and forbidden sexual nature. Eric Solomon, for instance, in his controversial article, "The Incest Theme in *Wuthering Heights*," offers evidence that Catherine and Heathcliff could have been half-sister and half-brother. Ellen Moers also emphasizes brother-sister relations, claiming that the Catherine-Heathcliff relationship reflects the common cruelties and eroticism of the nursery (106). Others, such as Richard Chase ("The Brontës, or Myth Domesticated") and Thomas Moser ("What Is the Matter with Emily Jane?"), see Heathcliff as an embodiment of the id, of pure sexual energy or potency, which Catherine both desires and fears.

From another angle, Philip Wion ("The Absent Mother") and Jeffrey Berman (*Narcissism and the Novel*) stress preoedipal separation issues in their psychoanalytic studies of the novel. Noting the preponderance of dead or dying mothers in the book, both critics see the death of Brontë's mother when Emily was three years old as the source of the novel's central concern with a deeply problematic maternal relationship. Berman draws on the theories of John Bowlby to discuss disturbances in attachment and the pathological mourning displayed by all of the novel's major characters. Wion views the relationship between Catherine and Heathcliff "as a displaced version of the symbiotic relationship between mother and child" (146). He offers abundant evidence throughout the work of the "fantasies and fears associated with the separation-individuation process" (146), such as a longing for primal oneness, a fear of regressive fusion or death, a confusion of boundaries between inner and outer worlds, and a primitive oral mode of relationship.

While a forbidden sexual or oedipal component certainly informs the Catherine-Heathcliff relationship, I think Berman and Wion are correct in stressing preoedipal separation issues as being stronger and more fundamental both to the relationship and to the novel as a whole. Wion's analysis, however, neglects a dimension crucial to the Catherine-Heathcliff identity/relationship and to the novel's overall psychodynamics—destructive rage. Berman points out the importance of narcissistic rage in the novel but does not pursue the text's representations of its intrapsychic consequences. Intense, primitive rage, directed both inward and outward, at self and other, and the consequent intrapsychic splitting that such rage occasions, fuels much of the novel's drama and determines its patterns. A psychological analysis of this rage can illuminate the dark dimension of the book that has so troubled readers and critics from Charlotte Brontë on—the violent aggression, cruelty, and pain interwoven throughout the novel's fabric. Such rage underlies what Wade Thompson has called the "perversity" of the book: the pervasive themes of sadism and infanticide, the numerous metaphors of the "killing of helpless animals" (70). Yet not only is infanticide a prevalent theme; so is its reverse: the killing of mothers by infants. The recurrent deaths of mothers in the novel may not only reflect loss or absence, mirroring Brontë's own loss; it may also be a projection of deep infantile rage directed at the mother.

Destructive rage is apparent in the Catherine-Heathcliff relationship from the beginning. Gilbert and Gubar's claim that initially Catherine and Heathcliff form an "undivided self" full of "joy" and vitality is simply not verified by the text. After Catherine's famous assertion that she *is* Heathcliff, for instance, she makes a point of telling Nelly that though he is always in her mind, it is "not as a pleasure, any more than I am always a pleasure to myself" (74). Even early on in the novel, Catherine frequently expresses irritation and anger with Heathcliff, and her behavior in general, from Heathcliff's initial arrival through to her death, betrays far more rage than joy. Consider, for instance, the early incident in which Catherine, without provocation, pinches and slaps Nelly, and then denies that she touched her, leaving Linton "greatly shocked" at both the "falsehood and violence which his idol had committed" (65). Far from expressing an "undivided self," Catherine and Heathcliff, I will argue, are projections of a single, but deeply divided self. Heathcliff is indeed Catherine's self, but specifically a projection of her enraged, "bad," instinctual self that she cannot fully accept or acknowledge, just as Catherine is a projection of Heathcliff's idealized "good" self that he cannot bear to lose. Psychoanalytic relational-model theories deal, like Brontë's novel, with the deep interconnectedness of love and identity, and can shed light on the novel's unconscious psychological structure.

Wion, drawing on the theories of Margaret Mahler, sees inadequate separation from the mother due to Brontë's "loss of her mother at a crucial point in her development" (146) and reflected in the deaths of mothers in the novel, as the key to understanding the novel's psychic and emotional tensions. Although the Catherine-Heathcliff relationship can be seen as a mother-child symbiosis, tragic and impossible because it can only lead to regressive refusion or death, it can also be seen, perhaps even more fruitfully, as the projected intrapsychic drama of a child who has been narcissistically wounded. The wound is due not only to loss or absence of the mother at an important developmental point, but to absence of the mother while she is present—to a mother who is herself narcissistically disturbed and incapable of empathy, of meeting and affirming the child's spontaneous, sensory and emotional self. The actual loss of the mother thus exacerbates a preexisting trauma and sense of loss; and what the novel seeks to recover is less an idealized symbiosis with the mother than the experience of a whole, authentic self. This interpretation also allows us to see an essential coherence between the first and second halves of the novel, and a clear developmental line connecting the first- and second-generation Catherines. Unlike Moser, who believes Brontë "loses control of the second half of her novel and writes insincerely" (13), I see the novel's second half as reflecting deep and authentic, if less powerfully expressed, insights about the growth of one's ability to love, and about the profound interconnection of loving self and loving others.

In *The Analysis of the Self*, Heinz Kohut argues that the development of a secure, cohesive self-structure is highly dependent on the appropriate functioning of the child's earliest relations with the parents. Because the mother is initially experienced as "part of the self," he refers to her as a "self-object" (xiv). In the earliest stages of development, the self-object needs to provide both "mirroring" and "idealizing" functions: the child needs to feel acknowledged and confirmed, reflected, as it were, by the approving "gleam in the mother eye" (116); and the child needs to be allowed to idealize the self-object and experience an empathic merger with it. Failure in either of these functions leads to a structural deficit in the self, to the deeply impaired self-esteem and underlying rage characteristic of pathological narcissism. Narcissistic persons are forever dependent on others to provide their missing self-esteem and ideals, and because of their structural deficit, they do not experience the other as other, but only as a missing part of the self, as a self-object. The Catherine/ Heathcliff relationship can be seen in these terms: each is a self-object for the other, a missing part of the self. Berman makes a similar argument about the narcissistic nature of the relationship: "Each remains incomplete without the other, unable to survive alone. Neither character recognizes the concept of otherness or object love" (92). As I will argue shortly, the novel also reveals massive failure in the empathic mirroring and approval responses of the maternal self-object and the consequent destructive rage.

Although the other leading theorist on narcissism, Otto Kernberg, differs substantially with Kohut in many respects, his theories are also rooted in the dynamics of the early mother-child relationship, and his ideas on narcissistic rage and splitting in particular can help illuminate Brontë's novel. Unlike Kohut, Kernberg retains the primary dual drives—

libidinal and aggressive—of classical Freudian theory. The infant originally internalizes or "introjects" the mother, or its most significant "object," under these two drive derivatives, and thus the object is initially split into "good" (libidinally determined) object and "bad" (aggressively determined) object. This splitting is first due to lack of integrative capacity of the early ego, but can later be used and maintained as a defense, causing severe ego weakness. According to Kernberg, the early ego must accomplish two essential tasks: differentiation of self-images from object images, and integration of libidinally and aggressively determined self-images and object images (*Borderline Conditions* 25–27).

Melanie Klein, an important influence on Kernberg, also stresses the initial splitting of the mother, and particularly the breast, into "good" (the source of libidinal gratification) and "bad" (as it frustrates or deprives libidinal needs). Every mother is inevitably experienced as both good and bad, but if the mother is especially withholding or frustrating, the internalized bad object will become intolerably threatening and the infant will attempt to project its badness outward (Segal 3–5). For both Kernberg and Klein, splitting can assume a defensive function by keeping the good object apart and protected from the dangerous bad object. Such defensive splitting can also result in excessive paranoia and feelings of persecution (due to the projection of the split-off bad object) and excessive idealization of self and object images (as a protection against persecution). Envy, hunger, and rage characterize this split condition, or what Klein refers to as the "paranoid-schizoid position." The second stage of development, however, the "depressive position," involves the integration of the good and bad objects and the tolerance of ambivalence. As Kernberg explains it, internal aggression is now "acknowledged rather than split off or projected," and the "tolerance of ambivalence implies a predominance of love over hate in relation to whole objects" (*Internal World* 30). Although splitting, envy, hunger, and rage form the most powerful psychological components of *Wuthering Heights*, the second half of the novel, as I will show, reveals a movement toward such acknowledgment and tolerance of internal rage and aggression, and toward a reintegration of self.

The central mother figure in *Wuthering Heights* is Nelly Dean, and an understanding of her character and function in the novel is key to uncovering the work's psychodynamic structure. Wion sees her as serving a dual purpose: she functions as a "reality testing" ego in the novel, and even more importantly, he believes, she provides an opportunity for Brontë "to recreate and to be, in fantasy, the mother she had lost" (162). If that were the case, however, one would expect a far more idealized, nurturing fantasy mother than Nelly presents. While Nelly Dean is not, as James Hafley argues ("The Villain in *Wuthering Heights*"), a malicious and calculating villain, neither is she a product of a wish-fulfilling fantasy. Rather, she is a reflection of Brontë's internalized experience of a mother who was not merely absent, but absent while present—distant, unempathic, unable to meet and affirm the child's physical, sensory, and affective life, particularly her angry and aggressive feelings. Consider the early scene between Catherine and Nelly in which Catherine wants to confide a troubling dream. Immediately Nelly cries, " 'Oh! don't, Miss Catherine!' " and then counsels her to " 'be merry, and like yourself!' " (72). Nelly is only comfortable with a "merry," "sweet," and compliant self, and is terrified of the unconscious bodily and emotional life that dreams express. When Catherine persists, Nelly becomes more adamant, " 'I won't hear it, I won't hear it!' " she insists. Finally Catherine holds her down and forces her to listen. This scene leads into the famous declaration, " 'Nelly, I *am* Heathcliff—' " and, as I will discuss more fully later, the entire scene is the single most important moment of self-exposure for Catherine, in which she tries to unearth to Nelly her deep, buried "true" self, with all its rage and pain. She ends by hiding her face in the folds of Nelly's gown. Nelly's response: " 'I jerked it forcibly away. I was out of patience with her folly!' (74).

Nelly is unable to empathize because she is unable to acknowledge or accept the instinctual, passionate life, both of her own unconscious and that of the children she mothers. This inability, as Kernberg has shown, springs from intolerable rage and aggression that must be split off or denied. Her failure of empathy is particularly apparent during Catherine's illness: she shows little concern for Catherine's suffering, disdainfully believing she "acted a part of her disorder" (104), and even lies to her that Edgar cares little for her suffering as well. As Hafley has shown, Nelly is often responsible for others' suffering in the novel. At one point she even admits responsibility, "passing harsh judgement on my many derelictions of duty; from which it struck me then, all the misfortunes of all my employers sprang" (220). Immediately, however, she qualifies and denies the statement: "It was not the case, in reality, I am aware; but it was, in my imagination, that dismal night, and I thought Heathcliff himself less guilty than I." Nelly's unconscious anger and aggression may indeed contribute to many of the tragic turns of events in the novel. When close to her death, Catherine in fact realizes that " 'Nelly has played traitor,' " and shrieks, " 'Nelly is my hidden enemy. You witch!' " (110). Nelly, however, is not as Hafley would have her, an evil, consciously manipulating Iago figure. Her limitations reflect a problematic selfhood that is mirrored on many levels throughout the novel.

Unable to tolerate any display of real pain or suffering, of anger or sadness, Nelly repeatedly charges both the elder and the younger Catherine to be merry and gay, to "put on a happy face," as it were, regardless of their real feelings. So, for instance, before the distraught younger Catherine visits the deathbed of her father, Nelly implores her "to say, she should be happy with young Heathcliff. She stared, but soon comprehending why I counselled her to utter the falsehood, she assured me she would not complain" (225). In her typical withdrawal from any scenes of genuine emotion, Nelly then relates how "she couldn't abide to be present at their meeting." She stands outside the door, and even later "hardly ventured near the bed." Such withdrawal, along with her emphasis on a compliant facade, exemplify what Winnicott has termed the "false self." This false self is a compliant social self developed to protect a "true" self; only the true self has the capacity to feel real. The true self is rooted in the infant's physical being, in its "sensori-motor aliveness" (*Maturational Processes* 149). If the mother is "good enough," she mirrors and approves the child's emerging self, acknowledging the child's full emotional and sensory life. As Alice Miller puts it, every "child has a primary need to be regarded and respected as the person he really is at any given time," and by this she means the child's "emotions, sensations, and their expression from the first day onward" (7). Without this regard or acceptance, the false self may set itself up as real, keeping the true self hidden through rigid defenses. This type of narcissistic pathology, Miller argues, can create a vicious cycle: a "false self" mother will invariably engender a "false self" or narcissistically disturbed child.

The relations of the true and false self, and particularly the struggle of the true self to break forth, create the underlying psychic drama of Brontë's novel. Not only is Nelly Dean unempathic and withdrawn from the sensory and emotional life of the children she raises, but so too are almost all of the parental figures in the novel. Even the seemingly kindly Mr. Earnshaw retreats from the emotional turmoil he creates by bringing

Heathcliff into the family. Further, Brontë makes a point of how he disappoints his children's expectations: before his trip he promises to bring them each a special gift, but on his arrival, the fiddle promised for Hindley is crushed, and the whip for Catherine is lost. Catherine immediately flies into a rage, spits at Heathcliff, and is promptly struck by her father (39). A child's sense of loss, disappointment, and rage in relation to mother or parent indeed pervades the book. The entire perspective of the novel—the much-discussed narrative distance—can in fact be understood not only as a psychological displacement, as Dorothy Van Ghent has suggested (160), but also in terms of the perspective of a narcissistically deprived child. The intense passions of Catherine and Heathcliff are only accessed after they are filtered through two levels of narrative, that of Lockwood and Nelly; the distance can reflect the child's sense of distance from its own authentic but dangerous emotional life, or, similarly, the mother's distance from the child's affective life. Furthermore, the first narrator, Lockwood, perfectly exemplifies the conventional and rigid "false self" who has "locked" and hidden away his "true" self, with all of its narcissistic rage. He is fittingly the novel's initial narrator: the false self is presented first, is most accessible to the reader or outside world, and is furthest from the explicit passions and rage of the Catherine-Heathcliff story at the novel's emotional core.

Lockwood's character, however, also reveals split-off rage and an underlying "true" self longing to emerge. At the beginning of the book, Lockwood presents a few curious facts about himself. First he states that his "dear mother used to say I should never have a comfortable home" (15), which he then immediately follows with an account of a previous romantic interest in a young woman. He was unable to express his feelings toward her explicitly—"I 'never told my love' vocally," he explains, but imagines that his "look" revealed all. When the young lady finally returned his look, however, he "shrunk icily" into himself, "like a snail; at every glance retired colder and farther" (15) until the woman retreated. Wion compares this incident to Lockwood's inability to relate to Heathcliff's dogs, particularly the "canine mother," and rightly connects these problems to his intensely ambivalent feelings toward that mother who predicted he would never find a comfortable home" (Wion 158). The mother's comment, however, needs still further analysis. From Wion's perspective, it would suggest that Lockwood, like Catherine and Heathcliff, will never find the ideal comfort and home of the womb, or the symbiotic reunion with the mother that he seeks. The ambivalence thus stems from both the desire and the fear of this refusion and is responsible for his fear of women in general. As I mentioned before, however, this perspective misses the psychodynamics of rage and splitting. A "comfortable home" is indeed connected with the mother, but also suggests being "at home" or at one with the self. Lockwood's restless traveling and avoidance of any real emotional relations or intimacy reflect a profound discomfort and disconnection with his own internal object relations. After first meeting Heathcliff, Lockwood immediately feels a "sympathetic chord within" that understands Heathcliff's "reserve" (15); Heathcliff is the novel's purest embodiment of narcissistic rage, and thus Lockwood's feeling of affinity with him implicitly asserts the connection between rage and Lockwood's withdrawal and fear of emotional expression.

The projection of unconscious rage may also be apparent in those ferocious dogs with whom Lockwood has such difficulty relating, and in the stormy, hostile nature that he is forced to battle. It is also a significant component in the two dreams Lockwood reports. These dreams have been submitted to a variety of critical interpretations, with the psychoanalytic readings again stressing the sexual imagery and oedipal fantasies. Ronald Fine sees the dreams of variations on the theme of incest and unpardonable sin that runs throughout the novel, and he highlights the castration fears the dreams express. While the sexual symbols throughout the book—the windows, locks, keys, pistols, and staffs—have oedipal associations, the oedipal issues are informed by even stronger, unresolved preoedipal conflicts revolving around dependency and autonomy, powerlessness and power, and by the fears and rage these conflicts evoke.

The presence of an enraged, buried child self is most evident in Lockwood's second dream, in which he is terrified by "a child's face looking through the window," wailing, " 'Let me in—let me in!' " (30). Explaining how "terror made me cruel," Lockwood describes how he rubbed the child's hand on the broken glass of the window until blood "ran down and soaked the bed-clothes." Van Ghent discusses the meaning of the window, here and elsewhere in the novel, as symbolic of a separation between the soul and its demonic "otherness" (160–63). Wion also sees the broken window as symbolic of a broken barrier between self and other, but in a convoluted and unconvincing interpretive leap, he argues further that the young child, by virtue of dream reversal, is representative of "the *older* female other most important to Lockwood, his mother" (159). A simpler, and as I see it, more logical interpretation involves a broken barrier *within* the self, and the child is neither the demonic "other" nor the mother, but that wounded and enraged child self or "true" self struggling to break through. The fact that the child is female and the ghost of Catherine does not undermine this view, for it reflects the essential underlying psychodynamic of all of the novel's major characters. As Kohut and Kernberg have shown, the result of narcissistic injury is violent, destructive narcissistic rage. So Lockwood refers to the child as a "little fiend" that probably would have strangled me!" (31); the child self is full of destructive fury, just as Lockwood is moved to violent, destructive behavior by the sound of its "melancholy" sobbing.

Lockwood's first dream begins with his trying to find his way home through a heavy snow. Joseph, his guide, reproaches him for not bringing a "pilgrim's staff," which he says he will need in order to get into the house. Lockwood considers "it absurd that I should need such a weapon to gain admittance into my own residence." He then finds himself not journeying home, but directed toward a chapel where the Reverend Jabes Branderham is preaching and "either Joseph, the preacher, or I had committed the 'First of the Seventy-First' [sins], and were to be publicly exposed and excommunicated" (28). Wion and others have pointed out the seemingly obvious oedipal fantasy here: the home represents the mother, which he needs a phallic "staff" to enter, and the forbidden nature of this "absurd" wish leads to the dream's theme of sin and guilt (Wion 159). While this may be, the emphasis of the dream, as Lockwood relates it, is on sin or "badness" and the ensuing eruption of diffuse, violent rage—all of which can be understood equally in preoedipal terms. Lockwood spends several paragraphs relating how long and tedious was the preacher's exhortation on sin. Finally, unable to stand it any longer, Lockwood erupts and enjoins the congregation to "drag him [the preacher] down, and crush him to atoms" (29). The deep sense of sin or "badness" the dream emphasizes can spring from the character's split-off but unconsciously recognized "bad" self, with all of its destructive rage. Like the helpless, narcissistically injured child, Lockwood feels defenseless, robbed of his own deep self and the power to assert that self, a power associated with the phallic staff (which he enviously tries to steal away from Joseph at the end). The diffuse, unfocused nature of the violent rage that concludes the dream also suggests a more primitive, preoedipal rather than oedipal source.

This same unconscious dynamic of a split-off or deeply buried self full of destructive rage and therefore "bad" also characterizes Catherine's dream. As mentioned earlier, Catherine forces Nelly to listen to her account of this dream: she describes how she was in heaven but "heaven did not seem to be my home; and I broke my heart with weeping to come back to earth; and the angels were so angry that they flung me out, into the middle of the heath on the top of Wuthering Heights; where I woke sobbing for joy (72). The goodness of heaven is associated with her false, "good" self; she is thus miserable in heaven because it is a betrayal of her "true" or real self, despite its destructive rage or "badness." Heaven is also associated with her impending marriage to Edgar— "I've not more business to marry Edgar Linton than I have to be in heaven" (72)—and thus we understand the marriage as an act of her compliant, false social self. Heathcliff we can now see as the projection of her true self—deprived, enraged, and envious, but also full of a primal physical and emotional vitality. This perspective allows us to make sense of Catherine's claims that "he's more myself than I am" (72) and that

if all else perished, and *he* remained, I should continue to be; and, if all else remained, and he were annihilated, the Universe would turn to a mighty stranger. I should not seem a part of it. My love for Linton is like the foliage in the woods. Time will change it, I'm well aware, as winter changes the trees. My love for Heathcliff resembles the eternal rocks beneath—a source of little visible delight, but necessary. (74)

Nevertheless, Catherine is unable to accept or embrace fully this part of herself—she tells Nelly that " 'it would degrade me to marry Heathcliff now' " (72). Knowing it is a betrayal of her true self, Catherine marries Linton anyway in an attempt to be a "good girl" and win the love and esteem of which she's always felt deprived—"he will be rich, and I shall like to be the greatest woman in the neighborhood, and I shall be proud of having such a husband" (70).

According to Klein and Kernberg, the split-off, angry, "bad" self in the unconscious world of the narcissist is counterbalanced by an idealized, grandiose, "all-good" self. This is precisely the role that Catherine plays for Heathcliff: she is a projection of his idealized "good" self, the feared loss of which would render him helpless to a consuming narcissistic rage. He thus sees her as perfect, as superior to everyone else: " 'She is immeasurably superior to them [the Lintons]—to everybody on earth, is she not, Nelly?' " (50). Heathcliff is least able to tolerate any sign of inferiority, of weakness or helplessness in himself or others. " 'It's odd,' " he exclaims, " 'what a savage feeling I have to anything that seems afraid of me!' " (215). Or again, " 'I have no pity! I have no pity! The more the worms writhe, the more I yearn to crush out their entrails!' " (128). A similar feeling motivates Lockwood's rage against the sobbing child at the window. As Alice Miller explains, "Contempt for those who are smaller and weaker is the best defense against a breakthrough of one's own feelings of helplessness: it is an expression of this split-off weakness" (67).

Such narcissistic splitting determines the unconscious structure of Brontë's characters and their relationships. Catherine and Heathcliff each reveal both self-contempt and grandiosity. Despite her feelings, as expressed in her dream, of being bad and undeserving of love or happiness, Catherine also reveals a fantasy of being universally beloved: when she begins to suspect Nelly's betrayal, she exclaims, " 'How strange! I thought, though everybody hated and despised each other, they could not avoid loving me—' " (104). In Catherine and Heathcliff's relationship, each primarily functions as a projected part of the other or, in Kohut's terms, as a self-object. This perspective can help us understand both characters' seeming lack of empathy or real care for the suffering of the other. On her deathbed, Catherine cries bitterly, " 'I wish I could hold you . . . till we were both dead! I shouldn't care what you suffered. I care nothing for your sufferings. Why shouldn't you suffer? I do!' " (133). And at her death, Heathcliff, with "frightful vehemence," screams, " 'May she wake in torment!' " and " 'Catherine Earnshaw, may you not rest, as long as I am living!' " (139). Their love for one another, though fierce, is not really a love of other but of a split-off or missing part of the self. Their relationship reflects the psychological structure of Klein's paranoid-schizoid condition of extreme splitting, envy, hunger, and rage.

This same structure underlies the novel as a whole. The hunger is apparent in the preponderance of oral imagery, which Wion does a good job of elucidating. Because the infant's first mode of relationship is oral, food and love maintain a primitive association. As Wion observes, "Nearly every social encounter involves food or drink," and even the secondary characters "tend to be imagined in oral terms" (149), from Hindley's drinking himself to death to Isabella's "fasting" and "pining" for love of Heathcliff. Hunger and oral rage are especially evident in Catherine and Heathcliff. For Catherine, relational issues are closely connected to food and eating. After Heathcliff has disappeared and Edgar has retreated to his books, Catherine expresses her feelings of outraged betrayal by refusing to eat. According to Nelly, "she fasted pertinaciously, under the idea, probably, that at every meal, Edgar was ready to choke for her absence" (103).

Like the narcissistically wounded child, Catherine is indeed starving for food/love, for a fundamental affirmation of her whole self. On the third day of her fast, she does ask Nelly for food and water, which she eats and drinks "eagerly." Immediately, however, she sinks back on her pillow, "clenching her hands and groaning. 'Oh, I will die,' she exclaimed, 'since no one cares anything about me. I wish I had not taken that' " (103). Her anger, expressed explicitly here in oral terms, reveals the primitive rage of a child who feels denied of the basic emotional nourishment it needs from its mother or first love object. Her perception of Edgar's behavior fits the narcissistically injured child's perception of its parent that we've seen repeated throughout the novel: he is present but absent, in the house but not attentive to her needs; he is unempathic and indifferent—" 'What is that apathetic being doing?' " (103) she demands to know from Nelly.

In her rage at such indifference, Catherine tears her pillow "with her teeth" (104), and the feathers evoke the memory of a lapwing she had once seen on the moors. The bird was trying "to get to its nest," which she finds later in the winter "full of little skeletons" (105). As Wion notes, "Catherine seems to identify both with the 'old' lapwing, which wants to get home but can't, *and* with the starved and abandoned little ones" (151). A child's experience of rejection and withholding of food/love is again associated with destructive rage in this memory/fantasy, and is projected, as usual, in the character of Heathcliff. There is confusion in Catherine's story as to whether Heathcliff actually shot the lapwing, but she does describe how he set a trap over the nest so "the old ones dare not come," and she concludes, " 'I made him promise he'd never shoot a lapwing after that, and he didn't. . . . Did he shoot my lapwings, Nelly?' " (105).

Heathcliff's character is indeed the novel's most powerful manifestation of a greedy and sadistic oral rage. James Twitchell has even devoted an entire essay to a discussion of "Heathcliff as Vampire." Wion too (149) points out the many references to Heathcliff as vampire or cannibal: Heathcliff exclaims that had Catherine ceased to care for Edgar, he "would have torn his heart out, and drank his blood!" (125); Catherine expresses fear that Heathcliff will "devour" Isabella (93); Isabella mentions " 'his sharp cannibal teeth' " (146) and describes how " 'his mouth watered to tear you with his teeth; because he's only half a man—not so much' " (149); and Nelly, at the novel's end, questions, " 'Is he a ghoul, or a vampire?' " (260). Such intense oral rage is often a consequence of abandonment and abuse (either physical or emotional) in childhood, a condition epitomized by Heathcliff's history. He is a foundling who at Mr. Earnshaw's death is forced to suffer degradation and humiliation at the hands of Hindley. Heathcliff embodies all the fury of the helpless, narcissistically injured child who feels empty, powerless, and alone. His character is driven by rage and envy, as well as by an obsessive desire to escape this empty, lonely state through a perfect fusing love with an idealized self-object.

Thus the Catherine-Heathcliff relationship dramatizes, with power and acuity, the interior relational world of the narcissistically wounded child—a world that is deeply divided, split between idealized all-good and contemptuous all-bad self and object images, and that harbors a fierce, destructive rage. Brontë's novel does not stop here, however, for in the second-generation Catherine-Hareton relationship it reveals a movement toward psychological healing: in this second relationship, the rage and loss are not split off, but acknowledged and accepted as part of oneself, and a whole, reintegrated self emerges. Catherine Earnshaw is literally and symbolically reborn. By marrying Hareton Earnshaw, Catherine Linton Heathcliff becomes again Catherine Earnshaw. Moreover, Nelly remarks how the eyes of young Catherine and Hareton " 'are precisely similar, and they are those of Catherine Earnshaw' " (254). Because, as I have argued, the entire novel reflects the internal object relations that result from wounded narcissism, the characters and relationships in the book's second half can also best be understood in terms of projections of a single personality. We can thus see the young Catherine and Hareton together as forming a single, cohesive self.

The second half of the novel reveals the psychic tasks that are necessary to achieving this reconstructed self. First, the younger Catherine (whom I will refer to now as Cathy) is able to love perhaps the novel's most unloveable, pathetic character, Linton Heathcliff. Even after his marriage to Cathy, Linton remains a sickly, whining, selfish child, so desperately needy that he is unable to consider anyone's needs but his own. He is perhaps the novel's most explicit portrait of that desperate, broken child clamoring beneath the surface of the self, the helpless, needy child that so many of the other characters are trying to defend against. Nevertheless, Cathy acknowledges and accepts him. She tells Heathcliff, " 'I know he has a bad nature, he's your son. But I'm glad I've a better, to forgive it; and I know he loves me and for that reason I love him' " (228). Unlike the elder Catherine, Heathcliff, or Lockwood, Cathy is able to embrace the frail, greedy child in the self, to forgive it, understanding that it only wants love and that it needs compassion.

Cathy has a more difficult time, however, learning to love and accept Hareton. While Linton is Heathcliff's biological child, Hareton, his foster-child, is more truly his son for he has inherited Heathcliff's raw and savage nature. He is, as has been commonly noted, a younger reflection of Heathcliff: Lockwood comments on his "rough and uncultivated" appearance and his "haughty" air (19), and Hareton is often described in animalistic terms. Like Heathcliff, Hareton projects the enraged, "bad," sensual and feeling self that Cathy at first rejects and treats with contempt. Ultimately, however, she comes to accept and even love him, and the terms she uses to inform Hareton of her changed attitude emphasize the fact that she is, in essence, coming to accept a part of herself. She does not simply tell Hareton that she has decided to like him, but " 'that I want—that I'm glad—that I should like you to be my cousin, now' " (247). She has decided to acknowledge their bond as relatives and to accept that he belongs to her—" 'I should like you to be *my cousin.*' " Just as she has decided to possess or own him, so she demands that he do the same with her: " 'Come, you shall take notice of me, Hareton—you are my cousin, and you shall own me' " (247). This perspective allows us to see the Cathy-Hareton relationship not as "a superficial stereotyped tale of feminine longings" (Moser 15), but as a genuine expression of emotional growth in the novel's underlying psychological narrative.

With Cathy's marriage to Hareton Earnshaw, Catherine Earnshaw re-emerges as a more complete, integrated whole. This reborn Catherine Earnshaw has learned to love even the unloveable parts of the self—the needy, helpless child and the enraged, "bad" destructive self. The internal aggression, in Kernberg's words again, is now "acknowledged rather than split off or projected" and this "tolerance of ambivalence implies a predominance of love over hate in relation to whole objects" (*Internal World* 30). Wion claims that Nelly is a " 'good enough mother' " for Cathy, which thus allows for her emotional development. Given Nelly's unempathic and "false self" character, however, that interpretation seems unlikely. Cathy's relationship with her father, on the other hand, although far from ideal, nevertheless presents the novel's strongest parent-child bond. Although Edgar is sickly and withdrawn throughout most of Cathy's life, she clearly feels a deep affection both for and from him, and is driven almost to madness when she fears Heathcliff will prevent her from attending his deathbed. Further, we are told that Edgar has strong nurturing and maternal qualities. He takes Nelly's place nursing Catherine in the last two months of her life: "No mother could have nursed an only child more devotedly than Edgar tended her" (113). Berman also points to Edgar as one of the only characters in the novel "who grows in stature" and is capable of a nonnarcissistic love: Edgar "adores his daughter but does not seek to possess or control her" (107). Edgar is perhaps the "good enough mother" who provides the underlying support for the psychological development reflected in the second half of the novel.

While the end of the novel achieves a restructuring and integration of self, the destructive rage is still a powerful presence. Catherine and Heathcliff's ghosts are still said to be stalking the moors. The narcissistic rage that fuels the novel remains a lurking force among the ghosts and dreams of the unconscious. Nevertheless, in the second half of the novel Brontë recognizes the need for empathy with one's own enraged self. Such empathy, as Miller has argued, is born out of mourning, out of confrontation with one's deep sense of loss. Mourning is the hallmark of Klein's depressive position and involves the acceptance—or, to use Cathy's word, the *owning*—of one's destructive as well as loving feelings, and the recognition that both are necessary to the experience of a whole, genuinely alive self.

Chapter 4

Gender, Self, and the Relational Matrix: D. H. Lawrence and Virginia Woolf

The problem of identity, of the cohesion and integrity of the self, has long been recognized as a predominant issue in the modern novel. Psychoanalytic relational-model theories can provide a lens through which to view this central problem. By seeing the core self as based on an interactional construct, the relational perspective can show how textual representations of intimacy, love, and sexual relationships are bound up with the question of identity. The works of Virginia Woolf and D. H. Lawrence, despite vast differences in style and aims, are equally fueled by intensely conflictual preoedipal relationships involving infantile dependence, merging, and separation. The novels of both writers reveal evidence of narcissistic injury and deep ambivalence toward the mother, along with attendant problems in self-cohesion and ego boundaries.[1] Feminist object relations theories, which focus on gender differences in the earliest preoedipal negotiations between self and m/other, can help us to understand both novelists' distinctive modes of addressing these problems and creatively recasting them in literary form.

In *The Reproduction of Mothering* Nancy Chodorow argues, "To the extent that females and males experience different interpersonal environments as they grow up, feminine and masculine personality will develop differently and be preoccupied with different issues" (51). For the boy, the original primary oneness with the mother may be an unconscious source of conflictual gender identity; the underlying sense of femaleness may undermine the sense of maleness. Masculinity thus becomes defined as "not female" or "not mother." Furthermore, the mother may experience a son as more "other" than a daughter, and thus the male self is based on a more fixed "me"–"not me" distinction than the female self. Because the girl's gender identity does not contradict her primary sense of oneness and identification with the mother, gender identity is less problematic for her. Preoedipal separation issues are not as tied up with sexual issues for the girl as they are for the boy. However, because a mother may experience a daughter as an extension of herself, and because preoedipal mother-love is prolonged for a girl, she may suffer greater problems of separation and autonomy than a boy.

These differing relational experiences with the mother, Chodorow concludes, account for fundamental differences in masculine and feminine personality:

Feminine personality comes to be based less on repression of inner objects, and fixed and firm splits in the ego, and more on retention and continuity of external relationships. From the retention of preoedipal attachments to their mother, growing girls come to define and experience themselves as continuous with others; their experience of self contains more flexible or permeable ego boundaries. Boys come to define themselves as more separate and distinct, with a greater sense of rigid ego boundaries and differentiation. The basic feminine sense of self is connected to the world, the basic masculine sense of self is separate. (169)

Carol Gilligan has applied Chodorow's theories in her study of gender differences in the ethical domain, and she comes to similar conclusions. She finds two differing male and female modes of seeing the self in relation to others and the world. Drawing on the texts of men's and women's fantasies and thoughts, Gilligan discovers that the male mode is dominated by images of hierarchy while images of web define that of the female. "Thus the images of hierarchy and web inform different modes of assertion and response: the wish to be alone at the top and the consequent fear that others will get too close; the wish to be at the center of connection and the consequent fear of being too far out on the edge" (62). Like Chodorow, Gilligan sees masculinity as defined through separation and femininity through attachment; thus male gender identity is threatened by intimacy and female gender identity by separation.

Patricia Waugh, in her study *Feminine Fictions*, also shares Chodorow and Gilligan's position that female gender identity is strengthened by a relational view while a male's is threatened by it. In her argument about the psychological consequences of this fact, Waugh uses Klein's two developmental positions—the "paranoid-schizoid" and the "depressive." A girl's longer preoedipal attachment to the mother, she believes, "means that ambivalence may be more successfully resolved through the reparations and integrations of the depressive position" (76). She thus argues that "it seems likely that the mobilization of the paranoid-schizoid defences of splitting (intense idealization and denigration), fragmentation, projection, and introjection is more likely to occur in the formal strategies of male writers. An expression of 'depressive' concerns and anxieties— the struggle to cope with ambivalence without splitting; fear of loss; recognition of guilt; desire for reparation and relationship—is more likely to occur in women's writing" (80). Waugh admits that this distinction is not absolute, and two of the other essays in this volume would indeed seem to argue expressly against it: the essay on Emily Brontë stresses the strong splitting defenses in her work, while the study of Wordsworth reveals the predominance of depressive, reparative, and relational concerns in his. In regard to Lawrence, though, I do agree with Waugh's view of gender as playing a determining role in the preeminent fear of regressive fusion and the need to control and separate that we find in this male writer's work.

Perhaps the distinctions that Chodorow and Gilligan draw should be considered more as indicators of general tendencies than as strict alternative categories in understanding the psychology of gender identity. This may be particularly important when considering the work of creative artists, whose ego boundaries are often more permeable and whose defenses may be less rigid than those of ordinary individuals.[2] Still, the works of Woolf and Lawrence illustrate the predominance of the kind of male/female pattern Chodorow and Gilligan describe: the metaphor of hierarchy (personal and sexual relationships conceived in terms of stratified levels of power) is highly characteristic of Lawrence's fiction; the metaphor of web (an insistence on unifying connections in human relations) is the prevailing motif in Woolf's work. Nevertheless, Lawrence's work also displays a yearning for connection and relationship, and Woolf's novels are not without a keen awareness of power dynamics in human and sexual relationships. The works of both writers reveal how gender and preoedipal relational issues affect and complicate each other, creating a level of intense emotional experience at the foundation of human identity.

Sons and Lovers and *To the Lighthouse* both revolve around powerful, ambivalently conceived maternal figures, and the structure of each work rides on the tensions and alternate rhythms of merging and separation. In Lawrence, the emphasis is on separation and autonomy. Intimacy with women threatens overdependence, possessiveness, total absorption or loss of self. In *Women in Love*, Birkin's "star balance," his idealized notion of an abstract, impersonal love, arises out of this fear of personal dependency and loss of self. In Lawrence's work, the relation between the sexes is generally perceived in terms of dominance and submission, as a continuous power struggle rooted in the first relational dynamic between helpless infant and omnipotent mother. In Woolf, intimacy and merging issues pose no threat to gender identity. The emphasis in her work is on connection and unity rather than on separateness and autonomy. The threat to the self lies not in the act of love, but in the state of isolation. In her work, when the conscious and exhausting effort at sustaining connections with others and the environment is relinquished, death—or the dissolution of self—is imminent.

Much has been made of the obvious oedipal dynamics in *Sons and Lovers*.[3] As both Chodorow and Dorothy Dinnerstein have argued, the oedipal triangle has a more powerful, primitive weight for the boy than for the girl since for him it is an extension of the earlier primitive tie to the mother. The oedipal is informed by the preoedipal, and in Lawrence's novel the specific psychodynamics of that more primitive infant-mother bond require critical attention. Lawrence's descriptions of Paul's relationship with his mother reveal a merged identity, a lack of boundaries or differentiation that extends well into Paul's adolescence and adulthood. He has no feeling, in any deep emotional or psychological sense, of his own separate reality, of any reality outside of his mother: "There was one place in the world that stood solid and did not melt into unreality: the place where his mother was. Everybody else could grow shadowy, almost non-existent to him, but she could not. It was as if the pivot and pole of his life, from which he could not escape, was his mother" (222). This passage reveals the essential Lawrencian ambivalence: his mother is for him both the source of all reality—of coherence and meaning—and the source of a suffocating bondage. The fierce self-assertion that so characterizes Lawrence's work, as well as the insistence on separateness and boundaries in his portrayal of sexual relationships, indeed grows out of this condition.

The roots of the condition lie in a particular relational dynamic between mother and son. Mrs. Morel brings to her mothering a desperate unhappiness with her life and marriage, and also a consuming guilt over Paul's birth: "She no longer loved her husband; she had not wanted this child to come. . . . With all her force, with all her soul she would make up to it for having brought it into the world unloved" (37). Indeed, Lawrence repeatedly makes the point in the early chapters that Paul was originally unwanted and unloved. Thus, behind Mrs. Morel's oversolicitous and overprotective love is guilt over an original antipathy or lack of love; at least this seems to be what is unconsciously experienced by the child. This can help account for Paul's hyperconsciousness of his mother: "His soul," Lawrence says, "seemed always attentive to her" (57).

Such extreme attentiveness arises out of the need to please the mother in order to gain or assure her love. If the mother's love was given freely and naturally, the child would have no need for such anxious and relentless attention. Jeffrey Berman (*Narcissism and the Novel*) makes a similar argument about Mrs. Morel. He claims that she is "alternately overloving and underloving" (205) and that beneath her fervent, overprotective love is underlying rejection and coldness. Berman compares her to the oversolicitous but essentially cold, unloving mother of "Rocking-Horse Winner" (209). In addition, Mrs. Morel projects onto her child the ambitions and intellectual aspirations she failed to achieve for herself, and she forces him to provide the love, understanding, and, in sublimated form, the sexual gratification she fails to receive from her husband. Chodorow claims that the mother's failure to recognize her child as other than an extension of herself may be more frequent with daughters; when it happens with sons, however, the threat to the boy's gender identity can incite acute unconscious rage and hostility.

As many critics have noted, the anger and aggression toward women in Lawrence's work is rooted in a fear of maternal absorption and consequent loss of masculine potency and autonomy. This deeply rooted fear, as Chodorow and others have argued, may be universal to the male psyche in a culture in which women are the primary caretakers. Ambivalence is unavoidable, but in Lawrence's case, that ambivalence is inflamed by the narcissistic nature of the mother-child bond; the mother's own boundary problems necessarily complicate boundary and differentiation issues for her son, a point that I do not think has been adequately made in the feminist psychoanalytic criticism of Lawrence's work. Lawrence's characters, furthermore, are often aroused to their most brutal and violent acts when they are confronted with any display of helplessness, dependency, or fragility, for they are responding with fury to that same condition in themselves. When Paul accidently breaks his sister Annie's doll, for instance, he devises a peculiarly sadistic ritual sacrifice of the doll:

He made an altar of bricks, pulled some of the shavings out of Arabella's body, put the waxen fragments into the hollow face, poured on a little paraffin, and set the whole thing alight. He watched with wicked satisfaction the drops of wax melt off the broken forehead of Arabella, and drop like sweat into the flame. So long as the stupid big doll burned he rejoiced in silence. At the end he poked among the embers with a stick, fished out the arms and legs, all blackened, and smashed them under stones.

"That's the sacrifice of Missis Arabella," he said. "An' I'm glad there's nothing left of her."

Which disturbed Annie inwardly, although she could say nothing. He seemed to hate the doll so intensely, because he had broken it. (58)

Margaret Storch and Daniel Dervin both interpret the doll in this episode as representative of the mother. According to Storch, "The body of the mother is, in fantasy, dismembered and destroyed, disintegrating in a flash of fiery consuming anger, and liquified into the wax and sweat of elemental fluids. . . . The scene is a vivid depiction of a child's sadistic fantasy against the mother" (99). Dervin sees the incident as the first crucial step in the emergence of Paul's creative and assertive self. The doll, he believes, is an example of Winnicott's "transitional object"; it contains projections of both the bad mother and the badness within Paul himself. The doll also represents, according to Dervin, a possessive and symbiotic bond with the mother that "must be smashed before the child can hatch out into separateness" ("Play, Creativity, and Matricide" 89). Dervin asks whether Paul hates the doll because, as Annie states, he had broken it, "Or did he break and burn it because of his hatred? The latter seems more probable" (85). I would argue that both motives are interrelated and equally true.

While I don't disagree with Storch and Dervin's view that the doll burning reflects Paul's enraged and destructive feelings toward the mother, I also think they do not give enough credit to Annie's assertion. Paul's original breaking of the doll indeed reflects inner rage and its potential to destroy. Paul is most incensed, however, by the doll in its fragile, broken state—he does hate the doll, as Annie says, *because* he shattered it. Paul is terrified of the power of his own unconscious rage— its ability to have hurt and destroyed the doll. The fragile, broken doll represents (I agree with Dervin in this sense) both his mother *and* himself. Paul's fear of his own destructive rage and the fragile vulnerability of mother/self, however, only incites him to further violence. Even Lawrence's female characters may become vicious and cruel at any reminder of infantile helplessness or vulnerability. Gudrun, for instance, despises Gerald for what she perceives as his infantile neediness: "Perhaps this was what he was always dogging her for, like a child that is famished, crying for the breast.... An infant crying in the night, this Don Juan. Ooh, but how she hated the infant crying in the night. She would murder it gladly. She would stifle it and bury it" (524).

The relation between the sexes in Lawrence's work always threatens to return to this state of the fragile, needy infant and the powerful mother, and thus all personal dependency must be stifled and maternal/female power resisted or destroyed. In *Sons and Lovers* Lawrence portrays Miriam as almost monstrous in her craving for an absorbing, suffocating intimacy and love. Paul watches in horror as she embraces her younger brother:

And, folding him in her arms, she swayed slightly from side to side, her face half lifted, her eyes half closed, her voice drenched with love.

"Don't!" said the child, uneasy—"don't Miriam!"

"Yes; you love me, don't you?" she murmured deep in her throat, almost as if she were in a trance, and swaying also as if she were swooned in an ecstasy of love.

"Don't!" repeated the child, a frown on his clear brow.

"You love me, don't you?" she murmured.

"What do you make such a fuss for?" cried Paul, all in suffering because of her extreme emotion. "Why can't you be ordinary with him?" (153)

Similarly, Paul is repelled by the intensity with which she smells a flower: "To her, flowers appealed with such strength she felt she must make them part of herself. When she bent and breathed a flower, it was as if she and the flower were loving each other. Paul hated her for it. There seemed a sort of exposure about the action, something too intimate" (173).

Lawrence repeatedly describes Miriam as wanting to "absorb" Paul, or, as Mrs. Morel complains, to "suck him up." Miriam "sat on the sofa absorbed in him. She always seemed absorbed in him, and by him, when he was present" (175), or again, "He felt that she wanted the soul out of his body, and not him. All his strength and energy she drew into herself through some channel which united them. She did not want to meet him, so that there were two of them, man and woman together. She wanted to draw all of him into her. It urged him to an intensity like madness, which fascinated him, as drug-taking might" (194). The analogy to drug taking is telling, for Paul is as attracted to the regressive merging that Miriam offers as he is repelled by it. There are indeed passages throughout Lawrence's fiction that celebrate fusion, as, for example, the following line from *Women in Love:* "There was no I and you, there was only the third, unrealized wonder, the wonder of existing not as oneself, but in a consummation of my being and of her being in a new one, a new paradisal unit regained from the duality" (417).

As Heinz Kohut has argued, a persistent unconscious desire for merging or fusion can result from an original frustration or deficiency in the mother-infant bond, particularly in the original mirroring relationship. Intersubjective theorists such as Daniel Stern and Jessica Benjamin see the obsession with merging as rooted in an original failure of infant-mother attunement. The intensity of Paul's repulsion to merging with women is also a product of the intensity of his unconscious wish. This wish arises out of lack—not the lack of an initial merged or symbiotic experience—but the lack of a primary facilitating or "attuned" relationship in which the self feels acknowledged and affirmed.

Lawrence recognizes, with intuitive psychological insight, that the desire for an all-absorbing intimacy or fusing loss of self in other indeed arises out of an inner deficiency or void. Paul accuses Miriam of being incapable of real love: "You don't want to love—your eternal and abnormal craving is to be loved. You aren't positive, you're negative. You absorb, absorb, as if you must fill yourself up with love, because you've got a shortage somewhere" (*Sons and Lovers* 218). And Miriam herself suspects the truth of this accusation, of the "shortage" or hollowness at the core of her being: "Perhaps she had not in herself that which he wanted. It was the deepest motive of her soul, this self-mistrust. It was so deep she dared neither realise nor acknowledge it. Like an infinitely subtle shame, it kept her always back" (221). To Lawrence's credit, he does not attribute this void or deficiency in the self solely to his female characters. Skrebensky in *The Rainbow* and Gerald in *Women in Love* suffer from this same condition. Incapable of real love, they smother and oppress their women in an attempt to absorb them, to compensate for their deep sense of emptiness and shame.

Ironically even Paul, so critical of Miriam, suffers from this same inner void, the same inability to love. The condition is a result of a breakdown in the earliest relations between self and primary other: the unsatisfactory and frustrating nature of the infant's first love relationship prohibits the growth of self-love or self-esteem. Psychoanalytic theorists vary on the specific nature of the self-other relational functions necessary to the development of healthy self-esteem. For Kohut, it is successful mirroring and idealizing functions; for Stern it is "affective attunement"; for Benjamin it is "mutual recognition" between self and mother as independent subjects.[4] Theorists agree, however, on the emotional and relational consequences if self-esteem has not been established. The inability to love oneself—the feelings of unworthiness, shame, and emptiness at the core of one's being—also precludes the ability to love others. Thus Paul complains, "You know, mother, I think there must be something the matter with me, that I *can't* love" (*Sons and Lovers* 350).

The closest he comes is with Clara Dawes, but he is attracted to her precisely because of her scornfulness and defiance of men. She thus confirms his own deep sense of worthlessness and shame. Unlike himself and Miriam, in whom neediness fuels a hot intensity, Clara is cold, and Paul perceives this coldness as strength: "He marvelled at her coldness. He had to do everything hotly. She must be something special" (265). Just as he accuses Miriam of "absorbing" him, so he at times feels absorbed by and merged with Clara. Lawrence describes one scene, for instance, in which Paul sits beside Clara at a play:

He was Clara's white heavy arms, her throat, her moving bosom. That seemed to be himself. Then away somewhere the play went on, and he was identified with that also. There was no himself. The grey and black eyes of Clara, her bosom coming down on him, her arm that he held gripped between his hands, were all that existed. Then he felt himself small and helpless, her towering in her force above him. (331)

The ambivalence is again clear: besides the pleasure of merging is also the feeling of being "small and helpless" beneath the woman's "towering" strength. Ultimately he must resist her power and domination. He accomplishes this partially by abstracting her, by stripping her of her individuality and making her symbolic of "woman" in their lovemaking, and partially by holding back and never truly giving of himself. Indeed, Clara accuses him of not really knowing or realizing her: " 'About *me* you know nothing,' she said bitterly—'about *me!*' " and she continues, " 'you've never come near to me. You can't come out of yourself, you can't' " (362). Interestingly, Paul accuses Miriam of the very same things, of never realizing *him* and never truly giving of herself. In the case of Miriam, Lawrence provides an explanation:

She knew she felt in a sort of bondage to him, which she hated because she could not control it. She hated her love for him from the moment it grew too strong for her. And, deep down, she had hated him because she loved him and he dominated her. She had resisted his domination. She had fought to keep herself free of him in the last issue. (296)

Thus at the same time that Miriam is characterized as exhibiting a merging or fusing love for Paul, she is paradoxically described as resistantly self-contained and withdrawn. The same may be said of Paul in his relationship with Clara. Paul and Miriam share a similar psychological condition, but perhaps Paul was too close to Lawrence's own self for him to undergo the same degree of psychological self-scrutiny that he achieves in the characterization of Miriam.

Lawrence's philosophy of heterosexual love, particularly as it is articulated by Birkin in *Women in Love*, grows out of his terror of being swallowed, fused with, and dominated by mother/woman. "Fusion, fusion," Birkin thinks, "this horrible fusion of two beings, which every woman and most men insisted on, was it not nauseous and horrible anyhow, whether it was fusion of the spirit or of the emotional body?" (348). Birkin's insistence on being "single in himself, the woman single in herself," on both being "two pure beings, each constituting the freedom of the other, balancing each other like two poles of one force, like two angels, or two demons" (223–24) may reflect, as both Dervin and Storch have argued, the intense ambivalence surrounding the infant's original symbiotic or merged experience with the mother. It could equally reflect, however, a *failure*, in Stern and Benjamin's terms, of "intersubjective" mutuality and recognition in that original mother-infant relationship.

Benjamin believes that healthy human relationships are founded on a crucial and "necessary tension between self-assertion and mutual recognition" (12); when that tension breaks down, power dynamics of domination and submission result. From this perspective, Lawrence's ambivalent obsession with merging and his aggressive domination of women are part of the same phenomenon: both reflect an original loss of tension and resulting omnipotence. "Omnipotence, whether in the form of merging or aggression, means the complete assimilation of the other and the self" (Benjamin 67). A mother who lacks a sense of her own agency and coherent selfhood—a condition enforced by a cultural denial of women's subjectivity—will make identity development problematic for her child. Drawing on Winnicott's ideas, Benjamin asserts, "Only someone who has achieved full subjectivity can survive destruction and permit full differentiation" (82). From this point of view, the destructive impulses toward women in Lawrence's texts could also be seen as attempts to restore a lost tension: only by destroying the mother can the infant hope to discover the mother's subjectivity as well as his own.

In Lawrence's fiction, the breakdown of tension and boundaries in the original love relationship leads to a depiction of all love relationships in terms of domination, possession, and control. Birkin's reflections on love again reveal this psychological configuration:

He wanted so much to be free, not under the compulsion of any need for unification, or tortured by unsatisfied desire. Desire and aspiration should find their object without all this torture, as now, in a world of plenty of water, simple thirst is inconsiderable, satisfied almost unconsciously. And he wanted to be with Ursula as free as with himself, single and clear and cool, yet balanced, polarized with her. The merging, the clutching, the mingling of love was become madly abhorrent to him.

But it seemed to him, woman was always so horrible and clutching, she had such a lust for possession, a greed of self-importance in love. She wanted to have, to own, to control, to be dominant. Everything must be referred back to her, to Woman, the Great Mother of everything, out of whom proceeded everything and to whom everything must finally be rendered up. (*Women in Love* 224)

Throughout the novel, women's love is invested with threateningly oral and maternal associations. Ursula, for instance, wants a different kind of love than Birkin: "She was not at all sure that it was this mutual unison in separateness that she wanted. She wanted unspeakable intimacies. She wanted to have him, utterly, finally to have him as her own, oh, so unspeakably, in intimacy. To drink him down—ah, like a life-draught. . . . He must be quaffed to the dregs by her" (299). And earlier, Lawrence describes Ursula as wanting to worship a man "as a woman worships her own infant, with a worship of perfect possession" (225).

While a merging love with a woman is always dangerous and abhorrent to Lawrence, he considers the same kind of fusing love with a man as desirable and vitalizing. A fusing bond with a man does not recall the ambivalence over fusion with the mother and thus does not threaten his masculine identity and potency. As Storch has shown, Lawrence's novels often portray the alliance between men as a kind of defiance of women, as in the case of Paul and Clara's estranged husband, Baxter Dawes, in *Sons and Lovers*, and Birkin's relationship with Gerald, which troubles Ursula in *Women in Love*. Storch in fact argues that only by forging an ideal image of masculine strength was Lawrence able to heal his internal split and assimilate the loving, "good" mother. This is similar to John Clayton's assertion that Lawrence "is able to imaginatively recreate his father into an image of male power with which he can then identify and from which he can take sustenance" (195). Clayton believes that this ability is what most distinguishes Lawrence from other modernist writers, permitting him "to identify with the center rather than long for the center, to assert knowledge rather than uncertainty" (195).

For Lawrence's male characters, then, merging with another man does not threaten their autonomy but rather fortifies their resistance to women and makes them feel strong and potent. In the wrestling scene between Gerald and Birkin, for instance, Lawrence states, "It was as if Birkin's whole physical intelligence interpenetrated into Gerald's body, as if his fine, sublimated energy entered into the flesh of the fuller man, like some potency, casting a fine net, a prison, through the muscles into the very depths of Gerald's physical being" (*Women in Love* 305). The desire for fusion or merging with an other, like the need to dominate and control, can be understood from Benjamin's perspective as a transformation and distortion of a fundamental desire for intersubjective recognition. Lawrence's short story "The Blind Man" makes this dynamic particularly apparent.

Maurice Pervin lacks visual consciousness but possesses what Lawrence describes as a vital physical, sensual consciousness—a "blood-contact with the substantial world" ("Blind Man," in *Complete Short Stories* 355). While the "rich suffusion of this state generally kept him happy, reaching its culmination in the consuming passion for his wife" (355), Maurice still suffers from dark depressions: "At times the flow would seem to be checked and thrown back. Then it would beat inside him like a tangled sea, and he was tortured in the shattered chaos of his own blood" (355–56). In other words, the lack of recognition of his innermost being or emotional core (the wife is apparently incapable of genuine recognition or contact on this innermost level) leaves Maurice deeply agitated and depressed. At the end of the story, Maurice attempts to make contact with a male friend of his wife. Bertie is a lawyer, a clever, intellectual man who is emotionally frigid and terrified of intimacy: he was "unable ever to enter into close contact of any sort. . . . At the centre of him he was afraid, helplessly and even brutally afraid. . . . At the centre he felt himself neuter, nothing" (359). Bertie finds himself alone with Maurice in the dark, sensual world of the blind man's barn. Maurice forces him to touch his eyes and face, and the physical contact between the two leaves Bertie feeling "annihilated" and "imprisoned," with "an unreasonable fear, lest the other man should suddenly destroy him" (364). Maurice, on the other hand, is deeply moved: " 'Oh, my God,' he said, 'we shall know each other now, shan't we? We shall know each other now' " (364). Such deep "knowledge" of each other—a mutual recognition—is craved but, as usual in Lawrence's fiction, it collapses into a power dynamic of domination and annihilation because of an original lack of mutual subjectivity: Bertie has no self with which to acknowledge Maurice. While the relationship here is between two men, Bertie is significantly associated with the maternal wife (she is pregnant) and her intellectual, nonsensual world.

An examination of the preoedipal relations in Lawrence's work, as Berman, Dervin, and Storch have also shown, allows us to understand more fully the misogyny that feminist critics have been so quick to condemn. Intimacy with women threatens the same overwhelming dependence and loss of agency as an original limitless infant-mother relationship. The threat is the same whether we consider that relationship as a normal mother-infant symbiosis or, as I am more inclined to see it, as a failure, in Stern and Benjamin's terms, of attunement and intersubjectivity. The characteristically male vision of hierarchy that Gilligan describes, that of perpetual power play between dominance and submission, indeed dictates Lawrence's conception of self-in-relation. The emphasis in his work on separateness and boundaries in love relationships, and his urgent demand for recognition of one's bodily, sensual, and sexual being, grow out of a feeling of threat to differentiated subjectivity and sexual identity. The origins of that threat lie in the infant's first ambivalent love relationship, a relationship complicated in Lawrence's case by a particularly intrusive mother whose own problematic subjectivity exacerbates boundary issues for her son.

Virginia Woolf's work is also characterized by a persistent threat to the integrity and viability of the self.[5] The maternal figures in her works are often, as Mrs. Morel is for Paul, the source of reality, meaning, and coherence for the other characters. Woolf describes Mrs. Dalloway as having the gift "to be; to exist; to sum it all up in the moment as she passed" (*Mrs. Dalloway* 264). She is invested with a magical quality: things come together, cohere, and gather meaning in her presence. For Peter Walsh, her unrequited lover, her mere being is a source both of terror and of ecstasy, and the novel ends with that assertion:

What is this terror? what is this ecstasy? he thought to himself. What is it that fills me with extraordinary excitement?
    It is Clarissa, he said.
    For there she was. (296)

Mrs. Ramsay has a similar function in *To the Lighthouse*. When she leaves a room "a sort of disintegration set[s] in": people disperse, things fall apart, and meaning dissolves. The most dramatic instance of this is the "Time Passes" section of the novel, in which we learn of Mrs. Ramsay's death. Without her presence, the house and the environment are rendered chaotic, empty, and indifferent. Even the trees and flowers are "standing there, looking before them, looking up, yet beholding nothing, eyeless, and so terrible" (203). For the infant or nascent self, the world without a primary caring m/other is a world without order or meaning; without the m/other's presence to behold and recognize one's being—to affirm one's reality—it is also a world without self (a condition Woolf returns to again at the end of *The Waves* when describing Bernard's deathly experience of an empty and indifferent world without self).

Woolf's portrait of these magical maternal figures who bestow meaning and order, however, is not without ambivalence. Both *Mrs. Dalloway* and *To the Lighthouse* convey a disturbingly distant, stern, and sealed quality about maternal love. Clarissa is described as cold and severe, and Mrs. Ramsay frustrates the other characters by what they perceive as her remoteness and inaccessibility. Lily's portrait of Mrs. Ramsay, the vision that frames the novel, captures the ambivalence. The picture is of Mrs. Ramsay and her son, as Lily sees them through the window. The vision is one of ideal maternal love, madonna and child, and yet it is also distant and detached, observed only from within a frame and behind paned glass. Unlike Lawrence's fiction, with its clamoring for boundaries, Woolf's work depicts a continual struggle to shatter boundaries so as to achieve greater union and identification with the mother. Lily's thoughts frequently express a fantasy of merging with Mrs. Ramsay. At one point she sits on the floor with her arms around Mrs. Ramsay's knees and reflects,

What device for becoming, like waters poured into one jar, inextricably the same, one with the object one adored? Could the body achieve, or the mind, subtly mingling in the intricate passages of the brain? or the heart? Could loving, as people called it, make her and Mrs. Ramsay one? for it was not knowledge but unity that she desired, not inscriptions on tablets, nothing that could be written in any language known to men, but intimacy itself, which is knowledge, she had thought, leaning her head on Mrs. Ramsay's knee. (*To the Lighthouse* 79)

Like the male, same-sex fusing fantasies in Lawrence's fiction, the fantasy of union here betrays its source in a passionate desire to know and be known by the beloved other: intimacy is knowledge. The merging Lily craves, however, is impossible: "Nothing happened. Nothing! as she leant her head against Mrs. Ramsay's knee" (79). She concludes that people are impenetrably "sealed."

Lily is finally able to identify with Mrs. Ramsay, however, in her role as artist. The artist makes connections and forges a permanent, ordered, and coherent whole, and this is indeed only another version of Mrs. Ramsay's maternal role: "Mrs. Ramsay saying, 'Life stand still here'; Mrs. Ramsay making of the moment something permanent (as in another sphere Lily herself tried to make of the moment something permanent)— this was of the nature of a revelation. In the midst of chaos there was shape.... 'Mrs. Ramsay! Mrs. Ramsay!' she repeated. She owed it all to her" (241). The end of the novel presents the resolution that Lily seeks: she completes her painting, her vision, at the moment that Mr. Ramsay and the children reach the lighthouse, the event that marks the culmination of Mrs. Ramsay's vision. This conclusion reflects, I believe, less a fantasy of merging than, in Stern and Benjamin's terms, a resonance or deep "attunement" between self and mother that is deeply satisfying.

In Woolf's fiction, merging fantasies are enforced, not threatened, by gender. A girl's sense of self is highly involved with her feeling of identification with her mother.[6] Nevertheless, merging and dissolution of self-boundaries in Woolf's fiction are rooted in a relational dynamic between self and mother that is just as ambivalent and problematic as it is in Lawrence. The problems are manifest in the ambivalent characterization of Mrs. Ramsay. She is identified with the lighthouse and the symbol captures her dual nature: she is a beacon, a figure who sheds light and order for the others; yet she stands alone, stark, exposed, and isolated (she is, to Lily's eyes, "an august shape; the shape of a dome"). The trip to the lighthouse, to bring gifts to the lighthouse keeper, represents an attempt to combat this condition of isolation and abandonment—of loss of human contact or connection—that Mrs. Ramsay perceives at the heart of life:

For how would you like to be shut up for a whole month at a time, and possibly more in stormy weather, upon a rock the size of a tennis lawn? she would ask; and to have no letters or newspapers, and to see nobody; if you were married, not to see your wife, not to know how your children were,—if they were ill, if they had fallen down and broken their legs or arms; to see the same dreary waves breaking week after week, and then a dreadful storm coming, and the windows covered with spray, and birds dashed against the lamp, and the whole place rocking, and not to be able to put your nose out of doors for fear of being swept into the sea? (11–12)

This passage begins by describing a condition of isolation that then escalates rapidly to a state of extreme violence and destruction. The movement reflects the intense destructive rage bound up with the infantile experience of loss, abandonment, and deprivation. The condition is similar to Mrs. Dalloway's feeling that "there was an emptiness about the heart of life; an attic room" (*Mrs. Dalloway* 45). As Ernest and Ina Wolf have argued about Mrs. Ramsay, and J. Brooks Bouson and Jeffrey

Berman about Mrs. Dalloway, the lack of a secure self-structure in the narcissistically deprived maternal characters themselves is integrally related to Woolf's overall vision of life as ultimate isolation and ever-threatening violence and disintegration.

Mrs. Ramsay, despite her husband's gross insensitivity, feels vitally dependent on the certainty and security that he provides:

> She often felt she was nothing but a sponge sopped full of human emotions. Then he said, Damn you. He said, It must rain. He said, It won't rain; and instantly a Heaven of security opened before her. There was nobody she reverenced more. She was not good enough to tie his shoe strings, she felt. (*To the Lighthouse* 51)

Although she is maternally protective of him, she "did not like, even for a second, to feel finer than her husband" (62) and is discomposed when he openly displays dependence, "for then people said he depended on her, when they must know that of the two he was infinitely the more important" (62). Mrs. Ramsay thinks of the "masculine intelligence" as a fabric of "iron girders . . . upholding the world, so that she could trust herself to it utterly" (159), like a child.

Woolf draws a distinction between masculine and feminine modes of thinking that corresponds strikingly with the differences Gilligan describes. The male role is abstract and hierarchical, and based on clear subject/object distinctions. Woolf describes Mr. Ramsay's way of thinking: "If thought is like the keyboard of a piano, divided into so many notes, or like the alphabet is ranged in twenty-six letters all in order, then his splendid mind had no sort of difficulty in running over those letters one by one, firmly and accurately, until it reached, say, the letter Q" (53). And when Lily asks Mr. Ramsay's son what his father's books are about, he replies, "Subject and object and the nature of reality" (38). She does not understand, so he continues, "Think of a kitchen table then, when you're not there." As Lily strolls out into the orchard, she pictures a bare, scrubbed kitchen table and wonders about minds that pass their days "in seeing of angular essences, this reducing of lovely evenings, with all their flamingo clouds and blue and silver to a white deal four-legged table" (38).

Lily and Mrs. Ramsay live mentally and imaginatively in a more empathic and weblike mode. They respond foremost to nuances of human feeling and they always think in terms of relationships and connections.

Although Lily's painting is abstract—Mrs. Ramsay is reduced to a purple triangle—it is based on essential relationships, on "the relations of masses, of lights and shadows," on "how to connect this mass on the right hand with that on the left" (82–83) so as to create a whole, unbroken unity. Elizabeth Abel has pointed out how the spatial relations in Lily's paintings also "articulate the boundary negotiations that shape the mother-infant bond" (*Virginia Woolf* xviii). Mrs. Ramsay's matchmaking, her continual efforts to bring people together, her dinner party, like Clarissa's parties, are all versions of the same attempt to make connections and create order, unity, and wholeness. These efforts spring from an underlying fear of boundary loss and chaos, from a menacing fragmentation of self and world.

Mrs. Ramsay sees life as the enemy that must be continually combated: "She must admit that she felt this thing that she called life terrible, hostile, and quick to pounce on you if you gave it a chance"; she sees herself on one side, and life on another, "and she was always trying to get the better of it, as it was of her" (*To the Lighthouse* 92). Her struggle with life is a solitary, lonely battle, "something private, which she shared neither with her children nor with her husband" (91). Her dinners and match-making are a form of protection against fragmentation and isolation: "She was driven on, too quickly she knew, almost as if it were an escape for her too, to say that people must marry; people must have children" (93). She wonders if all her social efforts and her constant solicitousness of others may not merely be shoring up her fragile self-esteem: "For her own self-satisfaction was it that she wished so instinctively to help, to give, that people might say of her, 'O Mrs. Ramsay! dear Mrs. Ramsay . . . Mrs. Ramsay, of course!' and need her and send for her and admire her?" (65).

Woolf nevertheless makes it clear that Mrs. Ramsay, whatever her motives, does succeed in bringing comfort and in creating moments of security and order for others. At the dinner party "they were all conscious of making a party together in a hollow, on an island; had their common cause against that fluidity out there" (147). As Mrs. Ramsay serves the meal, she thinks of the moment in the same terms as Lily thinks of her art: "There it was, all round them. It partook, she felt, carefully helping Mr. Bankes to a specially tender piece, of eternity; . . . there is coherence in things, a stability; something, she meant, is immune from change, and shines out. . . . Of such moments, she thought, the thing is made that endures" (158). It is not coincidental that such moments of unity often revolve around food and meals. In *The Waves*, the pivotal scenes of reunion among the characters (companions since childhood who periodically come together as they try to deal with the death of their friend Percival) always occur in a restaurant, around a table and food. The infant's first mode of union with the mother outside of the womb is oral, and this unconscious association again lends psychological resonance to the quest for unity and order in Woolf's work.[7] The most intimate form of order and unity is indeed one's own identity, the coherence and integrity of the self.

Formlessness and disintegration are always the dominant threat. While Lawrence fights this threat with a domineering insistence on boundaries and separateness, Woolf combats it by ceaselessly striving to make connections with others and with the environment. As Bernard in *The Waves* asserts, "it is the effort and the struggle, it is the perpetual warfare, it is the shattering and piecing together—this is the daily battle, defeat or victory, the absorbing pursuit" (203). Each of the characters in *The Waves* fights this battle in his or her own particular mode: Bernard with his words and phrases, Jinny with her body and sensuality, Louis with his commercial transactions and structures, Neville with his poetry and friendships, and Susan with her maternal earthiness. Rhoda has no form or structure with which to wage this battle, and the utter absence of boundaries and coherence in her experience of self leads inevitably to her death. Rhoda can be paralyzed by a mere puddle on the ground: "I came to a puddle. I could not cross it. Identity failed me. We are nothing, I said, and fell" (64). Life for Rhoda is perpetual struggle and pain, and the temptation to which she eventually succumbs is to abandon all effort and die: "Now I will relinquish; now I will let loose. Now I will at last free the checked, the jerked-back desire to be spent, to be consumed" (164).

Rhoda's condition is an extreme version of the psychological state underlying Woolf's work and informing all of her characters. Even the magical maternal figures are at times tempted to relinquish the effort of living, of tirelessly constructing connections to sustain themselves and others. Mrs. Dalloway thinks, "Death was defiance. Death was an attempt to communicate; people feeling the impossibility of reaching the centre which, mystically, evaded them; closeness drew apart; rapture faded, and one was alone. There was an embrace in death" (*Mrs. Dalloway* 281–82).

Death is conceived here in relational terms: it is a "defiance" of the enemy life, and it is "an attempt to communicate," an ultimate "embrace" or final loving union. Mrs. Dalloway is symbolically allied throughout the novel with the character of Septimus Smith, who does kill himself: "She felt somehow very like him—the young man who had killed himself"; yet his death frees her—"He made her feel the beauty; made her feel the fun. But she must go back. She must assemble" (283).

Mrs. Ramsay, too, in moments of solitude, abandons her usual effort and allows herself to retreat, to become a "wedge-shaped core of darkness" (*To the Lighthouse* 95). In this state, she also experiences a mystical embrace (much as Mrs. Dalloway conceives of death as embrace) with "inanimate things": "It was odd, she thought, how if one was alone, one leant to inanimate things; trees, streams, flowers; felt they expressed one; felt they became one; felt they knew one, in a sense were one" (97). Mrs. Ramsay feels herself merge with a stroke from the lighthouse: the light "seemed to her like her own eyes meeting her own eyes" (97). Again we see at the source of the merging or fusing fantasies the yearning to be known or recognized—to be seen by one's own eyes is indeed the ultimate recognition. Mrs. Ramsay's merging with the beam from the lighthouse (the symbol associated with her throughout the novel) is thus a kind of merging with herself—she "felt an irrational tenderness thus (she looked at that long steady light) as for oneself" (97–98). Woolf portrays the mother as being recognized and affirmed, in other words, by her own maternal gaze.

This is a singular fantasy, however; most of Woolf's characters do not experience merging and identity loss as affirmative. Rhoda is terrified when, as she says, "Identity failed me." Waugh interprets the lack of boundary distinctions and failures of identity in Woolf's fiction as part of a "postmodern awareness" (96) of the self's illusoriness. Incorporating Lacanian and postmodern perspectives into her Kleinian framework, Waugh states, "Woolf is clearly aware of the extent to which one's sense of self is a *theory* of the self constructed out of available social practices and discourses" (95). She believes, for example, that Bernard "recognizes the cultural constitution of subjectivity through language and thus the *illusoriness* of the self-determining, unified subject" (121). I find this argument unconvincing. Jane Flax has noted that the postmodernist view tends to confuse the notion of a "unitary subject" with that of a core, cohesive self (218), and I believe this applies to Waugh's argument as well. Awareness of the self as an indeterminate subject is not the same as the sense of utter fragility and the terror of disintegration that Woolf's texts expose. Such a postmodernist view of Woolf's work neglects the intense degree of narcissistic anxiety that permeates her fiction.

Unlike Mrs. Ramsay's experience, Bernard's experience of loss of self does not produce a sense of deep recognition and joy; on the contrary, it betrays profound feelings of abandonment, of negation and denial of self. In Bernard's vision, the world without a self is specifically a world without a confirming other. His vision reveals the utter lack of recognition at the heart of the self's relational experience, a lack or loss that Virginia Woolf's art itself persistently seeks to repair:

I waited. I listened. Nothing came. I cried then with a sudden conviction of complete desertion. Now there is nothing. . . . No echo comes when I speak, no varied words. This is more truly death than the death of friends, than the death of youth. . . . The woods had vanished; the earth was a waste of shadow. No sound broke the silence of the wintry landscape. No cock crowed; no smoke rose; no train moved. A man without a self, I said. A heavy body leaning on a gate. A dead man. With dispassionate despair, with entire disillusionment, I surveyed the dust dance. (*The Waves* 284–85)

Gradually Bernard's sense of identity returns, and with it the color and substance of the landscape. The return to identity, however, is a return to effort and battle: "Always it begins again; always there is the enemy; eyes meeting ours; fingers twitching ours; the effort waiting" (293). As Septimus Smith's death allows Mrs. Dalloway to feel the value of life, so Bernard's deathlike experience enables him to appreciate the rich complexity of reality and the value of the struggle to remain in it. The conclusion of the novel poses Bernard in an image of heroic defiance of death:

Death is the enemy. It is death against whom I ride with my spear couched and my hair flying back like a young man's, like Percival's, when he galloped in India. I strike spurs into my horse. Against you I will fling myself, unvanquished and unyielding, O Death! (297)

In Woolf's work, the maintenance of identity is a matter of sustaining connections, and it is always a supreme effort; the temptation to surrender that effort is a perpetual threat.[8] Her characters ceaselessly strive to make connections, to assemble, to unify, and to create a sense of order and permanence. In a sense, they approach their lives as works of art, and thus their fragile selves are bolstered through the creation of a cohesive artistic whole. Kohut has made this argument about creative artists in general: "The broken self is mended," he states, "via the creation of the cohesive artistic product" (Ornstein 781). Winnicott argues, however, that personal loss in the artists themselves can never be truly repaired through the artistic products alone: "The self is not really to be found in what is made out of products of body or mind, however valuable these constructs may be in terms of beauty, skill, and impact. . . . The finished creation never heals the underlying lack of sense of self" (PR 54–55). This seems to have been the case with Woolf herself. While creative work had a reparative function for her, in the end it was not enough, and the effort of living became too exhausting to continue.

The works of Lawrence and Woolf are deeply concerned with issues of boundaries and fusion, issues that dominate the earliest relations between self and m/other. Their novels both illustrate and transcend the gender distinctions described by Chodorow and Gilligan. Lawrence's novels emphasize boundaries and separateness as the primary means of fortifying the self. Fusion with women threatens male sexual and gender identity. Gender, identity, and relational issues were particularly complicated for Lawrence by an impinging and dominating mother. Woolf's novels emphasize unifying connections as the primary mode of constructing and fortifying the self. An apparently distant and inaccessible mother complicated gender identity and intensified relational concerns for Woolf. In both Woolf's and Lawrence's texts, we see how the mother's problematic subjectivity equally problematizes issues of identity and subjectivity for the child.[9]

The works of both writers, finally, display a need to construct and maintain a coherent selfhood, along with a simultaneous yearning for and terror of dissolution of self boundaries. While Freud saw this paradox as related to the death instinct, relational theorists attribute it to an underlying paradox of human relational needs: the need for deep contact with an other and the need to keep intact an inviolate core self—that "wedge of darkness" Mrs. Ramsay covets in moments of solitude. This is a paradox that Winnicott emphasizes, and that Benjamin recasts in her own terms as the contradictory needs to assert the self and to recognize (and be recognized by) the other. In their fiction, Woolf and Lawrence play out imaginatively complex variations of this fundamental relational paradox, providing insights into the deep dynamics that construct human and gender identity.

Chapter 5

Boundaries and Betrayal in Jean Rhys's *Wide Sargasso Sea*

Jean Rhys's *Wide Sargasso Sea* is a favorite for English literature survey courses. In its reworking of Charlotte Brontë's *Jane Eyre*, Rhys's novel makes the shift in literary sensibility from the nineteenth to the twentieth century particularly discernible. Rochester's lunatic first wife, Bertha Mason, the madwoman in the attic in Brontë's tale, assumes center stage in Rhys's version. Rather than the haunting "other" of *Jane Eyre*, the madwoman's searing subjectivity indeed defines Rhys's novel. The collapse of rational order, of stable and conventional structures on all levels, distinguishes Rhys's vision and places it squarely within the modernist tradition. Like many modernist works, Rhys's novel explores a psychological condition of profound isolation and self-division, a state in which the boundaries between the internal subjective world and the external object world have dissolved. Terror and despair form the corresponding affects. The condition is bound up with another of the novel's characteristically modernist themes: the conviction that betrayal is built into the fabric of life.

This conviction underlies all of Rhys's novels and plays a formative role, stylistically as well as thematically, in her literary art. Her works reveal a violation of trust at the foundation of human experience that serves to invest all human connection or intimacy with danger and threat;

at the same time, however, this early experience of betrayal only exacerbates the need for and dependency on others. Lack of basic trust in one's earliest human relations, as D. W. Winnicott and other object relations theorists have argued, can also impede the establishment of boundaries in which a reality is recognized as outside of and other than the self. This problematic relational dynamic informing Rhys's work is both personal and cultural: its roots are interpersonal and familial, but the family's economic and social position impacts upon those interpersonal dynamics; the familial relationships are influenced by the larger social network of relationships in which the family functions. The mother-daughter relationship in particular is complicated by the patriarchal culture in which it is embedded. The female experience in patriarchy is one of both forced dependency and exclusion. Thus for a girl, betrayal is indeed interwoven with dependency, troubling a girl's relational history from infancy through adulthood, and affecting her relationship with her own infant should she herself become a mother.

Elizabeth Abel has argued that women's helpless dependency in patriarchy can help account for the recurrent themes of madness, defeat, and passivity in so much twentieth-century women's fiction, and she suggests that "women's common experience can open almost imperceptibly into the pathological" ("Women and Schizophrenia" 169). Her point about Jean Rhys's fiction in particular is that the psychologically pathological, schizoid symptoms that Rhys's heroines exhibit—"impoverished affect, apathy, obsessive thought and behavior coupled with the inability to take real initiative, a sense of the unreality of both self and world, and a feeling of detachment from the body" (156)—are recognizable to women as an aspect of their common experience. Teresa O'Connor, in her critique of Rhys's West Indian novels, also ties the psychological and interpersonal to the cultural and historical. She sees an unresolved relationship with a rejecting mother, or "negative motherliness," that runs throughout Rhys's work as identified with the experience of British colonialism: "Maternal indifference and failure coincided with the failure of colonialism in developing a clearly defined and centered people . . . the mother country too failed to give sustenance and definition to its child colonies" (10).

Rhys's work has been submitted to a variety of other feminist and psychoanalytic readings, most of which connect the theme of madness to issues of female discourse and narrative strategy.[1] Judith Kegan Gardiner uses Heinz Kohut's self psychology to argue that "Rhys and many of her heroes manifest a 'narcissistic personality disorder' with a weak sense of self and difficulties with self-esteem. . . . Inadequately mothered, the narcissistic woman cannot be an empathic mother herself" (21). *Wide Sargasso Sea*, Gardiner claims, "replaces Jane's absent mother, typical of the nineteenth-century novel, with the more common twentieth-century figure of the rejecting mother whom the daughter fears becoming" (128). Her view lends support to John Clayton's thesis about the ruptured family relationships at the root of modernist angst in general. That angst, he claims, is a form of narcissistic anxiety—"the experience of being a fragile or empty self in an empty world" (6). Beneath such severe narcissistic anxiety, as Otto Kernberg has shown, is often a borderline personality organization, and this is precisely the diagnosis that Rhys biographer Carole Angier received when she took a summary of Jean's life and character to several psychoanalysts of various schools (657).

The use of such clinical diagnostic terms as "borderline," "narcissistic," and "schizoid" has the effect, I am aware, of immediately raising the hackles of some literary critics. That reaction reflects, I believe, a misconception about the point of clinical terminology in literary analysis. The use of such a diagnostic term does not necessarily imply that the critic is branding the work with a derogatory label and dismissing it as sick. From a psychoanalytic perspective, artistic creativity can always be understood as a response to and creative transformation of psychic loss and pain.[2] The pertinent issue in psychoanalytic literary criticism is not a question of whether the pain infusing the work is "sick" or not; rather, it is a question of how the suffering shapes the text and relates to the cultural context. The clinical concepts and definitions can help us chart the territory of emotional pain in the work—pain that is, in varying degrees and forms, intrinsic to human life.

While several critics, as mentioned above, have noted the schizoid, narcissistic, or borderline symptoms apparent in Rhys's character and that of her heroines, they have not psychoanalyzed any of her texts as a whole in terms of the dynamics, both interpersonal and intrapsychic, engendering those symptoms. A close reading of *Wide Sargasso Sea* from a relational perspective can reveal a coherent psychological patterning involved not only in the novel's characterizations but also in its imagery and narrative style. The novel's patterning, in turn, can illuminate the relational and emotional vicissitudes involved in boundary formation and the psychic construction of the self. None of the other psychoanalytic readings of Rhys's work has focused on this particular area—on the connection between trust and boundaries and its relation to Rhys's literary vision overall.

The power of *Wide Sargasso Sea* resides more in its evocation of a psychological and emotional state than in its plot or story; its force is more lyrical than narrative. Like a poem, it builds rhythmically through the repetition of images—such as fire and the color red—and words— such as "nothing." Words and names in the novel function poetically by assuming symbolic reality beyond their role as signifiers—such as when Antoinette insists that "names matter, like when he wouldn't call me Antoinette, and I saw Antoinette drifting out of the window" (180). Although part 1 of the narrative is told from Antoinette's point of view, and the majority of part 2 from Rochester's, the two voices are in many respects indistinguishable. Because all of the characters, as I will show, are projections or versions of a single subjective state, the real tensions of the narrative arise not out of the conflicts of different or competing characters, but out of a split or divided internal condition and the terrors it generates. The fact that all of the characters express a single sensibility is related to the tragically paradoxical conflict kindling the novel: a deep yearning for human contact with an other clashes with, and is ultimately defeated by, the self's subsuming of the other in its own subjectivity. A self without boundaries dooms the other to nonexistence since without delimiting borders, there is nothing outside of the self.

True contact with an other demands the recognition and acceptance of external reality. From a Freudian perspective, such recognition is always painful—external reality inevitably conflicts with desire. Winnicott, however, has stressed the "relief and satisfaction" that external reality affords: "In fantasy things work by magic: there are no brakes on fantasy, and love and hate cause alarming effects. External reality has brakes on it, and can be studied and known, and, in fact, fantasy is only tolerable at full blast when objective reality is appreciated well. The subjective has tremendous value but is so alarming and magical that it cannot be enjoyed except as a parallel to the objective" (*Through Paediatrics* 153). This is an insight that the alarming and magical world of *Wide Sargasso Sea* powerfully demonstrates.

Angier's biographical account of Rhys's infancy and childhood on the island of Dominica suggests some of the complicating factors in Jean's early emotional life. Prior to Rhys's birth, her parents lost a baby daughter to dysentery. Angier believes that "Jean was the baby they had to assuage their grief over the loss of her little sister" (11). She speculates that Jean's birth did not pull the mother out of her depression; a mourning mother, Angier argues, left Jean "with a lifelong sense of loss and emptiness, of being wanted by no one and belonging nowhere; of being nothing, not really existing at all" (11). Angier also points out that Jean was originally named Ella Gwen—both names of dead girls, the baby daughter and the mother's deceased sister. It is little wonder, Angier suggests, that Jean, like her heroines, often felt unreal, like a ghost, and that she attached peculiar importance to names.

When Jean turned five, her relationship with her mother was aggravated further by the birth of her sister Brenda. "My mother didn't like me after Brenda was born," Rhys wrote in her autobiography *Smile Please* (42). The father's role in her very early childhood seems minimal, and Angier also describes a sour and unfeeling nanny who Jean believed " 'couldn't bear the sight of me' " (Angier 12). Jean's feelings of rejection and marginality in relation to her family were only intensified by her experience of being a white colonial child on a West Indian island. As Angier discusses, she envied the black people for what she saw as their warmth, gaiety, and easy sense of belonging; she wanted to be like them, felt they " 'were more alive, more part of the place than we were' " (Angier 13).

How then does this early relational history figure into the composition of what most critics consider to be Rhys's masterpiece, *Wide Sargasso Sea*? The novel, first of all, took Rhys nine years to write, though Angier believes "its essence was there after four, perhaps even after one and a half" (495). The self-doubt that always plagued Rhys only intensified with age. She never felt the manuscript was ready and was terrified of having it seen. Angier describes how she fired a string of typists because once her work was typed, it looked too finished, too ready to be seen: "It was this terror of being seen which made her keep *Wide Sargasso Sea* back for nine years" (495). The terror of being seen is a product of shame, of a deep unconscious association of self-exposure with humiliation. Shame not only kept Rhys from publishing the manuscript for nine years, but, I would like to suggest, is also a central organizing affect of the novel.

Shame is a subject receiving increasing attention from psychoanalytic theorists, particularly as it is rooted in relational issues and intertwined with narcissistic disorder. Andrew Morrison (*Shame: The Underside of Narcissism*), working from a self-psychological perspective, sees shame sensitivity as both a reflection of a defective, incomplete self and a defense against such deficit or narcissistic vulnerability. Shame is elicited, he believes, by failures in the two vital relationships crucial to the early construction of the self—what Heinz Kohut has defined as the bipolar merging-mirroring and idealizing relationships with a primary other or selfobject. Shame is thus tied to a defective self-structure; it is bound up with poorly differentiated boundaries between self and other, and with conflicts over autonomy and merger.

Throughout *Wide Sargasso Sea*, shame forms a sort of leitmotif, affecting both characterization and plot structure. References are made repeatedly to an enraged fear of being laughed at, jeered, or scorned. This fear is expressed in relation to Antoinette, her mother Annette, and the Rochester character, and all at crucial points in the story; the dread of being laughed at, the shameful perception of oneself as exposed and humiliated, directs the narrative by playing a determining role in the characters' choices. At the beginning of the novel, Antoinette makes a point of how her mother was laughed at by the black people of the island: "the black people stood about in groups to jeer at her" (18) when her mother went riding; or when she walked along the terrace, "They stared, sometimes they laughed. Long after the sound was far away and faint she kept her eyes shut and her hands clenched" (20). The lines that immediately follow reveal how the mother's shame is inexorably tied to the daughter's. Antoinette describes the frown that would form between her mother's eyebrows: "Once I touched her forehead trying to smooth it. But she pushed me away, not roughly but calmly, coldly, without a word, as if she had decided once and for all that I was useless to her" (20).

The mother's final act of spirit, of self-assertion, before she succumbs to a state of complete inertia and mental decay occurs as the family estate is burning down. She wants to go back to save her pet parrot but is restrained by her husband. Only when Aunt Cora calls her name and snaps, "They are laughing at you, do not allow them to laugh at you" (41) does Annette stop fighting and submit to being "half supported, half pulled" away from the scene. Two other pivotal points in the story, moments when Antoinette has the chance to save herself by rejecting

Rochester, are also linked to the fear of being the target of others' laughter. The morning before the scheduled wedding, Antoinette balks. She explains to Rochester that there was a moment when he laughed and "I didn't like the way you laughed" (79). Later, after the marriage has deteriorated, Antoinette's beloved black caretaker Christophine advises her to "pack up and go," but Antoinette refuses: "No, I will not, then everyone, not only the servants, will laugh at me" (109). In the first instance, Rochester persuades her to go through with the wedding by insisting that he was not laughing at her, but at himself. He kisses her and proclaims, "I'll trust you if you'll trust me" (79). The novel only goes on to prove the bitter irony of that statement—the utter impossibility of such trust—and confirms Antoinette's worst fear that she is indeed so worthless and ludicrous that she must be kept hidden away in an attic room.

The same shameful fear of being the object of others' laughter, however, is also associated with Rochester at a turning point in the story. His rejection and betrayal of Antoinette are first triggered by a letter suggesting that he is a victim of her family's treachery: Antoinette's mother is mad, the letter explains, and he has been tricked into marriage with a girl with "bad blood," whose fate will assuredly be the same. The letter's author is Daniel Cosway, a boy of mixed blood who claims to be Antoinette's illegitimate half-brother (and thus he too feels victimized and betrayed by the family). After reading the letter, Rochester repeatedly describes his perception that the servant girls are laughing at him: Hilda "put her hand over her mouth as if to stifle laughter" (119); Amelie "smiled at me, and I felt that at any moment her smile would become loud laughter" (120); "Like Hilda she put her hand over her mouth as though she could not stop herself from laughing and walked away" (121). And Cosway too, when he pays Rochester a visit, tells him, "Must be you deaf you don't hear people laughing when you marry her" (125).

The extreme sensitivity to shame that the fear of being laughed at reflects is psychologically entwined with the novel's pervasive theme of betrayal. As O'Connor observes of the novel, "All the characters, early in their lives, have incorporated a sense of betrayal from the past: Antoinette by her mother; Antoinette's mother by the blacks; Daniel Cosway by his father and Rochester by his" (197). The maternal betrayal Antoinette suffers is particularly bitter and severe. From the beginning Antoinette portrays her mother as favoring her retarded brother Pierre.

When Antoinette wakes, for instance, from a terrifying nightmare (a recurring dream that I will return to later), her mother "sighed and covered me up. 'You were making such a noise. I must go to Pierre, you've frightened him' " (27). After the estate has burned and Pierre has died, Antoinette's reunion scene with her mother is devastating:

> She held me so tightly that I couldn't breathe and I thought, "It's not her." Then, "It must be her." She looked at the door, then at me, then at the door again. I could not say, "He is dead," so I shook my head. "But I am here, I am here," I said, and she said, "No," quietly. Then "No no no" very loudly and flung me from her. (48)

Antoinette's presence is said only to "make trouble" for her mother. At another attempted reunion, Antoinette describes how her mother "pushed me away and cried. . . . They told me I made her worse" (134). A child's sense of betrayal, of worthlessness and deep shame in relation to her first beloved other is at the crux of this novel. As O'Connor notes, "betrayal leads to madness, madness to betrayal; the two are barely separable" (197). I would like to explore this madness-betrayal connection more deeply, examining its intrapsychic dimensions and its effect on Rhys's vision overall. Mental disintegration or madness, from an object relations perspective, can indeed be understood as tied to betrayal, to a breakdown of trust in the primary self-other relationship. For the infant self, the lack of a reliable, loving, and "holding" other can impede the processes of integration and differentiation in which boundaries are explored and external reality—or the "not me"—is discovered.

Rhys's novels, particularly her earlier ones, have in fact been criticized for their solipsistic quality—for their failure to make any of the characters, other than the female protagonist, real. The psychological universe of the female protagonist, furthermore, is one that conforms quite closely to what Melanie Klein has described as the primitive, unintegrated, "paranoid-schizoid" position of early psychic life: her heroine's world is ruled by feelings of persecution, envy, shame, and self-pity, by a "hungry love"—a starving neediness—that is terrifying in its devouring ferocity. The hungry self experiences the object of its love as withholding and depriving; the destructive rage that experience provokes cannot be tolerated and is consequently projected outward—the external world is thus perceived as hostile and persecutory. Love itself is felt to be destructive and dangerous, and Rhys's novels reflect the futility and despair bound up with this condition.

In *Wide Sargasso Sea*, however, I agree with Angier that Rhys gains "artistic control over her demon of self-pity" (528). Unlike her earlier fiction, in this novel the oppressing, persecuting others are not mere shadowy, unreal figures: Antoinette's mother, and especially Rochester, are invested with their own inner lives, indeed with the female protagonist's own subjectivity. For the first time Rhys extends her pity to characters other than her alter-ego heroine. In a letter to Diana Athill, Rhys in fact describes what she considered a "Breakthrough" in her characterization of Rochester. She realizes that her initial portrayal of him as "a heel" was "all wrong":

Mr. Rochester is *not* a heel. He is a fierce and violent (Heathcliff) man who marries an alien creature, partly because his father arranges it, partly because he has had a bad attack of fever, partly no doubt for *lovely* mun, but most of all because he is *curious* about this girl—already half in love.

Then (this is good old Part II) they get to this lovely lonely magic place and there is no "half" at all. . . .

I have tried to show this man being magicked by the place which is (or was) a lovely, lost *and magic* place but, if you understand, a *violent* place. (Perhaps there is violence in *all* magic and *all* beauty—but there—very strong) magicked by the girl—the two are mixed up perhaps to bewildered English gent, Mr R, certain that she's hiding something from him. And of course she *is*. Her mad mother. (Not mad perhaps at all) So you see—when he gets this letter all blows sky high. (*Letters* 269)

Rochester is "magicked," Rhys says, just as Antoinette herself, and the island with which she is identified, is "lovely, lost *and magic.*" Magic involves an eradication of boundaries: inner wish becomes one with external reality. Magic is also associated with love in the novel. Antoinette secures a magic potion from Christophine in a final desperate attempt to win back Rochester's love. The potion, however, proves only to have the opposite effect and in fact seals her doom. The novel effectively demonstrates Rhys's belief that violence and destruction are inherent "in *all* magic and *all* beauty"—in all love and desire. Rhys succeeds in humanizing Rochester by investing him with the same tragic subjectivity as her heroine: both Rochester and Antoinette are trapped in a boundless magical state in which love is inseparable from enraged hostility, from violence and destruction.

Gardiner rightly argues that boundary issues of inclusion and exclusion are central to Rhys's fiction. "In Rhys's later work," she states, "inclusion comes to comprehend exclusion rather than be opposed to it, and the spatial and social aspects of inclusion/exclusion deepen to a concern for the moral and esthetic meanings of including other's experiences in one's own" (23). While I agree that such inclusion in *Wide Sargasso Sea* does represent a breakthrough for Rhys in relation to her earlier work, it still poses problems that Gardiner fails to recognize. The total inclusion of the other in one's own subjectivity still dooms the possibility of genuine relationship: the other needs to be recognized as both same *and* externally other. *Wide Sargasso Sea* plays out both the yearning and the despair that arise from such a totally inclusionary state in which the boundaries between self and other are missing.

Antoinette's recurring nightmare provides a microcosm of this terrifying subjective state and reveals the relational dynamics that are again at its root. The first time Antoinette has the dream, her description of it is terse: she is walking in the forest, but "not alone. Someone who hated me was with me, out of sight. I could hear heavy footsteps coming closer and though I struggled and screamed I could not move" (26–27). The context for the dream here is significant. Antoinette had been caught wearing the dress of her black friend Tia. Immediately preceding the dream, Antoinette relates how "all that evening my mother didn't speak to me or look at me and I thought, 'She is ashamed of me' " (26). She wakes from the dream to find "my mother looking down at me" (27) and is then admonished, as quoted earlier, for having frightened Pierre. The dream is encompassed, in other words, by the experience of shame and rejection in relation to the mother; and the dream itself reflects the psychic consequences: the narcissistic shame and rage are projected outward into a paranoid fantasy that the self is being followed, persecuted by a shadowy, unrecognizable other who renders the self helpless and paralyzed. The shadowy persecutor is of course associated with Rochester, who is significantly never actually *named* by Rhys. Despite the novel's breakthrough in granting him subjectivity in part 2, it never really prevails over Antoinette's underlying paranoid conception of the other—and of external reality—as unrealized and obscure, and as invariably destructive of the self.

The second time Antoinette has the dream she is in the convent, a place she experiences as a "refuge." Rochester, though, has begun to court her there, and following one of his visits, Antoinette expresses her sudden resentment of the nuns: "They are safe. How can they know what it can be like *outside?*" (59). The second version of the dream immediately follows this thought, illustrating even more elaborately her view of the outside—the world of the other and of love and desire—as alien and persecutory. This time she is following the man who is holding up the skirt of her dress:

It is white and beautiful and I don't wish to get it soiled. I follow him, sick with fear but I make no effort to save myself; if anyone were to try to save me, I would refuse. This must happen. Now we have reached the forest. We are under the tall dark trees and there is no wind. "Here?" He turns and looks at me, his face black with hatred, and when I see this I begin to cry. He smiles slyly. "Not here, not yet," he says, and I follow him, weeping. Now I do not try to hold up my dress, it trails in the dirt, my beautiful dress. We are no longer in the forest but in an enclosed garden surrounded by a stone wall and the trees are different trees. I do not know them. There are steps leading upwards. It is too dark to see the wall or the steps, but I know they are there and I think, "It will be when I go up these steps. At the top." I stumble over my dress and cannot get up. I touch a tree and my arms hold on to it. "Here, here." But I think I will not go any further. The tree sways and jerks as if it is trying to throw me off. Still I cling and the seconds pass and each one is a thousand years. "Here, in here," a strange voice said, and the tree stopped swaying and jerking. (60)

This version of the dream emphasizes again the hostility, contempt, and obscurity of the other (he is still shadowy and "strange") but also Antoinette's passive compliance and her sense of inevitability ("This must happen"), particularly the inevitability of corruption and contamination (her beautiful white dress gets sullied).[3] It stresses the betrayal of the familiar: the trees are suddenly different and unrecognizable, recalling Antoinette's panic while embracing her mother after the fire—" 'It's not her.' Then, 'It must be her.' " And the tree to which she tries to "cling" for protection "jerks as if it is trying to throw me off," evoking again that same embrace and her mother's having "flung" her away. The dream's associations with the mother are further enforced by the white dress, which Annette often wore, and also by an explicit connection Antoinette makes herself. After she wakes, one of the nuns offers her a chocolate drink, and Antoinette recalls having drunk chocolate at her mother's funeral. She reflects on how she was unable to cry at the funeral, and though she prayed, "the words fell to the ground meaning nothing. Now the thought of her is mixed up with my dream" (61).

The mother's rejection and betrayal, which from the child's perspective includes her death, leaves Antoinette with a profound sense of futility and nothingness, with a fatalism about all intimate relationships. Thus her "thought" of her mother—her mental identification and internalized relations with her—is indeed inextricably "mixed up" with her dream. The dream's representation of the other (and the external world) as a vague, threatening, and hostile presence is also echoed by the question the mother's parrot Coco repeatedly shrieks, "Qui est là? Qui est là?" Who is there? What menacing stranger lurks? The parrot is identified with both the mother and Antoinette. Coco too has been betrayed by men—his wings were clipped by Mr. Mason—and his death foreshadows Antoinette's. He dies in the fire in a final, brilliant self-exhibition: his "feathers alight," he falls as his clipped wings fail, "screeching" and "all on fire" (43).

The fatalistic view that desire and life are inevitably mixed up with and contaminated by hatred and destruction is one that Rochester expresses as well: "Desire, Hatred, Life, Death came very close in the darkness. Better not know how close. Better not think, never for a moment. Not close. The same . . . " (94). Jan Curtis has interpreted these lines as expressing a profound paradox at the heart of the novel, a "secret" that Rochester refers to when he says, "Only the magic and the dream are true—all the rest's a lie. Let it go. Here is the secret. Here" (168). Curtis compares Rochester's lines to a Zenlike embrace of paradox, of death-in-life and life-in-death, in which every boundary line is a "myth" (187). One problem with this interpretation is that the novel completely lacks the liberating serenity that should accompany such an enlightened acceptance of paradox. Hatred and death are not *integrated* with desire and life in balanced simultaneity or cyclical harmony in this novel; rather, hatred ultimately defiles desire, and death defeats life.

The same commingling of "Desire, Hatred, Life, Death" is also represented in the novel's many references to zombies and black magic. A child taunts Antoinette that her mother has "eyes like zombie and you have eyes like zombie too" (50). Finding a book on the island black magic known as "obeah," Rochester reads, " 'A zombi is a dead person who seems to be alive or a living person who is dead. A zombi can also be the spirit of a place, usually malignant but sometimes to be propitiated with sacrifices or offerings of flowers and fruit. . . . They cry out in the wind that is their voice, they rage in the sea that is their anger' " (107). Like the zombie spirit of the island swept by the wind and sea here, Antoinette and her mother embody an isolated death-in-life or life-in-death condition driven by pain and rage. The other character associated with zombies and obeah in the novel is Christophine. Many critics share O'Connor's view of Christophine as the novel's "most sympathetic and unflawed character" (208). O'Connor believes that Christophine, as "the only character who does not betray," encompasses a " 'reality principle' in a world in which most of the characters express difficulty in determining what is real" (197). Christophine may represent the novel's "reality principle," but that reality is still an uncertain and far from wholly trustworthy one.

There is a "hidden" dimension to Christophine's character, associated with obeah—with dark power and death—that even Antoinette, who loves her, deeply fears. While waiting in Christophine's room, Antoinette

was suddenly very much afraid. The door was open to the sunlight, someone was whistling near the stables, but I was afraid. I was certain that hidden in the room . . . there was a dead man's dried hand, white chicken feathers, a cock with its throat cut, dying slowly, slowly. . . . No one had ever spoken to me about obeah—but I knew what I would find if I dared to look. Then Chrisophine came in smiling and pleased to see me. Nothing alarming ever happened and I forgot, or told myself I had forgotten. (31)

Her qualifying the assertion that she forgot with the addendum "or told myself I had forgotten," suggests that the memory, and the fear, did in fact remain. This implies, again, a profound mistrust: hidden within the sunny room, as behind Christophine's smiling face, is a darker, more sinister reality. Though Christophine *is* good to Antoinette—she does try to help—her obeah love potion only vindicates Rochester's mistrust, turning his love irrevocably to hate: "No more false heavens. No more damned magic. You hate me and I hate you. We'll see who hates best" (170). Thus, despite good intentions, Christophine too is bound up with betrayal. After Antoinette secures the potion from her, she hears a cock crow and thinks, " 'That is for betrayal, but who is the traitor?' She did not want to do this. I forced her with my ugly money. And what does anyone know about traitors, or why Judas did what he did?" (118). In other words, Christophine is indeed associated with the novel's "reality principle"—the principle of betrayal as destiny. That principle in turn is connected to the novel's pervasive psychic reality: a boundless magical state in which love is polluted by rage and the self is trapped in its own perilous omnipotence.

Antoinette's relationship with another black character in the novel, Tia, is also ambivalent and psychologically complex. In the tradition of the double found in so much twentieth-century literature, Tia functions as a reflection or split-off projection of the protagonist herself. As the estate burns in part 1, Antoinette sees Tia and runs to her,

for she was all that was left of my life as it had been. We had eaten the same food, slept side by side, bathed in the same river. As I ran, I thought, I will live with Tia and I will be like her. Not to leave Coulibri. Not to go. Not. When I was close I saw the jagged stone in her hand but I did not see her throw it. I did not feel it either, only something wet, running down my face. I looked at her and I saw her face crumple up as she began to cry. We stared at each other, blood on my face, tears on hers. It was as if I saw myself. Like in a looking-glass. (45)

Despite being poor and black, Tia, from Antoinette's point of view, is in an enviable position: she is secure in her connection and identification with the island. In Antoinette's eyes, this connection also empowers Tia with an almost invulnerable strength: "Fires always lit for her, sharp stones did not hurt her bare feet, I never saw her cry" (23). Antoinette thus adores Tia for embodying what she herself lacks; in contrast to her own fractured and enfeebled state, Tia represents an idealized, impregnable wholeness.

Yet Tia is also explicitly cruel and treacherous. She throws the stone in the above incident, just as earlier she tricks Antoinette into doing somersaults under water in order to steal her pennies and dress. Tia, like Antoinette, is full of envy and enraged hostility. Unlike Antoinette, however, Tia *acts* on her anger; she is assertive and aggressive rather than helplessly passive and submissive. In this sense, Tia most accurately mirrors Antoinette's repressed "true" self—her enraged aggressive self that is clamoring for expression. This "true" self, however, is the very source of the rejection and shame Antoinette experiences in relation to her mother. She is significantly wearing Tia's dress that evening of her dream when her mother refuses to speak or look at her, convincing Antoinette that her mother is indeed "ashamed" of her.

Tia, however, is not the only character who functions as a double, mirror, or echo of the self in this novel. Antoinette and her mother Annette not only echo one another in their names, but they also share the same betrayed, bereft, and isolated condition—" 'Marooned,' said her [Annette's] straight narrow back, her carefully coiled hair. 'Marooned' " (26). Antoinette's fate of fire, madness, and death will equally mirror her mother's. Finally, Rochester, too, plays a similar reflecting role. Most feminist critics have interpreted Rochester as representative of the oppressive patriarchy with its rigid categories of rationality and logic. Like Abel, they see Antoinette and Rochester as embodying "two fundamentally different ways of ordering experience" ("Women and Schizophrenia" 173). O'Connor similarly believes that in this novel, "the male and female worlds are more completely and consciously polarized than in any of Rhys's other fiction" (181). Yet this interpretation neglects the profound similarities in vision and voice of these two characters.

Rochester, first of all, shares Antoinette's emotional history of betrayal by a parent who preferred a sibling. He writes to his father toward the end of part 2, "I know now that you planned this because you wanted to be rid of me. You had no love at all for me. Nor had my brother" (162). The father had indeed arranged the marriage, and for most of the short period leading up to the wedding, Rochester is sick and feverish. Like Antoinette, he passively submits to a destiny that has been arranged for him by others who are indifferent to his own desires or needs. Just as Antoinette's dream depicts her struggling along a path she is forced to follow, linked with a menacing stranger in an alien and ominous environment, so too Rochester finds himself living out a similar dream. He repeatedly describes the island as alien and menacing: "The trees were threatening and the shadows of the trees moving slowly over the floor menaced me. That green menace. I had felt it ever since I saw this place. There was nothing I knew, nothing to comfort me" (149). He too feels forced into connection with a stranger in an environment that threateningly pursues—"Those hills would close in on you" (69)—and pressures him on all sides: "Everything is too much, I felt as I rode wearily after her. Too much blue, too much purple, too much green. The flowers too red, the mountains too high, the hills too near. And the woman is a stranger" (70).

Nevertheless, Rochester hides his true feelings—"How old was I when I learned to hide what I felt? A very small boy" (103)—and assumes his expected role—"I played the part I was expected to play" (76). This is echoed in Antoinette's confession to Rochester that after the day she was caught in Tia's dress and "everything changed," she "learned to hide" her feelings of hatred and fear. Rochester recognizes the ruse, though, and responds, "You have never learned to hide it" (132). Yet in an important sense Rochester does experience Antoinette, and the island itself, as hiding its secret truth—its essential being—from him. He refers repeatedly to the "secret" of the place: "What I see is nothing—I want what it *hides*—that is not nothing" (87). He hates the place, he says:

I hated its beauty and its magic and the secret I would never know. I hated its indifference and the cruelty which was part of its loveliness. Above all I hated her. For she belonged to the magic and the loveliness. She had left me thirsty and all my life would be thirst and longing for what I had lost before I found it. (172)

This same thirst for what was lost before it was found applies equally to Antoinette. Christophine tells Rochester that Antoinette "love you so much. She thirsty for you" (157), and the phrase "she thirsty for you" echoes in his head again later, though he thinks bitterly, "She thirsts for *anyone*—not for me" (164–65).

Both Rochester and Antoinette suffer from a raging, "thirsty" love that ultimately overpowers its object, negating the other's subjectivity. Feminist interpretations of Rochester stressing the rigid and controlling aggressor have missed this underlying dynamic. Rochester craves the same recognition of his being, of his singular subjectivity, as Antoinette, and feels equally as denied. Toward the end of part 2, he thinks,

I'll watch for one tear, one human tear. Not that blank hating moonstruck face. I'll listen. . . . If she says good-bye perhaps adieu. . . . If she too says it, or weeps, I'll take her in my arms, my lunatic. She's mad, but *mine, mine*. What will I care for gods or devils or for Fate itself. If she smiles or weeps or both. *For me.* (165–66)

Rochester's feelings here mirror Antoinette's rage and despair when Rochester calls her "Bertha," a name she feels is not her own—is not *her*. Both characters are furious at being *unrealized* by the other. Each expresses the same feeling that the world of the other is "unreal," like a dream. Antoinette asks if "England is like a dream? . . . a cold dark dream," and thinks, "Yes a big city must be like a dream." Rochester, however, responds, "that is precisely how your beautiful island seems to me, quite unreal and like a dream" (80–81). If the other is unreal, then the self too remains unrealized and trapped in its own powerful dream. Wounded at the core by the experience of a betraying other, both Rochester and Antoinette suffer the same enraged, thirsty love that dooms the other to nonexistence. Only their reactions to this condition differ. Antoinette totally surrenders to her dangerous love and, as Rochester notes about her after lovemaking, is "lost and drowned" (92). She yields to her need for a total, fusing love, knowing that it ultimately means death. Rochester seeks to dominate rather than merge, or in Christophine's words, to "break up" the wounding, threatening other. He will rob the other of all passion, rendering her powerless: "I will destroy your hatred. Now. My hate is colder, stronger, and you'll have no hate to warm yourself. You will have nothing" (170). Rhys shows that within both the oppressor and the oppressed are the same yearning and despair. In this novel both absolute surrender and absolute domination spring from the same disruption in the fundamental self-other experience.

At the end of part 2, Rochester observes a "nameless boy" leaning against a tree, crying in "loud heartbreaking sobs." Antoinette explains that when they first arrived on the island, the boy had asked "if we—if you—would take him with you when we left. He doesn't want any money. Just to be with you." The reason, she continues, is that "he loves you very much." He is crying because he has learned that Rochester will not take him, though originally Antoinette had said that he would (171). The nameless boy with his heartbreaking sobs expresses the deep pain—the core experience—at the heart of this novel: the experience of a child who feels mortally betrayed by the one he most admires and loves. The fact that he is "nameless" reflects the lack of self-identity or "I-ness"—the sense of the self's nothingness—bound up with this experience.

Rochester significantly responds to the boy with fury and contempt: "I could have strangled him with pleasure" (170). The contemptuous rage with which he responds to his own pain and helplessness mirrored in the boy allows us to understand why he responds similarly to Antoinette, who evokes these same feelings; he must strangle and destroy her as well. Rhys refers to Rochester in her letter to Athill as a "Heathcliff" man and the comparison is apt: both react to their buried loss and rage with the same violent contempt. Like Heathcliff in relation to Catherine, Rochester is less Antoinette's polar opposite than a vital part or projection of her. Part 2 ends with Rochester's observation, "That stupid boy followed us. . . . Who would have thought that any boy would cry like that. For nothing. Nothing" (173). The boy is crying for love—love that is once again equated with "nothing." It is the same "nothing" Antoinette feels at her mother's funeral, the same emptiness at the core of the self.

The final, brief part 3 of the novel returns to the original setting of *Jane Eyre.* Antoinette is locked in the attic of Thornfield Hall, and most of part 3 consists of her impressionistic account of the experience, along with a dream that precedes and predicts her burning of the estate. This last highly imagistic section provides one more version of the nameless boy scenario above; it creates a final tapestry of the controlling emotional and psychological threads running throughout the novel. Antoinette's associative musings reveal the dominant pattern. At one point she observes the tapestry hanging in the room: "Looking at the tapestry one day I recognized my mother dressed in an evening gown but with bare feet. She looked away from me, over my head just as she used to do" (180). This leads to the thought that she wouldn't tell this to her caretaker, Grace Poole: "Her name oughtn't to be Grace. Names matter, like when he wouldn't call me Antoinette, and I saw Antoinette drifting out of the window with her scents, her pretty clothes and her looking-glass." The looking-glass association is then elaborated in the paragraph that follows:

There is no looking-glass here and I don't know what I am like now. I remember watching myself brush my hair and how my eyes looked back at me. The girl I saw was myself yet not quite myself. Long ago when I was a child and very lonely I tried to kiss her. But the glass was between us—hard, cold and misted over with my breath. Now they have taken everything away. What am I doing in this place and who am I? (180)

Antoinette's thought of her mother looking away and typically not "seeing" her leads to her feeling of withdrawal, of wanting to keep her thought hidden ("I wouldn't tell Grace this"). This flows into her reflection on names—Rochester's refusal to name her properly and her resulting sense of self-dispersal—and finally to her past and present lack of identity—to her inability to "see" or know herself in any meaningful way. The original lack of recognition from the other (Rochester's failure repeats the mother's) leaves the child hidden and withdrawn, unable to recognize and affirm herself, to make contact with any authentic sense of her own being. As with the "hard, cold" glass of the mirror, contact with an authentic self is obstructed. Furthermore, both self and other are blurred, obscured by an inescapable solipsism: the mirror fails to reflect because it is "misted over with my breath." The locked attic room itself also typifies this sense of entrapment in one's own mental world and its nightmare projections.

These same dynamics fuel the imagery of Antoinette's final dream. Prior to the dream, Antoinette pulls down her favorite red dress: "Does it make me look intemperate and unchaste?" she asks Grace Poole (186). Throughout the novel the color red is associated with her passionate, intemperate (Tia) self. She writes her name, for instance, in "fire red" (53) on the needlepoint tapestry she cross-stitches at the convent. The red also associates with the fire of the dream and the actual burning of Thornfield that it forecasts. The fire in the dream both protects and scorches: "There was a wall of fire protecting me but it was too hot, it scorched me and I went away from it." The sky in the dream "was red and all my life was in it." Images from her life at Coulibri pour forth, and the dream ends with these lines:

Tia was there. She beckoned to me and when I hesitated, she laughed. I heard her say, You frightened? And I heard the man's voice, Bertha! Bertha! All this I saw and heard in a fraction of a second. And the sky so red. Someone screamed and I thought, *Why did I scream?* I called "Tia!" and jumped and woke. (190)

The scream is an impassioned cry of the wounded, divided self, and the call for Tia (still associated with laughter and the feeling of shame) is a final attempt at self-contact and wholeness. The passionate Tia-self, however, like the fire, ultimately cannot be tolerated; the self cannot survive its full expression. As the fire both protects and scorches, so the buried passion that signifies salvation of her true self is a scorching love that finally obliterates the self. Gardiner believes that Antoinette "achieves her identity" and "fulfills herself" through her dream (131). Abel too interprets the ending positively—the burning of Thornfield represents a "liberating form of self-assertion" ("Women and Schizophrenia" 174). Antoinette and the novel as a whole, however, never break out of the imprisoning equation of self-assertion with annihilation, of love with inevitable destruction. The ending does not portray an act of free, spontaneous self-expression; rather, it merely enacts a preordained destiny— the destiny of fire, madness, and death set by both the mother and the mother text, *Jane Eyre*. It is difficult to see the ending as liberating when it only confirms Antoinette's original nightmare: pursued by a menacing stranger, she has climbed the steps that led inexorably to her own destruction. The novel indeed reflects the terror and despair of a condition in which one cannot escape the omnipotence of one's own dreams.

Wide Sargasso Sea exposes, finally, the psychic pain and disintegration that result from a collapsing relational network. The interpersonal betrayals in this novel are continuous with the encompassing cultural and historical betrayals. The breached and distorted relations between men and women and between blacks and whites in a patriarchal, colonial society are inseparable from the breaches and distortions in the relationships of these particular characters. The mother's betrayal of her daughter is intertwined with her subjection to and betrayal by men, and her ambivalent position in relation to the blacks of the island. Similarly, Rochester's betrayal of Antoinette is indissoluble from his betrayal by his father and his subjection to the constraints of the economic system. The fractured interpersonal relations have intrapsychic repercussions: boundary construction is impeded—both self and world feel unreal—and love and hate remain unintegrated—hate is projected out, and love is felt to be dangerously destructive. Cultural and personal pathology, in other words, are interlinked.

The psychic condition that Rhys's novel depicts—the portrayal of an alienated, illusory self in relation to an incoherent, unreliable world—is considered from a Lacanian and postmodernist perspective as normative. While I believe that it does represent a modernist norm, I do not think it presents a "normal" condition of subjectivity, nor an inevitable or necessary relationship between self and external world. The condition is historically specific—grounded in a relational instability characteristic of the culture and the time. That *Wide Sargasso Sea* depicts a pathological psychic state does not mean, however, that it is without aesthetic or social value. The novel accesses, with great lyrical force, the intense emotions, the primal self-other relations and unconscious mental dynamics common to early psychic life. Nor is the pathological ever wholly alien to the normal. As Winnicott has pointed out, much sanity "has a symptomatic quality, being charged with fear or denial of madness, fear or denial of the innate capacity of every human being to become unintegrated, depersonalized, and to feel that the world is unreal. Sufficient lack of sleep produces these conditions in anyone" (*Through Paediatrics* 150). Winnicott appends a note to this statement with which I would like to conclude: "Through artistic expression we can hope to keep in touch with our primitive selves whence the most intense feelings and even fearfully acute sensations derive, and we are poor indeed if we are only sane."

Chapter 6

Updike, God, and Women: The Drama of the Gifted Child

One of the most prominent features of Updike's fiction, and a topic equally prominent in the critical discussions of his work, is the conjunction of sex and religion. "Not many authors," quips Frederick Crews in a review of *Roger's Version*, "get to please the horny and the sanctimonious at one stroke" (7). When asked in an interview if it was not perhaps a mistake to connect sex with religion, Updike, as Brooke Horvath notes, "offered an implicit 'no,' responding that 'to have a woman or man love you is about like saying that the universe, appearances to the contrary, loves me. So maybe the same kind of people tend to be sexy and religious' " (73). This notion of a love relationship as fundamental not only to the sexual but also to the religious impulse is in fact the central assumption of current revisionist psychoanalytic studies of religion. Working from relational model perspectives, these studies view the self, as James Jones explains, as "but one pole of the relationships through which we sustain ourselves" and thus "religion would be defined not primarily as a defense against instincts or a manifestation of internalized objects but rather as a *relationship*" (63).

The relationship with God or the sacred grows out of, and is congruent with, the relationships—particularly the first, primary relationship between infant and mother—that shape and support the self. Issues of

105

dependency and autonomy, of helplessness and power, are highly involved in the psychology of religion. The religious thread in Updike's fiction is intertwined with a narrative of dependency and power in relation to women; the representations of God and women are interconnected and relationally determined. A psychoanalytic inquiry into the relational dynamics behind the erotic and religious in Updike's work can shed light on other aspects of his fiction as well: the underlying nihilism that many critics have noted, the strangely disdainful attitude toward moral goodness or virtue, the distancing and denigration of a central character, and even the linguistic dazzle of his style.

Apparent throughout Updike's writing, in the essays as well as the fiction, is a scorn for liberal humanistic religion and a conception of God, drawn from the theology of Karl Barth, as a "God men do not invent," as "*totaliter aliter*—Wholly Other" (*Assorted Prose* 273). Crews defines Updike's religious stance as "Christian-existential," characterized by "a fear (bordering on phobia) of eternal nonbeing; an attempt to reconcile both spiritual and erotic striving with awareness of the implacable heartlessness of the natural world; and a resultant struggle to believe in the grace of personal salvation" (7). As Updike's career has progressed, Crews argues, "he has radically divorced his notion of Christian theology from that of Christian ethics" (7), and Crews is severely critical of that dissociation. The separation between faith and ethics, I would argue, is not only progressive in Updike's oeuvre, but is there from the beginning: faith has always represented a flight from the human, an escape from what is intolerable and threatening in human relationships and human consciousness. "Faith," Updike declared in a 1966 interview in *Life* magazine, "is a leap out of total despair" (Howard 80). That despair is bound up with what Updike identifies in an essay on Denis de Rougemont as "our fundamental anxiety"—that "we do not exist—or will cease to exist" (*Assorted Prose* 283).

There seems little question, as critic Bernard Schopen as well as Crews has argued, that when the minister Tom Marshfield in *A Month of Sundays* calls "ethical passion the hobgoblin of trivial minds" (192), he is expressing Updike's own views. "What interests us," Marshfield proclaims, "is not the good but the godly. Not living well, but living forever" (192). Similarly, at the end of the story "Pigeon Feathers," which I will discuss more fully later, the central character, David, experiences a revelation after discovering the elaborately patterned feathers of the pigeons he has killed: he feels rapturously certain "that the God who had lavished such craft upon these worthless birds would not destroy His whole Creation by refusing to let David live forever" (105). In an interview with Richard Burgin, Updike again suggests "some deep alliance between the religious impulse and the sexual. Both are a way of perpetuating our lives, of denying our physical limits" (Burgin 10).

God is not a positive, felt reality in Updike's fictional world; the terror of disintegration and the dread of nothingness are the overwhelming realities in response to which God is projected in desperate counteraction. Faith becomes a denial of helpless dependency and, as Freud believed, an identification with the limitless power and being of God. The alliance with an established source of indifferent, implacable power is precisely what Crews finds so ethically despicable in Updike's work. Quoting again from one of Marshfield's sermons—"Somewhere, Barth says, 'What shall the Christian in society do but attend to what God does.' What God does in the world is Caesar"—Crews then comments, "Only by full acquiescence in established power, in other words, can the salvation-minded Christian ready himself for 'a way out of the crush of matter and time' " (10). The result of such an attitude is not Christian compassion for the weak or disadvantaged in society, but rather, contempt, and Crews points to several examples of this in *Roger's Version* (14). The construction of religious faith in Updike's work is, again, founded not in the conviction of God's presence or reality, but, contrarily, in the experience of absence, in the feeling that any significant or meaningful reality is alien from the self—"Wholly Other"—and inaccessibly remote. In an essay on Melville, Updike writes, "the awful absence of God . . . becomes, in a way, God" and this absence is "a horror so awesome as to excite worship" (*Hugging the Shore* 97–98).

This same sense of alien otherness, of remote and indifferent power, is also apparent in Updike's attitude toward women and female sexuality. Kathleen Verduin, for instance, points out the connection between Updike's "totaliter aliter" God and the line from his poem "Pussy": " 'Your pussy, it is my pet, it is my altar, totaliter / aliter: unknowable, known, and wild, subdued' " (310). If faith and sex are both leaps out of the despair of nothingness and death for Updike, they nevertheless seem only to lead him right back to a void. In *The Centaur*, Updike's alter ego, Peter, kneels before his girlfriend and discovers "a fact monstrous and lovely: where her legs meet there is nothing. . . . This then is the secret the world holds at its center, this innocence, this absence" (184). The experience of absence, though common to Updike's relations to both women and God, nevertheless arouses such extreme ambivalence that he strives to keep those relationships as separate as possible; the relationship with God needs to be protected from the intense rage that the experience of absence incites and that so conflicts his relations with women.

The following passage from the minister's sermon in *Of the Farm* expresses the radical division between woman and God, between the physical and the spiritual, that is reflected throughout Updike's writing:

Man, with Woman's creation, became confused as to where to turn. With one half of his being he turns toward her, his rib, as if into himself, into the visceral and nostalgic warmth wherein his tensions find resolution in dissolution. With his other half he gazes outward, toward God, along the straight line of infinity. He seeks to *solve* the riddle of his death. Eve does not. In a sense she does not know death. Her very name, *Hava*, means "living." (152)

This passage reveals a characteristic Updike paradox: while proclaiming that women are the essence of life, of the "living," it also implies that they are a source of inner "dissolution" and connected with the death or nothingness that must be fled or "solved" through the pursuit of God. In recent years feminist critics in particular have commented on this dualistic aspect of Updike's work. Suzanne Uphaus, for instance, argues that women (and the physicality they represent) always pose a threat to male spiritual aspiration in Updike's fiction. The dominating power of women, she says, "brings about the loss of supernatural yearning and the myth by which it seeks expression" (49).

Mary Allen makes the same argument even more censoriously. She sees the women in his fiction as absolutely excluded from any spiritual or mental life: "For the woman who would be anything more than a vegetable-wife, this writer is the cunning enemy" (69), and she concludes that "only the woman as a comfortable blank is to be desired and accepted by individual men and by society. Women who do not fit this standard are not really human and must be rubbed out of the world" (95). Like Uphaus, she points to all of the encircling images of nets and traps in the *Rabbit* novels, their association with female sexuality, and the threat of suffocation and constriction they inevitably represent. Many critics have indeed noted the ubiquitous alliance between women, nature, and death in Updike's work. "It had all seemed like a pit to him then, her womb and the grave, sex and death," thinks Rabbit Angstrom in *Rabbit Redux* (27). Or again, in *Rabbit Is Rich*, Rabbit looks at the weeds in his lawn and proclaims "Nature such a cruel smotherer" (47). "The natural," Updike asserted in the *Life* interview, "is a pit of horror" (Howard 80).

Kathleen Verduin argues that in *The Witches of Eastwick*, Updike struggles to come to terms with these dualities of nature and the supernatural, of male and female, and in fact resolves or transcends them. By making the Lucifer of the novel, Darryl Van Horne, openly contemptuous of the physical, organic world, Verduin maintains, Updike is implicitly rejecting this view since it is "of the Devil's party" (308). Furthermore, she argues, Updike grants his female witches masculine qualities and powers. Sukie's body is " 'boyish' "; Jane's upper lip is " 'slightly hairy' "; and the witches not only seek "to wield the masculine power to kill" (308), but they also reveal a "quest for transcendence and supernature" (311) that is usually reserved for men. When the character Brenda shouts "Pray!" at one point in the novel, Verduin notes that this is a "cry to a supernatural plane" rare for Updike's women and, moreover, it is uttered in " 'a hollow man's voice' " (314). Verduin's argument is to my mind unconvincing since I cannot understand how making females masculine is in any way resolving the dualism. It seems to me only another form of denial or dismissal: only by denying the women their femaleness and their separateness can he then abide or empower them.

Psychoanalytic relational model theories can offer a map for exploring in the texts the sources of his dualistic attitude; such a map, furthermore, can bring into relief a complex of interconnections in the fiction, a psychologically determined order or design that might not otherwise be visible. Recent psychoanalytic studies of religion, as mentioned earlier, stress the relational character of faith. John McDargh, in reference to the theology of Reinhold Niebuhr, writes, "The response which is evoked by the object of faith is the response of a self receiving and accepting recognition from another self, regardless of whether the locus of value and trust is conceived of as a person" (26).

These recent theorists on religion all stress the self's need for recognition and reflection by an other as the core experience in self development and in the formation of religious faith. Ana-Maria Rizzuto in her influential study *The Birth of the Living God* indeed argues that we all harbor some form of unconscious God representation derived from our early relational needs and experiences, though that representation may be repressed or denied. The mirroring or recognition of oneself by the m/other, she claims, "is the first direct experience the child has which is used in formation of the God representation" (185). William Meissner similarly maintains that "the mirroring components of the God representation find their first experience in eye contact, early nursing, and maternal personal participation in the act of mirroring" (188). Furthermore, if the child "has not found himself in the reflection and the object behind the mirror, he will maneuver defensively and fantasize elaborations to compensate by feeling 'like God' " (188).

D. W. Winnicott, on whose work these psychoanalytic theorists on religion often draw, has argued that insufficient mirroring can block apperception and the experience of "a significant exchange with the world" in which self and other hold both depth and meaning. "If the mother's face is unresponsive," he adds, "then a mirror is a thing to be looked at but not to be looked into" (PR 113). Common to both Updike's conception of God and his configurings of women is the image of a blank, obdurate surface that defies the probing or penetration of consciousness, that cannot "be looked into." The failure of the mother to provide adequate mirroring for her baby, Winnicott suggests, is due to her own narcissistic deprivations as a child and the consequent rigidity of her defenses. This vicious cycle is the subject of Alice Miller's *Drama of the Gifted Child*, and the drama she describes is highly pertinent to the dynamics of Updike's fictional world.

Miller's book is about what she calls "the loss of the self" due to the child's early emotional adaptation to an insufficiently responsive parental environment. By "gifted" child she means the particularly sensitive child who is alert to the subtle cues and unconscious emotional needs of the parents. Drawing primarily on the theories of Winnicott, Mahler, and Kohut, Miller argues that the crucial prerequisite for "healthy narcissism" or self-esteem is the fulfillment of the child's "primary need to be regarded and respected as the person he really is at any given time, and as the center—the central actor—in his own activity" (7). The "person he really is" refers to the child's "emotions, sensations, and their expression from the first day onward," which form the "core of the self... the crystallization point of the 'feeling of self' around which a 'sense of identity' will become established" (7). Parents, however, who did not grow up in this emotional climate themselves, who are emotionally insecure at the core, will seek gratification through their children—imposing their own feelings on them, using them to feel strong and important, seeing themselves mirrored in their children's love and admiration.

The gifted child who grows up in such an environment will lack access to his or her "true self," to a sense of authentic emotional life and the feeling of being truly alive. Instead, the child will cultivate an idealized, conforming false self and will often express contempt or derision for the needs and emotions that were denied. Such children frequently are high achievers with well-developed intellectual defenses, ever desirous of winning respect and admiration by way of their intellectual achievements. Beneath their successes, however, "lurks depression, the feeling of emptiness and self-alienation, and a sense that their life has no meaning" (6). Along with the depression resides "unconscious (or conscious but split off) fantasies of grandiosity. In fact, grandiosity is the defense against depression, and depression is the defense against the deep pain over the loss of the self" (38).

The above drama is enacted repeatedly in Updike's fiction. Leo Schneiderman refers to Updike's Roger Lambert in *Roger's Version*, for instance, as being "in search of a mirroring self-object that he can make part of his own inert and empty self. Such an undertaking is bound to fail because it is a matter of emptiness crying out to emptiness" (218). In many of the novels, the vacillation between depression and grandiosity is apparent in the alternation of nihilism and contemptuous superiority that Crews has pointed out in regard to Updike's religious stance. Most of Updike's central male characters, furthermore, are essentially childlike—relating to women and the world as wounded, angry children. Brooke Horvath has described Rabbit as the perpetual "kid with a grudge"; he is constantly represented, she argues, "mnemonically, psychologically, symbolically— as a child" (81). The autobiographical *Of the Farm* indeed ends with the Updike-character's mother and wife both referring to him as "a good boy" (173). The narcissistic nature of the mother-child relational dynamic at the root of this drama is especially apparent in Updike's early autobiographical stories and novels—*Of the Farm* and *Pigeon Feathers*, in particular—and in a more recent 1990 story published in *The New Yorker*—"A Sandstone Farmhouse," based on the death of his mother. The remainder of this essay will concentrate on these works, which from a psychoanalytic perspective are far more revealing of the author's highly conflictual, formative relationships than his overtly autobiographical memoir, *Self-Consciousness*.

Both the 1965 *Of the Farm* and the story "A Sandstone Farmhouse," published twenty-five years later, revolve around the central character Joey's return to the Pennsylvania farmhouse where he grew up and where his mother, alone and in ill health, still resides. In *Of the Farm*, Joey brings along his second wife, Peggy, and her stepson, and the tension between the two women in the house quickly accelerates to an angry boil. Joey, meanwhile, alternates in his allegiances, revealing his own anger and his resentful dependency on both of them. Intense ambivalence also characterizes Joey's final visit with his mother before she dies in "A Sandstone Farmhouse." The ambivalence is represented by a paradoxical state that is repeatedly evidenced—imagistically and thematically—throughout Updike's fiction: mother/woman is experienced at once as overwhelming and remote, smothering and distant, intrusive and yet hopelessly elusive. In relation to the self, the mother is felt to be suffocatingly invasive while simultaneously closed off, inaccessible, "wholly other." In "A Sandstone Farmhouse," Joey thinks, "He knew he and his mother were regarded as having been unusually, perhaps unnaturally close; when in fact between themselves the fear was that they were not close enough" (44–45).

Joey's paradoxical bind can be understood in terms of the the child's entanglement in the mother's unconscious, narcissistic world. As in the drama Miller describes, the mother experiences the child only as a projection or extension of herself, using him to bolster her own grandiosity. This deeply affects the child's own experience of himself; unrecognized as a separate being in his own right, he feels unreal, trapped in her dream. The mother's lack of boundaries gives rise to the child's experience of being terrifyingly overwhelmed, suffocated, or smothered. Joey indeed suffers from asthma, which is always reactivated when he returns to the farm (Updike writes about his own struggles with asthma and his fears of suffocation in *Self-Consciousness* 88–102). On the other hand, the mother, closed off from her own authentic emotional life or "true self," will also be experienced by the child as closed off, distant, and withholding. While he runs from her, he will also be perpetually in pursuit of her; on her elusive "reality" depends the sense of his own reality or authentic being. Joey and his mother are indeed "unnaturally close" in that the natural boundaries between them are missing; at the same time, however, as Joey realizes, they are "not close enough."

The mother's narcissism is apparent in the descriptions both of her and of the farm, the symbol of her world. It was, Joey describes, "as if in being surrounded by her farm we had been plunged into the very territory of her thoughts" (*Of the Farm* 13). Similarly, in "A Sandstone Farmhouse," Updike writes, "She loved the old house; she loved the *idea* of it. For most of her life . . . she happily inhabited an idea" (37). In both the novel and the story, we learn, furthermore, that the move to the farm was *solely* the mother's idea—both her husband and Joey opposed it. Joey and his passive father, however, are caught up in the mother's idealized fantasies, in the dominating projections of her mental world. The farmhouse is the same house she had lived in as a young child with her parents, and her buying it back represents an attempt to recapture the *idea* of her childhood, particularly an idealized relationship or connection with her parents: "This was the private paradise, then, to which she attempted to return, buying back the old sandstone farmhouse that her parents . . . had sold while she was innocently off at normal school" ("Sandstone Farmhouse" 37).

The mother felt betrayed by her parents' selling of the farmhouse, but there is evidence, particularly in the short story, that she had felt betrayed—narcissistically wounded—by her own mother long before, and thus buying back the farm is an attempt to recover a paradise that never existed. Though she moves back to the farm, she never really succeeds in recovering the lost childhood self that it represents. Her own child will in turn suffer the consequences of her relentless search for self; Joey indeed feels that she had "betrayed him with the farm and its sandstone house" (46) and is jealous of the farm itself: "He was determined to impress his mother—to win her back, since here on this farm he for the first time encountered something she apparently loved as much as she loved him" (39).

References are made throughout "A Sandstone Farmhouse" to the difficulties in the mother's relationship with her own mother, providing glimpses into the originating circumstances of her impaired self-esteem. Her mother, we are told several times, was a "little woman," while she herself was "big." Her birth had been long and agonizing, and Joey believed it "shaped her relations with her own mother into, it seemed, a ferocious apology, a futile undying adhesion in an attempt to make amends" (40). We learn that she nursed her mother during her equally long and agonizing dying, but "not always patiently, or tenderly," which added to her pattern of self-blame: " 'I spent my whole life,' she concluded, 'trying to please my mother, and never did' " (40). She also believes that her husband admired her mother more than herself, that he indeed married her only for her mother's sake: "He really admired my mother, that style of little woman. . . . But admiring Mother was no reason to marry me. I was *big*. It was a mistake, and we both knew it" (46). She tells Joey, in addition, that little women "have the best of it, and take the men from the big women like herself, big women who have tortured their little mothers in the birthing" (46–47).

Joey reflects that "behind these formulations there was something— about sex, he believed—that he didn't want, as a boy or a man, to hear" (47). The message was nevertheless communicated to the boy in a deep and visceral way. The mother's shame and contempt for her own physicality—her bodily, sexual self—may be one of the contributing factors in the contempt for the physical and the ambivalence toward female sexuality reflected throughout Updike's fiction. Joey even wonders "if women had not quite been his thing all along. He had always felt most at ease, come to think of it, in the company of men, especially those who reminded him of his father" (39). Anger, shame, and self-contempt rule the mother's inner life, an inner life to which the boy Joey is acutely attuned: "Even as a very small child he had been aware of a weight of anger his mother carried; he had quickly evolved—first word, first crawl—an adroitness at staying out of her way when she was heavy with it, and a wish to amuse her, to keep her light" (47). His negotiations with his mother's rage, in other words, set the parameters for his own evolution; his first words and movements, the whole direction of his being, aimed at appeasing her.

Joey is never more than a narcissistic object for the mother or, in Heinz Kohut's terms, a "selfobject"—an object "used in the service of the self" or "experienced as part of the self" (Kohut xiv). From Winnicott's perspective, the mother fails to provide an appropriately responsive, mirroring experience for the boy. Never having felt "real"—as a separate, whole, and loved being in his own right—in relation to the mother, Joey is ever in pursuit of his own reality, returning to his mother again and again for the recognition that she is incapable of giving. In "A Sandstone Farmhouse," Joey complains that the characters on the television comedies his mother faithfully watched " 'seem realer to you than I am' " and his mother "did not deny it" (42). After listening to his mother give an account of his birth, of how delighted she was that the doctor "treated her as a normal woman and not as the monstrous product of her own mother's agony," Joey suddenly realizes "that his own self . . . was lovable to her above all as a piece of her body, as a living proof of her womanhood" (42).

We learn that Joey's mother had had literary aspirations herself, and thus her promotion of Joey's literary ambitions is a cultivation of her own fantasy. She carefully collects and preserves each award he wins, each token of his achievement. With a passion Joey finds curious, she hoards the pictures, papers, all the symbols of his life. "Her passion for mementos of me," Joey reflects in the novel, "had begun before I realized that I had truly left" (16). Being the mother's grandiose selfobject, however, arouses deep ambivalence in the boy that continues into his manhood and affects his relations with women. The short story "Flight" in the *Pigeon Feathers* collection reveals the psychological repercussions of this central ambivalent relationship.

The story begins, "At the age of seventeen I was poorly dressed and funny-looking, and went around thinking of myself in the third person. 'Allen Dow strode down the street and home.' . . . Consciousness of a special destiny made me both arrogant and shy" (49). Alternate shame and arrogance define the emotional poles of this character, the Updike alter ego in the story, who feels so oddly disconnected from his own being that he thinks of himself in the third person. Allen's "special destiny" relates to his mother's pronouncement early on in the story that unlike herself and their friends and neighbors, who will remain in their small town of Olinger forever, " 'you, Allen,' " she says, " 'You're going to fly' " (50). Allen feels that "his most secret self had been made to respond, and I was intensely embarrassed" (50).

Allen's own grandiosity indeed reflects and responds to his mother's, though he complains that she does not consistently perform this idealizing function for him: "That she continued to treat me like an ordinary child seemed a betrayal of the vision she had made me share. I was captive to a hope she had tossed off and forgotten" (50). Allen suffers from the mother's own ambivalence and inner split; he must bear the projections of her self-contempt as well as her grandiosity. She yells at him at one point, " 'You'll never learn, you'll stick and die in the dirt just like I'm doing. Why should you be better than your mother?' " (51). Nevertheless, the grandiose fantasy prevails: "The entire town," Allen believes, "seemed ensnarled in my mother's myth, that escape was my proper fate" (67). As a result, Allen remarks that he had always felt "simultaneously flattered and rejected" by the town; this simultaneous flattery and rejection again mirrors his deepest experience in relation to his mother. His conflicting feelings toward her are repeated in his ambivalent treatment of his female classmate, Molly, with whom he becomes romantically involved in the story: "Even in the heart of intimacy, half-naked each of us, I would say something to humiliate her" (69). He torments her to please his mother, who of course believes Molly is not good enough for him—"Don't go with little women, Allen. It puts you too close to the ground" (65).

Allen's "most secret self" certainly agrees with his mother about Molly and his own superiority, and yet he is also profoundly resentful of his mother's power and dominance over him. Thinking back, he believes Molly may have been "the one person who loved me without advantage" (69). As the story ends, he and his mother are arguing about the girl when they hear Allen's grandfather first singing, and then coughing, in the room above them: "His voice broke into coughing, a terrible rending cough growing in fury, struggling to escape, and loud with fear he called my mother's name. She didn't stir. . . . I felt intensely angry, and hated that black mass of suffering, even while I realized, with a rapid, light calculation, that I was too weak to withstand it" (72). The grandfather's struggle is an overt expression of Allen's own inner turmoil: the feelings of suffocation, fear, and fury in relation to the mother who fails to respond. Allen himself, however, does not respond to the grandfather's suffering with compassionate empathy, but with intense anger and resentment. This response exposes the deep contempt with which Allen relates to his own pain and neediness; it reveals the roots of the shame and self-contempt that so many of Updike's male characters display, as well as their scorn for any display of helplessness or neediness in others. In *Of the Farm*, we learn that as a child, Joey "would torment his toys . . . trying to make them confess" (136), and that he cruelly teased a puppy that had once been trapped in a drainpipe by repeatedly threatening to push her in again. Such childish sadism can be understood as the child's attempt to master and control his own deep feelings of helplessness, entrapment, anger, and guilt.

Following Allen's hard and dry recognition of his own weakness at the end of "Flight," he says coldly, " 'All right. You'll win this one, Mother; but it'll be the last one you'll win" (72). That sentence leads into the story's concluding paragraph:

My pang of fright following this unprecedentedly cold insolence seemed to blot my senses; the chair ceased to be felt under me, and the walls and furniture of the room fell away—there was only the dim orange glow of the radio dial down below. In a husky voice that seemed to come across a great distance my mother said, with typical melodrama, "Goodbye, Allen." (72–73)

The terror and dissolution—the falling away of reality—that follows Allen's expression of rage toward his mother is related to the generalized fears of death and dissolution that haunt Updike's characters throughout his fiction. Allen describes to Molly "the steep waves of fearing death that had come over me ever since early childhood." This fear, a "dense, lead-like sea," makes him think that "it would take great courage to be an atheist" (62). Everywhere in Updike's fiction, the terror of death and the counteractive belief in God are tied to a terrifying inner rage that poses an ever-present threat of dissolution and annihilation.

The final image of Allen's ascendancy is also fraught with ambivalence and bitter irony. On the one hand, he is flying from his mother, escaping her, as he tries to dismiss her with his final repudiating words. On the other hand, his flight is precisely what his mother predicted, indeed commanded of him; the last thing he hears, her "melodramatic" voice saying "Goodbye," is only a reminder of the theatrical destiny she had always planned for him. However much he tries to flee, he is still "ensnarled in [his] mother's myth."

The intensely conflicting feelings involved in this original maternal relationship inform all of the relationships with women in Updike's fiction, and thus the erotic in his work is always heavily invested with aggressive and destructive feelings. "What man can exempt, from his purest sexual passion and most chivalrous love," Updike has written, "the itch to defile?" (Introduction, *Soundings in Satanism* x). The wish to defile the beloved can only be due to a deep resentment of her—resentment, in Updike's case, of what is felt to be her pure, obdurate impenetrability and superior power over the self. Updike's men continually seek remote, inviolably self-contained women, and then become furious at them for those very qualities. The remoteness is desirable, however, not only because it duplicates a quality experienced in relation to the ever-desired mother but also because it is felt to protect against the more serious threat of suffocation and entrapment.

In *Of the Farm*, Joey refers to Peggy as "withdrawn and cool," and describes his sense of her "composure" as a kind of "non-commital witnessing that preserves me from claustrophobia through any descent however deep" (47). He says he never felt this way in relation to his first wife, Joan, but the imagery he uses to describe her suggests otherwise: "I think I married Joan because, when I first saw her wheeling her bicycle through the autumnal dusk of the Yard, she suggested, remote and lithe and inward, the girl of 'The Solitary Reaper' and, close-up, seemed a cool Lucy whose death might give me cause to sing" (109). The remote, cool quality of the woman is again connected with a death fantasy. Similarly, when Joey returns home from church toward the end of the novel and finds Peggy unexpectedly absent, her absence provokes a violent fantasy that she has been raped and assaulted. As he imagines the scene, he is bemused by the fact that he feels more pity for Peggy's son, "a pitiable witness, more pitied by me, more clearly pictured in his helpless bright-eyed onlooking, than his mother my wife, the actual victim, the mangled nude" (160). Like the boy, Joey feels excluded, small and helpless in relation to mother/wife, and the fantasy plays out the angry, vengeful consequences—the woman's mangled body.

These same dynamics are also apparent in the attitude toward nature, earth, and physical matter in general. Joey's description of his mowing strategy in *Of the Farm* illustrates once again the fusion of the erotic and the destructive in his mind: "Mine was to slice, in one ecstatic straight thrust, up the middle and then to narrow the two halves, whittling now at one and now the other, entertaining myself with flanking maneuvers acres wide and piecemeal mop-ups" (58). While mowing, he would get "so excited by destruction" that at one point he feels "a swelling which I idly permitted to stand, thinking of Peggy. My wife is a field" (59).

The commingling of desire and destructiveness towards mater/matter is, again, rooted in the inadequate mirroring and responsiveness of that original relationship between self and m/other. The oedipal is thus informed by the preoedipal; desire is fused with rage, and sexuality becomes an angry attack on the nonresponsive other. In the brief story, "A Crow in the Woods," Jack watches a "huge black bird" swoop towards the woods: "His heart halted in alarm for the crow, with such recklessness assaulting an inviolable surface, seeking so blindly a niche for its strenuous bulk where there was no depth. It could not enter. Its black shape shattering like an instant of flak, the crow plopped into a high branch and sent snow showering from a quadrant of lace" (*Pigeon Feathers* 226).

The imagery here betrays the essential relational dynamic shaping so much of Updike's fiction. Mother/woman/nature is experienced as "an inviolable surface" with "no depth"; the child/man's "assaulting" efforts at penetration or union lead to a fear of "shattering" or disintegration. This fear is far more primitive and intense than the ordinary castration fears that typically accompany the oedipal fantasy. At the conclusion of the crow scene, Jack's "heart overflowed" and he cries his wife's name. The story ends with these lines: "The woman's pragmatic blue eyes flicked from his face to the window where she saw only snow and rested on the forgotten food steaming between his hands. Her lips moved: 'Eat your egg' " (226). The wife is figured in the same terms in relation to the man as the woods in relation to the crow: referred to impersonally as "the woman," she is hard, "pragmatic," and unresponsive. Just as the woods ultimately defeat the crow, so the story ends with the wife's icy, imperious command.

Not only is sex an assault on the inviolable surface of the female other, but language and religious faith perform a similar function in Updike's world. In *Of the Farm*, the minister gives a sermon in which he speaks of language as "an act of husbandry, a fencing-in of fields," and proclaims, "language aerates the barren density of brute matter with the penetrations of the mind, of the spirit" (151). We thus see the relational source of those dualities of the physical and the spiritual, of female and male, noted earlier. Language, mind, and spirit are associated with the male, phallic effort to penetrate the "barren density" of female matter, an effort that again reflects both desire and destructive rage. The obdurate and unreflecting female realm must be countered and combated; belief in an omnipotent spirit that transcends the physical, as well as the exaltation of the mental and linguistic domain over the material, becomes the armament of the self. Both language and religious faith serve as weapons for an offensive self-assertion in the battle against dissolution or suffocation in relation to "brute" mater/matter.

The story "Pigeon Feathers" offers perhaps the clearest illustration of how religious faith in Updike's work is rooted in relational and narcissistic issues. The fourteen-year-old protagonist, David, has trouble, like Allen Dow in "Flight," feeling himself the central agent of his own activity— he felt himself "more moved than a mover" (117). He tries "to work off some of his disorientation" (117) by prowling in his mother's book collection. The books, acquired mostly in his mother's youth, are "obscurely depressing to him" because they suggest "the ominous gap between himself and his parents, the insulting gulf of time that existed before he was born" (117). We are immediately reminded, in other words, of the originating narcissistic injury—the feeling of nonexistence in relation to the mother. David then comes upon a book by H. G. Wells that gives an account of Jesus not as a divine being, but as a man who freakishly survived his own crucifixion. David experiences this denial of Christ's divinity as a devastating narcissistic blow—as a denial of his own grandiosity. His own deep fears of extinction and nothingness are reactivated, and he thinks that if this blasphemy were true, then it "collapsed everything into a jumble of horror" (119).

David struggles with this "horror," this "formless dread," throughout most of the story, though he experiences it most profoundly in one particular scene that occurs in the outhouse. The prelude to that scene is significant. At dinner with his parents and grandmother, David watches mutely as his parents argue and his mother insults her mother: " 'Mother, put your waggler *away!'* . . . For some reason, the sight of her bad hand at the table cruelly irritated her daughter. . . . David's mother began, without noise, to cry. His father did not seem to have eyes at all; just jaundiced sockets of wrinkled skin" (122–23). The castration anxiety reflected in both the grandmother's impaired hand as well as the father's eyeless sockets is here associated with the mother's rage. The anxiety, while imaged in bodily, sexual terms, is not confined to the sexual domain; the castration images also contain a broader, more generalized fear of disintegration and loss of self, evident in the outhouse scene that immediately follows. While sitting on the toilet, David

was visited by an exact vision of death: a long hole in the ground, no wider than your body, down which you are drawn while the white faces above recede. You try to reach them but your arms are pinned. Shovels pour dirt into your face. There you will be forever, in an upright position, blind and silent, and in time no one will remember you, and you will never be called. . . . And the earth tumbles on, and the sun expires, and unaltering darkness reigns where once there were stars. (123–24)

Death is significantly figured, once again, in terms of suffocation in the earth. Desperate but unable to reach out for human contact, the self is rendered "blind and silent," ultimately dissolving into a general state of universal nothingness. This vision is connected psychologically both to the mother's anger of the preceding scene and to the terrifying rage within David himself; they are indeed interrelated. As in "Flight," the desire and rage in relation to mother are inextricably bound up with a terrifying dissolution, a loss of self and reality. The fact that David's vision occurs on the toilet is very likely, as Donald Greiner has pointed out, an allusion to Martin Luther's epiphany while seated on the privy (Greiner 114), but the allusion does not exclude other associations and psychological implications. Melanie Klein, in a letter to Marion Milner, has described some of the unconscious relational dynamics that might be bound up in the act of excretion: "The pouring out of love and hatred, urine, faeces, products of the body, implies a projecting out first of all into the mother. . . . The dangers implied in an ejaculatory projection of that kind are a losing of the ego into the other person, 'the total merging' and a fear of not being able to retrieve it. This is a cause of great ego disturbance" (Milner 109).

While David feels that "nowhere in the world of other people would he find the hint, the nod, he needed to begin to build his fortress against death," he does recognize an ally in his depressed father: "Indeed, in the man's steep self-disgust the boy felt a kind of ally. A distant ally" (*Pigeon Feathers* 139). In much of Updike's early fiction, the father is figured as a rather ineffectual, pitiable person suffering, like his son, under the mother's domination. As the object of the mother's scorn, the father is unavailable as a figure of positive identification for the boy, and his attitude toward the father vacillates between secret admiration and contempt. In "Pigeon Feathers," however, father and son unite in their anger and "self-disgust," forming an alliance in hostile opposition to the mother's world:

Even on weekends, he and his father contrived to escape the farm; and when, some Saturdays, they did stay home, it was to do something destructive—tear down an old henhouse or set huge brush fires that threatened, while Mother shouted and flapped her arms, to spread to the woods. Whenever his father worked, it was with rapt violence;... He was exhilarating to watch. (141)

"Pigeon Feathers" ends with David's own act of exhilarating, rapt violence. Asked by his mother and grandmother to kill the pigeons roosting in the barn, David is at first reluctant—"I don't want to kill anything especially" (143), he says—but the act of killing the birds ultimately liberates him from the stranglehold of his own terror of extinction. After the first few birds fall, he felt "fully master now... like a beautiful avenger" (146). In the act of destruction, David discovers his own creative self-expression: "He had the sensation of a creator; these little smudges and flickers that he was clever to see and even cleverer to hit in the dim recesses of the rafters—out of each of them he was making a full bird. A tiny peek, probe, dab of life, when he hit it, blossomed into a dead enemy, falling with good, final weight" (147). Destructive fantasies, as Winnicott has argued, are indeed bound up in the creative process. Most often, however, Updike's characters are paralyzed, not liberated, by their destructive rage. Perhaps the identification with the father in this story (when David's mother enters the barn, she snaps, "Don't smirk. You look like your father") defends against the fear of retribution and the annihilation fantasies that usually accompany the rage.

David digs a deep hole in which to bury the birds, which recalls his own death vision of being buried in the earth. Now, however, he is the avenger, not the victim. Before he buries the birds, David observes his mother as she returns to the house, and the image of her indeed suggests a birdlike association: she "held her head rigidly, tilted a little, as if listening to the ground" (149). As quoted earlier, the story's final lines at once reaffirm David's religious faith and his own grandiosity. After marveling at the intricate designs of the pigeons' feathers, "he was robed in this certainty: that the God who had lavished such craft upon these worthless birds would not destroy His whole Creation by refusing to let David live forever" (150). Despite the authorial irony (of course David will not live forever), the character's reassertion of faith—faith in God's grace and his own everlasting soul—rises out of the momentary triumph over his inner objects and the terror and fury they provoke.

The roles of God and women in Updike's fiction, finally, follow an underlying script: they are part of the drama, in Miller's terms, of the gifted child. An almost perfect parable of that drama is contained in a story that Joey tells his stepson Richard in *Of the Farm*. The story concerns a frog who "heard rumors of a wonderful treasure stored deep in the dungeon of his guts, where he had never been" (130). The frog burrows deep down into himself until he is sure he's reached the dungeon, and then disappears. Joey explains that the frog had not died. "He just became so small he couldn't find himself. He was hibernating." Eventually, he climbs back up, "threw open the lids, and looked out" (131). The treasure is the "true" self—the experience of authentic being—that has been buried or suppressed, locked away in a "dungeon." Sadly, in this story, the treasure is never found; the search for the self becomes a disappearance and retreat, and the final image of the frog opening its eyelids like shutters and looking out suggests a deep self-alienation, a disconnection between the inner self and the outer, bodily self that functions in the world. This self-alienated condition contributes to that dualism of spirit and body so prominent in Updike's work.

The true self is relationally bound to the mother, who is also experienced as remote and retreating as she pursues her own narcissistic search for self. Thus in "A Sandstone Farmhouse," as Joey attends his mother's funeral, the one image that Joey recalls, the image that finally moves him to tears, is the image of his mother running:

His tears came and kept coming, in a kind of triumph, a breakthrough, a torrent of empathy and pity for that lost young woman running past the row houses, under the horse-chestnut tree, running to catch the trolly. . . . There was something amazing, something immortal to him in the image of her running. . . . Trying to do the right thing, the normal thing, running toward her farm, her death. In his vision of her running she was bright and quick and small, like an animal in a trap. This was the mother he had loved, the mother before they moved, before she betrayed him with the farm and its sandstone house. (45–46)

The image of his mother here—trapped and desperately running—is also an image of himself, the empathy for her also a rare breakthrough of empathy and pity for himself. The act of fleeing or running distinguishes many of Updike's male characters—it indeed forms the central motif of the first Rabbit novel.

Back in Manhattan at the end of "A Sandstone Farmhouse," Joey feels as if his "own uncluttered rooms, suspended above Manhattan's steady roar, . . . were flying somewhere. He felt guilty, anxious, displaced. He had always wanted to be where the action was, and what action there was, it turned out, had been back there" (48). Joey has always been suspended in the paradoxical dilemma of wanting to flee both from and to his mother, but in either direction, the "action" eludes him. The experience of authentic being—the "action"—is perpetually elusive and is projected onto the quest for a God who is "Wholly Other" and whom "we cannot reach." This psychological dynamic also underlies Rabbit's feeling, expressed in a line found in both the first and last *Rabbit* novels, that "somewhere behind all this there's something that wants me to find it" (*Run* 237; *Rest* 136). The "it," like the frog's treasure, cannot be reached; it is buried deep within the dungeon of the self.

This condition accounts, I believe, for the ultimate hollowness and nihilism of Updike's literary vision. Even Joyce Carol Oates, an Updike admirer, has noted the "terrifying nihilism" (459) that emerges when Updike's comic vision crumbles. Other critics share John Aldridge's view that beneath "the rich, beautiful scenery of the descriptive prose . . . Mr. Updike has nothing to say" (13). The hollowness or lack of depth— particularly moral depth—is rooted in an original failure of significant exchange between self and m/other. In Winnicott's terms, the mirror has become "a thing to be looked at but not to be looked into." The glut of surface detail in Updike's fiction, however precisely or beautifully rendered, may be related to Winnicott's observation that when mirroring fails, "perception takes the place of apperception, perception takes the place of that which might have been the beginning of a significant exchange with the world, a two-way process in which self-enrichment alternates with the discovery of meaning in the world of seen things" (PR 113). Updike's characters have trouble looking into themselves or exploring any deep or meaningful moral experience because "good" and "bad" in relation to both self and mother still represents an intolerable, ambivalent split. Thus God too must be divorced from morality; "ethical passion," as Marshfield believes, afflicts only "trivial minds."

The relation of Updike's characters to the pain and rage of their inner lives is, as we've seen, generally characterized by contempt rather than compassion; the rage is projected, or denied and scorned, rather than owned. This same dynamic is also apparent in the authorial relationship with the characters. Particularly in the later novels, Updike seems to back away from his central characters—from Rabbit, Roger Lambert, or Colonel Ellellou, for instance—and maintain a cynical distance. Crews believes the "extreme denigration of a narrator" in Updike's later fiction serves as a "cover" for expression of what Crews sees as the author's own mean-spirited and contemptible views (12). The hard-hearted views themselves, however—the scorn for moral rectitude, compassionate service, or "good works"—are part of the same psychological defense as the distancing and denigration of the character: both are attempts to distance the inner life and its painful, needy claims.

In an interview on National Public Radio, Terry Gross asked Updike about Rabbit's lack of moral fiber, about Rabbit's never feeling any remorse in *Rest*, for instance, about his affair with his daughter-in-law. Usually in literature, she pointed out, the moment of death is portrayed as a time of revelation or moral awakening. She asked Updike to comment on the fact that Rabbit exhibits his blind prejudices and petty grievances up until the very end, never expressing regret for having wronged others, particularly his wife. Updike seemed surprised and somewhat taken aback by the question, but after a moment's pause, suggested that Rabbit's sins in relation to his wife were mitigated by the fact that his wife holds the superior position—has "one-up on him" throughout the novel—since she, after all, is alive and healthy while he is dying. This is a curious response indeed to the question of Rabbit's moral culpability. From a psychological perspective, however, it betrays the familiar emotional scenario in which the feeling of intractable female power or superiority justifies aggressive vengeance on the part of the male. It suggests again how strongly moral development is linked to that first relational dynamic between self and m/other.

Updike's prose style, itself, in the relationship it sets up with the reader, also represents a repetition of that original relationship. The reader is dazzled by a glittering display of linguistic agility—by rhythmic, polished sentences and a skillful play of image and metaphor. The reader may also be dazzled by the audacity of the opinions the central characters express, as well as by scenes of extended, explicit sexuality. The reader is dazzled, finally, but not allowed to care; we are rebuffed from an empathic identification with the characters by a contemptuous authorial distancing. The pattern repeats the child's experience in relation to the tantalizingly desirable, but essentially cold, narcissistic mother. As we saw in the minister's sermon in *Of the Farm*, language for Updike is a primary means of self-assertion, a weapon with which to penetrate the "barren density of brute matter." The highly developed use of language can become an assertive, almost exhibitionistic form of self-display in Updike's fiction. Ultimately, however, such display forms a surface that is just as dense and barren for the reader as mater/matter is for Updike's characters. This is particularly true of the later novels. In Updike's early autobiographical fiction, and in "A Sandstone Farmhouse," there is less distancing of the central character, less denial of the inner pain and loss.

Thus Harold Bloom calls Updike a "minor novelist with a major style" (7), and Garry Wills accuses him in *Rabbit at Rest* of "succumbing to his own stylistic solipsism" in which "description makes up for analysis; detail for design; inclusiveness for rigor; and mere length for moral heft or grip" (14). The experience of authentic being, and the moral consciousness that accompanies it, can seem as elusive to the reader of Updike's fiction as they do to Updike's characters. His work nevertheless presents a vivid reflection of contemporary American culture—a culture that prizes stylish, seductive surfaces and that also harbors deep-rooted ambivalence towards women. In a time in which so many complaints psychiatrists hear concern feelings of unreality and emptiness, it is not surprising that Updike's fiction resonates with such a silvery ring.

Chapter 7

Internal World and the Social Environment: Toni Morrison's *Beloved*

Toni Morrison's *Beloved* penetrates, perhaps more deeply than any historical or psychological study could, the unconscious emotional and psychic consequences of slavery. The novel reveals how the condition of enslavement in the external world, particularly the denial of one's status as a human subject, has deep repercussions in the individual's internal world. These internal resonances are so profound that even if one is eventually freed from external bondage, the self will still be trapped in an inner world that prevents a genuine experience of freedom. As Sethe succinctly puts it, "Freeing yourself was one thing; claiming ownership of that freed self was another" (*Beloved* 95). The novel wrestles with this central problem of recognizing and claiming one's own subjectivity, and it shows how this cannot be achieved independently of the social environment.

A free, autonomous self, as Jessica Benjamin argues in *The Bonds of Love*, is still an essentially relational self, and is dependent on the reccognizing response of an other. *Beloved* powerfully dramatizes the fact that, in Benjamin's words, "In order to exist for oneself, one has to exist for an other" (53); in so doing, it enacts the complex interrelationship of social and intrapsychic realities. For Morrison's characters, African-Americans in a racist, slave society, there is no reliable other to recognize and affirm their existence. The mother, the child's first vital other, is made unreliable or unavailable by a slave system that either separates her from her child or so enervates and depletes her that she has no self with which to confer recognition. The consequences for the inner life of the child—the emotional hunger, the obsessive and terrifying narcissistic fantasies—constitute the underlying psychological drama of the novel.

"124 was spiteful. Full of a baby's venom." The opening lines of the novel establish its psychic source: infantile rage. A wounded, enraged baby is the central figure of the book, both literally, in the character of Beloved, and symbolically, as it struggles beneath the surface of the other major characters. Even the elderly grandmother is significantly named Baby, and the ferocity of a baby's frustrated needs colors the novel's overt mother-child relationships as well as the love relationship between Sethe and Paul D and that between Beloved and her sister Denver. "A baby's frustrated needs" refers here not to physical needs but to psychic and emotional ones. The worst atrocity of slavery, the real horror the novel exposes, is not physical death but psychic death. The pivotal event, or crisis, of the novel is Sethe's murder of her baby daughter Beloved. The reader is allowed to feel, however, the paradoxical nature of the murder. Sethe, having run away from the sadistic slavemaster Schoolteacher, is on the verge of being recaptured. Her humanity had been so violated by this man, and by her entire experience as a slave woman, that she kills her daughter to save her from a similar fate; she kills her to save her from psychic death: "If I hadn't killed her she would have died and that is something I could not bear to happen to her" (200).

Psychic death, as the novel makes clear, involves the denial of one's being as a human subject. The infant self has an essential, primary need to be recognized and affirmed as a whole being, as an active agent of its own legitimate desires and impulses, and the fulfillment of this need is dependent on the human environment, on other selves. The premise of object relations theory, as Jessica Benjamin notes, is that "we are fundamentally social beings" (17). Human beings are not innately sexual or aggressive; they are innately responsive and relational. As Harry Guntrip explains, the "need of a love-relationship is the fundamental thing" in life, and "the love-hunger and anger set up by frustration of this basic need must constitute the two primary problems of personality on the emotional level" (*Schizoid Phenomena* 45). The experience of one's cohesiveness and reality as a self is dependent on this primary relationship, on the loving response and recognition from an other. This issue is repeatedly illustrated and explored in Morrison's novels. *Sula*, for instance, speaks of the two most formative experiences of her life: the first concerns her overhearing her mother state matter-of-factly that she simply didn't "like" her (Sula), and the second involves her having thrown a child, seemingly by accident, into the river to drown. "The first experience taught her there was no other that you could count on; the second that there was no self to count on either. She had no center, no speck around which to grow" (*Sula* 118–19). These experiences are intimately related: the lack of an affirming, reliable other leads to an unconscious, murderous rage and the lack of a coherent, reliable self.

In *The Bonds of Love*, Benjamin modifies object relations theory along the lines of Daniel Stern's "intersubjective theory." She maintains the primacy of relationship in self development, but argues that the self grows through relationship with another *subject* rather than through relations with its object. The child has a need to see the mother, or his/her most significant other, "as an independent subject, not simply as the 'external world' or an adjunct of his ego" (23). The intersubjective view, which Benjamin sees as complementary to intrapsychic theory, conceives of self and other "as distinct but interrelated beings" (20) who are involved in an intricate dance of assertion and recognition. The essential need is for *mutual* recognition—"the necessity of recognizing as well as being recognized by the other" (23). Benjamin also emphasizes the concept of attunement, a "combination of resonance and difference" (26) in which self and other are empathically in tune while maintaining their distinct boundaries and separateness. When the boundaries break down and the necessary tension between self and other dissolves, domination takes root. The search for recognition then becomes a struggle for power and control, and assertion turns into aggression.

Beloved does not delve into the roots of white domination, but there is a suggestion of fear and inadequate selfhood underlying the problem. The white farmer Mr. Garner, while still sharing in the cultural objectification of blacks, nevertheless boasts that his " 'niggers is men every one of 'em.' " When another farmer argues that there " 'ain't no nigger men,' " Garner replies, " 'Not if you scared, they ain't. . . . But if you a man yourself, you'll want your niggers to be men too' " (10). A self wants the recognition of another self; this form of mutuality is more desirable, Garner implies, than mastery of an object. Garner, however, dies—his perspective cannot prevail in a world in which domination and the denial of recognition are built into the social system.

Beloved explores the interpersonal and intrapsychic effects of growing up as a black person in such a system, one in which intersubjectivity is impossible. How can a child see self or mother as subjects when the society denies them that status? The mother is made incapable of recognizing the child, and the child cannot recognize the mother. As a young girl, Sethe had to have her mother "pointed out" to her by another child. When she becomes a mother herself, she is so deprived and depleted that she cannot satisfy the hunger for recognition, the longed-for "look" that both her daughters crave. The major characters in the novel are all working out of a deep loss to the self, a profound narcissistic wound that results from a breakdown and distortion of the earliest relations between self and other. In the case of Beloved, the intense desire for recognition evolves into enraged narcissistic omnipotence and a terrifying, tyrannical domination.

The infantile rage in the novel is a form of frustrated, murderous love. The baby ghost of Beloved wreaks havoc in Sethe's home, prompting Denver to comment, " 'For a baby she throws a powerful spell,' " to which Sethe replies, " 'No more powerful than the way I loved her' " (4). The power of Beloved's rage is directly linked to the power of Sethe's love. The intimacy of destructive rage and love is asserted in various ways throughout the book—Sethe's love for Beloved is indeed a murderous love. The violation or murder of children by their parents is a theme that runs throughout much of Morrison's work, from Cholly raping his daughter in *The Bluest Eye* to Eva setting fire to her son in *Sula*, and in these cases too the acts are incited by feelings of love.[1] If the infant is traumatically frustrated in its first love relationship, if it fails to receive the affirmation and recognition it craves, the intense neediness of the infant's own love becomes dangerous and threatening. The fear, as Guntrip and others have discussed, is that one's love will destroy. The baby's enraged, destructive love is also projected outward onto the parent, which suggests one perspective on the strain of destructive parental love in Morrison's novels.

Because the first physical mode of relationship to the mother is oral, the earliest emotional needs in relation to mother are also figured in oral terms in the child's inner world. Frustration in this first oral stage of relationship leads to what object relations theorists call "love made hungry," a terrifying greediness in which the baby fears it will devour and thus destroy mother, and conversely, that mother (due to projection) will devour and destroy the self (Guntrip, *Schizoid Phenomena* 35). A preponderance of oral imagery characterizes Morrison's novel. Beloved, in her fantasies, repeatedly states that Sethe " 'chews and swallows me' " (213), while the metaphor of Beloved chewing and swallowing Sethe is almost literal: "Beloved ate up her life, took it, swelled up with it, grew taller on it" (250). Denver's problems of identity and self-cohesion, too, are often imaged in oral terms: leaving the house means being prepared to "be swallowed up in the world beyond the edge of the porch" (243). When Denver temporarily loses sight of Beloved in the shed, she experiences a dissolution of self—"she does not know where her body stops, which part of her is an arm, a foot or a knee"—and feels she is being "eaten alive by the dark" (123). Beloved, in the second part of the novel, is said to have two dreams: "exploding, and being swallowed" (133). Everywhere in the novel, the fantasy of annihilation is figured orally; the love-hunger, the boundless greed, that so determines the life of the characters also threatens to destroy them.

Sethe repeatedly asserts that the worst aspect of her rape was that the white boys " 'took my milk!' " (17). She feels robbed of her essence, of her most precious substance, which is her maternal milk. We learn that as a child, Sethe was deprived of her own mother's milk: "The little whitebabies got it first and I got what was left. Or none. There was no nursing milk to call my own" (200). Sethe was not physically starved as a baby—she did receive milk from another nursing slave woman—but she was emotionally starved of a significant nurturing relationship, of which the nursing milk is symbolic. That relationship is associated with one's core being or essence; if she has no nursing milk to call her own, she feels without a self to call her own either. Thus, even before she was raped by the white farm boys, Sethe was ravaged as an infant, robbed of her milk/essence by the white social structure.

Beloved's first appearance in her incarnated form is marked by her excessive drinking, by her downing "cup after cup of water" (51), while Sethe, suddenly feeling her "bladder filled to capacity," lifts her skirts and "the water she voided was endless" (51). The dynamic suggests a mother being drained by the child's greedy, excessive need. Sethe's voiding is also associated with her own child-self in relation to her mother: "Not since she was a baby girl, being cared for by the eight-year-old girl who pointed out her mother to her, had she had an emergency that unmanageable" (51). One might rather expect Sethe to experience thirst upon seeing her mother, but perhaps that thirst is so extreme, so potentially violent and destructive, that the more urgent need is to void, to empty oneself completely of this unmanageable hunger and rage. Sethe must drain herself in order to avoid draining, and therefore destroying, her mother. This is the fearful fantasy so central to the book; it is precisely what Beloved almost succeeds in doing to Sethe. The nursing dynamic also characterizes Denver and Beloved's relationship: "So intent was her [Denver's] nursing" of Beloved that "she forgot to eat" (54), and she hides Beloved's incontinence. Paul D, as I will discuss more fully later, also plays a maternal, nurturing role in relation to Sethe. When he arrives, Sethe feels "that the responsibility for her breasts, at last, was in somebody else's hands" (18).

The primal nursing relationship is so fraught with ambivalence that frequently in the novel satiation leads to disaster. The most obvious example is the grand feast Baby Suggs prepares for ninety people— "Ninety people who ate so well, and laughed so much, it made them angry" (136). The feast is the prelude to the abandonment of the community, the return of Schoolteacher, and Sethe's consequent murder of her baby. Melanie Klein has discussed the baby's extreme "envy" of the withholding breast (Klein 183), and this projected envy may underlie the anger of the neighbors at the maternal bounty of Baby Suggs—she had "given too much, offended them by excess" (138). Similarly, the overture to Beloved's appearance in the flesh and the ensuing disruption of Sethe's relationship with Paul D is the festive plentitude of the carnival at which Paul D plies both Sethe and Denver with candy and sweets. Paul D's abandonment of Sethe, too, is preceded by a special dinner that Sethe, feeling confident that "she had milk enough for all" (100), prepares for him.

The rage and ambivalence surrounding the love-hunger in the novel is illustrated again in the scene in which Sethe, while sitting in the Clearing associated with Baby Suggs and her sermons on love, experiences fingers touching her throat. The fingers are first soothing and comforting, but then begin to choke and strangle her, and the hands are associated with those of both Baby Suggs and Beloved, of both mother and child. When Denver accuses Beloved of choking Sethe, Beloved insists that she "fixed" Sethe's neck—" 'I kissed her neck. I didn't choke it' " (101). The incident, of course, parallels Sethe's murder of Beloved by sawing through her neck, the oral associations once more enforced by mention of the "teeth" of the saw (251) having chewed through the skin. After denying that she choked Sethe's neck, Beloved adds, " 'The circle of iron choked it' " (101), and the image recalls the collars locked around the necks of the black slaves. Her statement is thus true in that the slave system has choked off the vital circulation between mother and child so crucial to the development of the self. Some of the most vivid, disturbing passages in the novel describe the experience of having a horse's bit forced in one's mouth; the sense of deep, searing injury to one's humanity that these descriptions evoke is perhaps compounded by unconscious resonances of violation at the earliest oral roots of our human identity.

The oral imagery in the novel is also closely associated with ocular imagery, with images of eyes and seeing. Sethe is described as being "licked, tasted, eaten by Beloved's eyes" (57); when Sethe lies hidden in the field, anticipating the approach of one of the white boys, she "was eager for his eyes, to bite into them. . . . 'I was hungry,' she told Denver, 'just as hungry as I could be for his eyes' " (31). For Denver, "looking" at Beloved "was food enough to last. But to be looked at in turn was beyond appetite; it was breaking through her own skin to a place where hunger hadn't been discovered" (118). In the logic of the unconscious world, the desire to get and "drink in" with the eyes is akin to the oral wish to consume. Heinz Kohut has written about the oral-visual relationship. If the mother is physically and emotionally distant from the child, if she withholds her body, he says, the visual will become "hypercathectic" for the child (116). One can also understand the connection from Benjamin's perspective in that the real hunger in this first relationship between self and other is the hunger for recognition—the desire to be, in Denver's words, "pulled into view by the interested, uncritical eyes of the other" (118). The gaze of the beloved other recognizes and affirms the wholeness and intrinsic value of one's being. Denver describes the quality of being looked at by Beloved: "Having her hair examined as a part of her self, not as material or a style. Having her lips, nose, chin caressed as they might be if she were a moss rose a gardener paused to admire" (118). The look takes Denver to a "place beyond appetite," to where she is "needing nothing. Being what there was" (118). To be recognized by the beloved is all the nourishment one needs; it brings one into coherence, into meaningful existence. Before Beloved's arrival, Denver craved this look from Sethe: none of the losses in her life mattered, she felt, "as long as her mother did not look away" (12).

Sethe's eyes, however, are described as "empty"; Paul D thinks of Sethe's face as "a mask with mercifully punched-out eyes. . . . Even punched out they needed to be covered, lidded, marked with some sign to warn folks of what that emptiness held" (9). Her eyes reflect the psychic loss and denial of self she has experienced on all levels in her life. The face of Sethe's mother was also masklike, distorted into a permanent false smile from too many times with the bit. Sethe comments that she never saw her mother's own smile (203). Sethe's mother, deprived of her authentic selfhood, her status as a human subject, cannot provide the recognition and affirmation that her child craves. The cycle is vicious, and thus Sethe's children, Beloved and Denver, will suffer the same loss. Beloved's eyes too are remarkable for their emptiness: "Deep down in those big black eyes there was no expression at all" (55).

The craving for mutual recognition—for simultaneously "seeing" the beloved other and being "seen" by her—propels the central characters in the novel. Beloved says she has returned in order to "see" Sethe's face, and she wants "to be there in the place where her face is and to be looking at it too" (210). When, as a child, Sethe is shown the brand burnt into her mother's skin and is told that she will be able to "know" her by this mark, Sethe anxiously responds, " 'But how will you know me? How will you know me? Mark me, too. . . . Mark the mark on me too' " (61). Love is a form of knowing and being known. Beloved repeatedly commands Paul D, " 'I want you to touch me on the inside part and call me my name' " (116). The hunger is to be touched, recognized, known, in one's inner being or essential self. This yearning is poignantly captured in the image of two turtles mating. Denver and Beloved observe the turtles on the bank of the river:

The embracing necks—hers stretching up toward his bending down, the pat pat pat of their touching heads. No height was beyond her yearning neck, stretched like a finger toward his, risking everything outside the bowl just to touch his face. The gravity of their shields, clashing, countered and mocked the floating heads touching. (105)

The yearning of Beloved, Sethe, and Denver to touch faces with the beloved other, to know and be known, is, like that of the turtles, obstructed and mocked by the shields or shells each has constructed. The shell, however, is a necessary defense; it attempts to preserve the self from a culture that seeks to deny it. As Joseph Wessling argues in an article on narcissism in *Sula*, narcissistic defenses, such as "self-division" and an inability to empathize or experience human sympathy, may be "the price of survival" (286) in an oppressive, unjust society. The shell also serves to protect the self and its boundaries from the intensity of its own frustrated desire. The hunger for recognition, as discussed, may be so overwhelming that it threatens to swallow up the other and the self, destroying all boundaries in one total annihilation.

The novel as a whole is characterized by a fluidity of boundaries, by a continuously altering narrative perspective that slides in and out of characters' minds, by a mutable, nonsequential time structure, and by an absence of the conventional lines between fantasy and reality. Such fluidity, as Nancy Chodorow and Carol Gilligan have argued, is characteristic of female, as opposed to male, modes of perception and expression. It derives from the preservation of an original identity and preoedipal bondedness between self and mother. The series of monologues by Beloved, Sethe, and Denver in part 2 of Morrison's novel, however, suggests something more extreme and dangerous than mere fluidity of boundaries: the monologues reveal an utter breakdown of the borders between self and other, a collapse that is bound up with incorporative fantasies. Sethe's section begins, "Beloved, she my daughter. She mine" (200). Denver's opens, "Beloved is my sister. I swallowed her blood right along with my mother's milk" (205), and Beloved's with the line, "I am Beloved and she is mine" (210). After that sentence, Beloved's monologue is marked by a total absence of punctuation, highlighting the fantasy of merging and oneness—"I am not separate from her there is no place where I stop her face is my own"—at the essence of her plaintive ramblings. Her words reveal the psychic loss—the denial of recognition—at the core of the fantasy:

there is no one to want me to say me my name . . . she chews and swallows me I am gone now I am her face my own face has left me . . . Sethe sees me see her and I see the smile her smiling face is the place for me it is the face I lost she is my face smiling at me doing it at last a hot thing now we can join a hot thing. (212–13)

A similar merging fantasy also figures prominently in *Sula*, in the relationship between Sula and Nel. The two characters are described as so close that "they themselves had difficulty distinguishing one's thoughts from the other's" (83); for Nel, "talking to Sula had always been a conversation with herself" (95); and Sula eventually realizes that neither Nel nor anyone else "would ever be that version of herself which she sought to reach out to and touch with an ungloved hand" (121). Each is compelled continually to seek the self through an other, and such blurring of boundaries can lead to one of the forms of domination and submission Benjamin describes: the self can surrender totally to the will and agency of the other, or the self can consume and appropriate the other as part of itself, as an object of its possession.

The repetition of the word "mine" in the monologues of Sethe, Denver, and Beloved suggests exactly this sort of possession and incorporation of the other as an object. "Mine" is the haunting word that Stamp Paid hears surrounding Sethe's house in ghostly whispers, and is stressed again in a lyrical section following Beloved's unpunctuated monologue. In this section the voices of Beloved, Sethe, and Denver are joined (the identity of the speaker in each line is sometimes unclear) while at the same time each voice remains essentially isolated (the voices speak to but not *with* each other):

> Beloved
> You are my sister
> You are my daughter
> You are my face; you are me
> I have found you again; you have come back to me
> You are my Beloved
> You are mine
> You are mine
> You are mine (*Beloved* 216)

This form of possessing and objectifying the other, however, cannot satisfy; it imprisons the self within its own devouring omnipotence, its own narcissism. True satisfaction or joy, as Benjamin explains, can only be achieved through "mutual recognition" between self and other, between two subjects or selves.

Both sides of the power dynamic, both surrender to and incorporation of the other, are apparent in the relationship between Sethe and Beloved. Toward the end of the novel, Sethe relinquishes herself completely to the will and desire of Beloved. She neglects to feed or care for herself and becomes physically drained and emotionally depleted. Sethe literally shrinks while Beloved literally expands and swells; both are caught up in a mutually destructive, frighteningly boundless narcissism. The prelude to Sethe's decline is an incident that again stresses lack of recognition at the source of this narcissistic condition. Sethe has been abandoned once again, this time by Paul D (her previous abandonments include those of her mother, her husband Halle, Baby Suggs, and her two sons), and to cheer herself, she takes Denver and Beloved ice skating on the frozen creek. The three are unable to keep their balance, and as they fall on the ice, they shriek with both pain and laughter. The scene is evocative of childhood and of childlike helplessness. "Making a circle or a line, the three of them could not stay upright for one whole minute, but nobody saw them falling" (174). The phrase "nobody saw them falling" becomes the dominant motif of the scene; the line is repeated four times in the two-page description. Sethe's laughter turns into uncontrollable tears, and her weeping in the context of the scene's refrain suggests a child's aching sense of loss or absence, specifically the absence of the confirming, legitimizing gaze of the other.

Once it is asserted that "nobody saw" her falling, that there is no "other" to confer the reality of her own existence on her, Sethe falls prey to a consuming narcissism. Suddenly she consciously recognizes Beloved as the incarnation of her dead child and surrenders herself totally to her. Sethe now feels that "there is no world outside" her door (184) and that since her daughter has come back, "she can sleep like the drowned" (204). In psychological terms, she retreats from external reality and succumbs to her destructive, narcissistic fantasies, to her murderously enraged child-self as well as her insatiable need to make reparation for her murderous love. Paul D recognizes, and fears, the narcissistic nature of Sethe's love: "This here new Sethe didn't know where the world stopped and she began. . . . more important than what Sethe had done was what she claimed. It scared him" (164). Paul D is the one character in the novel who has the power to resist and disrupt the destructive, narcissistic mother-child dyad. Sethe recalls, "There was no room for any other thing or body until Paul D arrived and broke up the place, making room, shifting it, moving it over to someplace else, then standing in the place he had made" (39). Sethe also tells Beloved that she would have recognized her "right off, except for Paul D" (203). Paul D is the external "other" who triangulates the dyad, as the image of the "three shadows" of Sethe,

Denver, and Paul D "holding hands" as they walk to the carnival (47) emphasizes. The excursion to the carnival is Sethe's first venture into the community since the murder; Paul D has the capacity to lead Sethe out of her narcissistic isolation and into relationship with the external world. The claims of the angry baby Beloved, however, are still too powerful to allow for these other attachments: she makes her first appearance in the flesh immediately following the excursion.

While Paul D plays the role of the saving other in contradistinction to Beloved and the narcissistic dyad, he does not represent the typical world of the father. He is not, for instance, a token of male rationality countering the irrationality of the female world. He too is deeply affected by Beloved's irrational power—she literally "moves" him, making him physically restless and forcing him to sleep with her in the shed outside the house. His power lies precisely in his maternal, nurturing quality; he is that "other" with the power to recognize and affirm the inner or essential self. He is described as "the kind of man who could walk into a house and make the women cry. Because with him, in his presence, they could" (17). The women see him and not only want to weep; they also want to confess their deepest secrets, to expose all the pain and rage bound up with their true selves. Sethe thinks of how he "cradled her before the cooking stove" and is deeply comforted by "the mind of him that knew her own" (99).

Paul D has the power to satisfy the craving that fuels the novel, the craving to be "known," to have one's existence sanctioned by the empathic recognition of the other. That Morrison bestows this quality on an African-American male character is an interesting, and unusual, point. A common criticism of black women novelists is that their portrayals of black males are often flat, stereotypic, or unempathic. For Morrison, the maternal, nurturing quality is a form of love that is not restricted by gender; this view expands the possibilities, and is a liberating factor, for her characters. Yet Paul D, too, is not a totally reliable other: he temporarily retreats when learning of Sethe's murder of her child. Like all of the other black characters in the novel, he must work out of a condition of psychic fragmentation—his selfhood has been severely impaired, his status as a human subject denied by the slave culture. He feels that even the old rooster, Mister, was allowed an essential integrity of being denied him: " 'Mister was allowed to be and stay what he was. But I wasn't allowed to be and stay what I was. Even if you cooked him you'd be cooking a rooster named Mister. But wasn't no way I'd ever be Paul D again, living or dead' " (72).

Only Denver does not see Paul D as the other women do; for her he does not play the same nurturing role. She sees him only as a threat, an intruder into her intense and deeply ambivalent relationship with her mother. Denver is terrified of Sethe's murderous love: she has "monstrous and unmanageable dreams about Sethe" (103) and is afraid to fall asleep while Sethe braids her hair at night. In her fantasies, "She cut my head off every night" (206). For Denver, the idealized, saving other is her father Halle, whom she calls "Angel Man." Yet the father is significantly incapable of playing the savior role. The "other"—whether represented by mother or father—is always untrustworthy in Morrison's world, rendered thus by the social environment. As a result, the self remains trapped within its own destructive narcissism.

Sethe regards Halle as the ultimate betrayer: he witnessed her rape, she learns, but did not protest or try to protect her. His absent presence is worse than mere absence for it confirms an essential hollowness and undependability of the other and of love. Yet Halle is not simply a "bad guy"; Morrison extends her compassion equally to her male characters. The reader is allowed to see Halle too as a deeply wounded child. Traumatized by the rape of Sethe and the maternal violation that it also represents, Halle literally loses his mind—his selfhood shatters. Paul D observes him later squatting by a churn, with butter all over his face. He smeared that butter all over his face, Sethe thinks, "because the milk they took is on his mind" (70). The image of Halle here recalls Beloved and the image at the psychological base of the book: it is the picture of a lost, greedy child whose ravenous hunger/love is out of control.

Ultimately Denver is able to escape the narcissistic vacuum, and she is helped not by Halle, as she had fantasized, but by another maternal figure in the novel, Mrs. Jones. Denver is first propelled out of the house by literal hunger, for Sethe, locked in her obsession with Beloved, has become oblivious to food and to all external or physical considerations. Denver realizes that "it was she who had to step off the edge of the world and die because if she didn't, they all would" (239). Excluded from the Beloved-Sethe dyad, Denver is forced into the role of the outside other, and assuming that role is her salvation. She goes first to her former teacher Lady Jones, an old woman of mixed race who has long struggled with the contempt of the black community and, equally, with her own self-contempt. Lady Jones thus has a special "affection for the unpicked children" (247), an empathy with those, like Denver, who have never been recognized or "picked," who have never had their existence validated or confirmed. After Denver asks her for food, Mrs. Jones compassionately croons, " 'Oh, baby," and that empathic recognition of the hungry baby within finally frees Denver from the trap of her infantile needs: "Denver looked up at her. She did not know it then, but it was the word 'baby,' said softly and with such kindness, that inaugurated her life in the world as a woman" (248).

With this recognition, Denver for the first time begins to experience the contours of her own separate self. When Nelson Lord, an old school acquaintance, affectionately says, " 'Take care of yourself, Denver,' " Denver "heard it as though it were what language was made for," and she realizes that "it was a new thought, having a self to look out for and preserve" (252). Self-recognition is inextricably tied up with self-love, and this is precisely the message of the sermons that Baby Suggs preaches to her people in the Clearing. In a white society that does not recognize or love you, she tells them, you must fight to recognize and love yourself:

"Here," she said, "in this here place, we flesh; flesh that weeps, laughs; flesh that dances on bare feet in grass. Love it. Love it hard. Yonder they do not love your flesh. They despise it. They don't love your eyes; they'd just as soon pick em out. . . . Love your hands! Love them. Raise them up and kiss them. Touch others with them, pat them together, stroke them on your face 'cause they don't love that either. *You* got to love it, *you*!" (88)

Baby Suggs continues to enjoin her people to love every appendage, every organ in their bodies, and especially to " 'love your heart.' " This is the crucial lesson, but it cannot be learned in isolation; self-love needs a relational foundation and a social context. Thus even Baby Suggs is unable to sustain her convictions and heed her own teachings. After Sethe's murder, Baby Suggs retreats and ceases to care about herself or others, showing interest in nothing except "colors."

Morrison's novel, however, is not hopelessly bleak or despairing. Her characters are wounded, but not all of them are ruined. Denver and Paul D, by courageously facing their inner terrors—Denver leaves the house even though she expects to be "swallowed up," and Paul D returns to Sethe and her fearful, murderous love—are able to salvage out of the wreckage a bolstering faith in both self and other. Paul D tries to pass this faith on to Sethe at the end. He assumes again a maternal, nurturing role. He holds Sethe, calls her "baby," and gently tells her not to cry. Beloved is gone and Sethe feels bereft and lost: " 'She was my best thing,' " (272) she tells Paul D. He "leans over and takes her hand. With the other he touches her face. 'You your best thing, Sethe. You are.' His holding fingers are holding hers" (273).[2] While the word "thing" still suggests a sense of self as object (an objectification of self that perhaps no black person in the slave culture could ever totally escape), the scene between Sethe and Paul D at the end comes closest to that state of mutual recognition and attunement that Benjamin describes. Paul D's gently touching Sethe's face recalls the touching faces of the mating turtles; the relationship here is not one of merging nor of domination, but of resonating "likeness" and empathic understanding. Paul D recalls Sixo's description of his mistress, the "Thirty-Mile Woman": " 'She is a friend of my mind. She gather me, man. The pieces I am, she gather them and give them back to me in all the right order. It's good, you know, when you got a woman who is a friend of your mind' " (272–73). The beloved other has the power to give to the self its own essential wholeness. The role of the other here is neither as an object to possess nor even as a mirror for the self; as a "friend of (the) mind," the other is a subject in its own right, with an inner life that corresponds with that of the self. In such correspondence, in that mutuality of inner experience and suffering, lies the self-confirming and consoling power of the relationship.

Paul D tells Sethe in this final scene that "he wants to put his story next to hers" (273). Throughout the novel, stories and storytelling are associated with the self and with the primary oral relationship at its root.[3] Beloved is tireless in her demand, in "her thirst for hearing" Sethe's stories: "It became a way to feed her . . . Sethe learned the profound satisfaction Beloved got from storytelling" (58). Denver too feeds Beloved's craving for stories about Sethe, "nursing Beloved's interest like a lover whose pleasure was to overfeed the loved" (78). Denver's storytelling, because of the empathic identification it involves, also allows her to feel a closer bond and oneness with her mother. As she narrates the tale of Sethe's escape to Beloved, "Denver was seeing it now and feeling it—through Beloved. Feeling how it must have felt to her mother" (78). Paul D does not want to merge or incorporate Sethe's story into his own at the end; rather, he wants to "put his story next to hers." This suggests again an essential maintenance of boundaries, a balance of two like but separate selves, an attunement.

The novel does not end, however, with the scene between Sethe and Paul D, but with one last lyrical section on Beloved. The refrain of the last two pages is the line, repeated three times, "It was not a story to pass on." The final section arouses a deep sense of pathos for that un- recognized, ravenously needy infant-self that is Beloved:

> Everybody knew what she was called, but nobody anywhere knew her name. Disremembered and unaccounted for, she cannot be lost because no one is looking for her, and even if they were, how can they call her if they don't know her name? Although she has claim, she is not claimed. In the place where long grass opens, the girl who waited to be loved and cry shame erupts into her separate parts, to make it easy for the chewing laughter to swallow her all away.
> It was not a story to pass on. (274)

The poignancy of Beloved's story/self is that it is *not* a story/self. She has been denied the narrative of her being, the subjectivity and continuity of inner experience that should be everyone's birthright. Beloved's des- olation, her sorrow, is a more extreme version of the same sorrow that all of the black characters in the novel experience. Thus Baby Suggs, finally freed from slavery, expresses not the elation of freedom, but the deep sadness of not knowing her self, of not being able to read her own story: "The sadness was at her center, the desolated center where the self made its home. Sad as it was that she did not know where her children were buried or what they looked like if alive, fact was she knew more about them than she knew about herself, having never had the map to discover what she was like" (140). In the end, the novel is more about Beloved than Sethe. Beloved's character frames the book, and it is her story—or her desperate struggle to know and experience her own story— that is the pumping heart of the novel. Beloved's struggle *is* Sethe's strug- gle; it is also Denver's, Paul D's, and Baby Suggs's. It is the struggle of all black people in a racist society, Morrison suggests, to claim themselves as subjects in their own narrative.

Beloved demonstrates, finally, the interconnection of social and in- trapsychic reality. The novel plays out the deep psychic reverberations of living in a culture in which domination and objectification of the self have been institutionalized. If from the earliest years on, one's fundamental need to be recognized and affirmed as a human subject is denied, that need can take on fantastic and destructive proportions in the inner world: the intense hunger, the fantasized fear of either being swallowed or exploding, can tyrannize one's life even when one is freed from the external bonds of oppression. The self cannot experience freedom without first experiencing its own agency or, in Sethe's words, "claiming ownership" of itself. The free, autonomous self, *Beloved* teaches, is an inherently social self, rooted in relationship and dependent at its core on the vital bond of mutual recognition.

Chapter 8

Ann Beattie and the Culture of Narcissism

Ann Beattie's fiction has been hailed for its trenchant portrayal of the baby boom generation struggling to make sense of life after Woodstock. Her world of aging postwar children is marked by both passivity and restlessness, by a profoundly apathetic as well as an anxiously obsessive quality. Her representation of contemporary life lends credence to Christopher Lasch's diagnosis of contemporary American society as a "culture of narcissism." In his controversial book of that title, Lasch argues that individual character structure reflects the structure of the society or culture at large. Every society in every age, he believes, develops its own particular form of pathology: post-1960s America manifests pathological narcissism.

Lasch points to certain narcissistic traits—such as the lack of deep personal attachments and commitments, and the need for approval and power to validate self-esteem—as the very traits that make for success in our bureaucratic and corporate world. The general "warlike conditions that pervade American society" (64), he maintains, foster narcissistic fears of disintegration and breakdown, as well as feelings of futility and despair. He cites a general dependence on social institutions and bureaucratic organizations as reinforcing infantile helplessness and narcissistic dependence on external validations of the self. Our mass media's cult of celebrity, furthermore, serves only to intensify grandiose fantasies of fame and glory.

Beattie's vision confirms Lasch's view: her world is one of boredom, emptiness, and paralyzing passivity; her characters experience no real connections with one another nor any sense of continuity in their lives. They are fascinated with celebrity, and develop idealized fixations on others that they hopelessly, ineffectively pursue. As Ann Hulbert has remarked, "With characters so convincingly lacking in spirit, it has been natural to assume that her real subject is the spirit of the time: she has been our expert at taking the weak pulse of the anticlimactic Seventies and the soulless Eighties" (33). Beattie's fiction over the past two decades, despite its careful chronicling of surface changes in the cultural environment, has continued to manifest the same underlying narcissistic condition. Though her work of the seventies depicts posthippies in communal houses and her late eighties and early nineties fiction features successful professionals with summer homes, the pervasive sense of isolation and impending disintegration endures. Her fiction can offer a glimpse into the psychodynamic sources of the narcissistic anxiety that continues to plague our time.

Although the two leading theorists on pathological narcissism, Heinz Kohut and Otto Kernberg, differ in their ideas about the origin and development of the condition, both connect it with the failure to achieve a securely structured or integrated self. Due to traumatic separation or empathic failure in the earliest self-other relationship, the infant self is unable to integrate its rage or to feel loved, "good," and whole. The absence of a coherent self-structure can give rise to a generalized sense of incoherence in life, to fears of disintegration, and to feelings of emptiness and boredom. According to Kernberg, the narcissist experiences the past as lost, and due to the failure to accumulate an internal life, he or she lives in an "eternal present" (*Internal World* 138). Lasch connects this to the "waning of a sense of historical time" (3) that he finds so characteristic of our culture.

Beattie's 1980 novel *Falling in Place* typifies the general sense of discontinuity, emptiness, and boredom pervading her world. The novel focuses on the unhappy members of a suburban Connecticut family and the people around them. Although we are presented with family, lovers, and friends, no one is fully connecting with anyone else. If the Knapp family is a unit, it is bound only by the accidents of birth and a mutually felt anger and frustration. The characters not only fail to understand each other; they cannot understand, much less control, their own real feelings or the patterns that their lives have taken. John Knapp tries to express his exasperation to his children: " 'Don't you think I might already realize that my existence is a little silly? Do you think I had visions of working at an ad agency dancing in my head like sugarplums? Everybody I work with . . . is stoned on Valium all day' " (82). Knapp's bored, aloof daughter, Mary, responds, " 'I haven't finished the book, but that's what *Vanity Fair* is like. Things just fall into place' " (83). Knapp thinks this a remarkable insight and wonders how his daughter could be failing English. He also realizes, though, that if she truly thought this from reading the book or "from what she knew of life," then why should she make the effort to succeed? "Of course, if that was what she thought, then there wasn't much point in her trying to organize her life or in any of the things he had believed about getting ahead, the necessity of getting ahead, when he was her age" (85–86). Many of Beattie's characters cannot imagine a future that they have a role in shaping; they cannot think through the consequences of their actions or, as a result, feel any meaning or purpose in their present lives.

In Beattie's first novel, *Chilly Scenes of Winter* (1976), the sense of futility and empty boredom is best exemplified by the daily encounter between the central character, Charles, and a blind man who runs a concession stand. Charles routinely picks up a candy bar and the blind man routinely asks, "What have you got?" At one point Charles reflects, " 'What have you got?' The blind man there every day to remind him that, at the close of the day, he has nothing. It adds insult to injury to have to answer, 'A peanut butter cup' " (142). The last line is typical of Charles's, and Beattie's, ironic, self-deprecating humor. Yet the humor has a bitter edge, and irony always implies a distance from its subject. Charles's detached self-reflection is characteristic of the general sense of detachment the novel conveys, a detachment the characters feel from one another as well as from themselves. Life for Charles is as predictable and meaningless as his daily routine with the blind man. "Predictable. Everything is predictable" (31), he thinks, and the thought becomes a motif that runs throughout the text. His stepfather, Pete, accuses him of never having done anything exciting in his life and Charles replies, " 'There's not much exciting to do' " (88). Life, excluding his obsession with his unattainable former girlfriend, Laura, holds no meaning or promise; the world, like the blind man, is a blank presence that cannot recognize or affirm his existence and that can offer nothing more than a peanut butter cup.

In *Love Always* (1985), one character quits the job that had defined his life for several years and videotapes himself cleaning out his office: "Everything might have been anyone's. Looking at the videotape, he was convinced, long before it was over, that he had never been there at all, in spite of all the things he saw himself lugging away" (246). Another character feels "sorry for all the people who didn't realize that their world could change in a second" (213). Lack of continuity distinguishes both the physical and emotional lives of Beattie's characters. The title *Love Always* refers to the closing of an ambiguous love letter one of the characters receives. The letter's recipient, Lucy, ponders whether the words are flippant or sincere, finally feeling "unsure of what was or ever had been true" about their relationship, about her lover's feelings, or about her own.

The one connection that Beattie's characters do seem to feel is to the celebrities of the popular culture. In *Falling in Place* a character proudly relates, "I have a friend who knows Linda Ronstadt, and my aunt went to school with Joan Kennedy. A girl who lived in my building once went to a beach party and jumped on a trampoline with David Nelson" (35). In *Chilly Scenes of Winter*, references to rock musicians form another of the novel's running motifs. One woman tells Charles of a friend whose daughter "thought Dylan was coming for her. She had substantial proof from the last two records" (135). The rock celebrities are idealized, glamorous figures with whom the characters yearn to identify. Attaching oneself in fantasy to those who radiate power, glamor, and charisma can be a method of compensating for one's own missing self-esteem. Idealization is indeed one of the prime narcissistic defenses, protecting against fragmentation and against the sense of inner "badness" and worthlessness. The rock figures in *Chilly Scenes of Winter*, however, are also associated in Charles's mind with aging and death, and with the loss of an idealized past. "Elvis Presley is forty" (13), he reminds himself after hearing one of his songs. "Janis Joplin is dead," is another of the novel's refrains. "Janis Joplin is dead. Jim Morrison's *widow* is dead" (20).

Beattie's characters often look back to the sixties as an ideal time now past. In *Chilly Scenes*, one character exclaims, "Everybody's so pathetic. ... What is it? Is it just the end of the sixties?" (215). These sixties characters would like to believe that that is the simple reason, but their idealization of the past decade is part of a larger narcissistic pattern of idealization and disillusionment. Charles is fascinated with the rock stars and yearns for the idealized sixties for the same reason that he yearns for his inaccessible ex-girlfriend, Laura—they are all associated with a lost, idealized self. Laura, first of all, exists more in Charles's imagination than elsewhere (she actually appears in the novel only twice, briefly toward the beginning and again at the end), and he even admits "that he wasn't that wild for her when he had her" (73). Both Laura and the celebrity figures are, in Kohut's terms, idealized selfobjects that Charles experiences primarily as projections or extensions of himself. The idealization of Laura also reveals roots in a deeply ambivalent maternal attachment.

Charles relates to most of the women in the novel, in fact, as a child to a mother. He fantasizes, for instance, about his sister Susan: "He would like to be smaller, and her child instead of her brother, and then he would curl up and shut his eyes, and everyone would think he was being good, instead of being bad" (32–33). He wants her to tell him "what to do" (69). He relates to Laura in the same way. He feels he needs her because she knows how to take care of him and can explain things for him. He is entranced when he learns that she bakes cookies and bread in her role as "room mother" for the elementary school class of her stepdaughter, Rebecca. He is, in fact, jealous of Rebecca: "She [Laura] is a devoted stepmother. She is devoted to everybody but him. He envies Rebecca" (45). Charles's real mother is portrayed as a ridiculous crazy woman who dances naked with broomsticks and tries to kill herself with laxatives. Since the death of Charles's father, she has been in and out of mental institutions. Charles thinks that she purposely went crazy, that it makes things easier for her that way. The narrative presentation of her shares Charles's view and is utterly devoid of sympathy.

Like Charles, most of Beattie's characters are essentially terrified children desperately seeking an idealized maternal love. John Knapp, for instance, is obsessed with his mistress Nina, and his obsession betrays roots in an infantile fear of maternal abandonment:

He would get obsessed with calling her. At night, in New York, he would tear himself away from her, and then he would stop to call three times before he got back to Rye and then call again from the dark hallway, whispering like a criminal who had broken into the house. He would talk to her about love, standing in the dark of his mother's house, feeling like a child who couldn't possibly know what he was saying. (258)

Sometimes he would have nothing to say and remain silent, then panic at the thought of her hanging up. Not only does his "standing in the dark of his mother's house, feeling like a child" connect his anxious love for his mistress with a child's frustrated attempts to make contact with its mother, but his feeling "like a criminal" also underscores the preoedipal content. Just as Charles expresses the desire to curl up like a baby on his sister's lap so people would think he was "being good, instead of being bad," many of Beattie's characters feel, at bottom, criminally "bad," unworthy and unlovable. The sense of badness stems from rage over narcissistic injury; the characters feel "bad" because they harbor a good deal of unconscious anger and hostility.

Throughout *Chilly Scenes* Charles reveals such unconscious rage. He is afraid, for instance, of falling asleep in public. "He thinks that he will scream. He doesn't even close his eyes on buses any more. In fact he has started driving to work instead of taking the bus so he won't be tempted to fall asleep" (30). Or again, while waiting in his car for Laura, "He opens his eyes, convinced that he will fall asleep and scream, that she will walk up to his car and he will be screaming inside" (44). Charles is obviously terrified of losing control, of relaxing his defenses and regressing to a state of boundless rage. That rage and the guilt associated with it are also at the root of Charles's various other terrors. He is paranoid, for instance, of policemen. He takes his hands out of his pockets when a policeman passes—"he thinks that the policeman might think that he's hiding something" (63). He recalls being stopped for a routine speeding ticket and afterward experiencing a wild, uncontrollable shaking fit. He had finally managed to pull himself together and driven to a friend's house where he had immediately, and unaccountably, gone into the bathroom and taken a shower. The "badness," the rage and guilt that Charles is hiding and fears may be discovered, makes him feel criminal and unclean. It is also the source of his hypochondria, nightmares, and fantasies of impending doom.

Charles repeatedly expresses anxieties about death and disease that expose frightening fantasies of narcissistic disintegration. He remembers being in the hospital once and overhearing the doctor inform his roommate that he (the roommate) had inoperable melanoma. The phrase "inoperable melanoma" becomes another of the novel's repeated strains, a reminder of the self's helpless subjection to arbitrary, destructive forces. Feeling tired, Charles thinks that he "should have a checkup. He doesn't want to. They will find out he has an inoperable melanoma" (77). As a child, Charles had read an article about leprosy and had "thought that his limbs were going to fall off, go clunk on the sidewalk. . . . For a long time he went around expecting to hear a clunk" (237).

A similar note often sounds following fantasies about Laura. He dreams, for instance, about going to Bermuda with Laura, running on the beach and drinking rum. Then he thinks, "He would be eaten by a shark; Laura would get an inoperable melanoma. . . . He and Laura would probably be blown up in the plane flying them there" (225). Charles projects his own destructive rage onto the world at large. Like his fragile self, the world is unstable and untrustworthy. This is the essential vision informing all of Beattie's work. In the story "You Know What" from her 1991 collection *What Was Mine*, a father learns that his child's teacher has been hit by a truck: "She was struck from behind. . . . She was out getting groceries. It seems clear that that is so often the way. That in some very inconspicuous moment, a person can be overwhelmed" (153). In *Falling in Place*, one of the characters, Spangle, is disturbed by dreams about fireballs, fiery nightmares of annihilation. He explains to his girl-friend Cynthia that he loves her because of "the impression she gave of being at peace—no nightmares about fireballs" (313). Beattie's men may turn to their idealized women for maternal protection, but the women are revealed to be no more grownup or secure than they. Cynthia loves Spangle, she determines, because he would "hold her hand for a minute before she went in and faced a root canal. What she had done for him in return, was to say that there was no fireball when there was" (341). Even Laura in *Chilly Scenes* "liked to be rocked; she liked to pretend to be a child again" (220). The women, moreover, prove to be dangerously bound up with the underlying terrors and hostility.

In *Chilly Scenes* Charles frequently fantasizes the deaths of the women around him. He remembers an old girlfriend who fell asleep on his shoulder while they were sitting together on a park bench: "He couldn't believe that she'd fallen asleep. Policemen kept walking by, and he was terrified that she was dead, and that eventually he would have to call out to one of the passing policemen that the woman next to him was dead" (62). A friend of his sister's disappears and Charles thinks, "She will be dead somewhere. Twisted and dead. And the police will find his fingerprints on her coat . . . and they will come to work and arrest him" (119). Such irrational fears suggest an unconscious wish and a profound ambivalence toward women. Laura accuses him at one point of not trusting her, and Charles admits that it's probably true (46); he often questions the veracity of things she's told him. His mistrust perhaps also accounts for his inexplicable rejection of former girlfriends. He wonders, "Why had he left any of them? Surprisingly, he left as many of them as had left him" (60). He also reveals a discomfort with female bodies. He remembers being in dancing school with girls who had "big breasts he was afraid to touch" (113). His mother also made him dance with her and he recalls, "She towered over him—no chance of running into her breasts, thank God" (113–14).

The deep ambivalence, the mistrust of women and female sexuality that runs throughout Beattie's fiction, emphasizes the point that such unconscious dynamics are not exclusive to the male psyche in our culture. The ambivalence toward women and sexual relationships is most strikingly revealed in one of Charles's nightmares:

Thinking of Bermuda, he falls asleep and has a dream of a jolly fat man, water-skiing. He must be the fat man, because the fat man is wearing his clothes. . . . He is water-skiing down a narrow, wavy line—not the real ocean at all, but a line that has been drawn. There are boundaries to Bermuda—to the left and right there are concrete walls, and if the fat man isn't careful he will smash into one of them. There is nothing on the other side of the walls. The fat man is so jolly that he pays no attention, comes within a fraction of an inch of crashing into walls. (229)

Charles wakes up in a sweat, then falls back asleep. This time he and Laura are swimming in the ocean. They are turning somersaults, but "Laura doesn't come out of her somersault, but keeps sinking, bent in half, sinking deeper than he can go. He tries to make his body heavier, to sink with her, but he is light, buoyant, he can't follow." He wakes again, falls back asleep, and "this time the jolly fat man is following Laura down, laughing, cackling. There are bubbles as the fat man sinks. He can no longer see Laura, only the fat man's head, grown immense, and the gush of bubbles." Once again he wakes and falls back asleep. Now he "is trying to catch the fat man's arm, to hold him back, but he is sinking fast, and Charles is buoying upward, frightened, realizing that he has no air tank, that he will drown. He has to get to the top fast. . . . What does the fat man want with Laura? Why isn't he floating?" (230).

The imagery of the dream sequence, first of all, arises out of his Bermuda fantasy with Laura. Love and desire, in other words, lead to disastrous chaos, to drowning and annihilation. The consecutive dreams again betray Charles's characteristic fears of losing control and imminent destruction. They are symbolic expressions of his deepest terrors and so threatening they cannot be sustained: he keeps waking and falling back asleep. The self-representations, furthermore, are split: he is the manic, jolly fat man and he is also Charles attempting to save the fat man from sinking at the end with Laura. The image of the fat man suggests that Charles feels his love for Laura is greedy, and it is this greedy love that wants to incorporate its object that is so potentially dangerous and destructive. In one sequence he tries to sink and drown with Laura but is unable to follow her; as in reality, she is inaccessible and the merging or union he desires, impossible. In the last sequence, however, as the fat man, he experiences the terror of self-annihilation that his desire really signifies. The regressive nature of his greedy love implies a passive refusion, a submerging or loss of the self. The novel contains a few other instances in which Charles exposes the same desire for such regressive merging or extinction of self. He dreams of falling asleep in the snow, sinking in the "deep white" (213). Another time he expresses a wish to drown (213).

The desire for merging, and the ambivalence associated with it, are apparent throughout much of Beattie's work. In *Falling in Place*, Spangle is afraid to commit himself to a relationship with Cynthia because "the realization that he did not have a private, separate existence from her began to bother him" (269). As in Charles's dream about the fat man, the merging and ambivalence often reveal oral/maternal associations. Charles's frightening fantasy, mentioned earlier, of falling asleep and screaming while waiting in the car for Laura, immediately follows a memory of her standing before him, having playfully put two grapefruit under her sweater.

Charles indeed admits to himself that "he thinks about food too much" (57), and his thoughts about Laura frequently involve his craving for a particular dessert she used to make for him—a souffle made with cognac and oranges. Although he has the recipe, he won't make it himself because "he wants to think of it as magic" (24). When Laura finally allows him to meet with her at the end of the novel, he exclaims, "Jesus. . . . I'm going to get that dessert." When she tells him that she doesn't understand why he loves her, he replies again, "The orange souffle" (317). Doubtless this is not meant to be taken literally; nevertheless, the association of food with Laura, and with mothers in general, is psychologically significant. Another maternal figure in the novel—Rebecca's natural mother—is, like Charles's mother, in a sanitarium. She makes her ex-husband and Laura bring her packages of junk food, which she eats in enormous amounts and in gross combinations: "She would eat olives with Tootsie Rolls, and then drink grape soda. The foods Laura named made a great impression on Charles; he has trouble forgetting them" (36).

In *Falling in Place*, one of the children, John Joel, is grossly overweight, and it becomes clear that his obesity is connected to an unappeasable hunger and rage. His fat both shields him from a world in which he feels excluded and also expresses an angry hostility toward that world. John Joel is pleased, for example, that his obesity upsets his father. In the novel's climactic scene, he shoots his sister with a pistol he didn't think was loaded or aimed. He is genuinely baffled when she falls. The rage that surfaces in Beattie's work is indeed never understood nor even directly experienced by the characters. As in a dream, it is given a symbolic form, and always it is related to a larger sense of abandonment and isolation.

In the short story "Distant Music" (*Secrets and Surprises*), for instance, a young woman's boyfriend runs off to California to become a pop singer. The woman's dog, which the couple had formerly shared, suddenly becomes inexplicably mean and ferocious. The woman herself expresses no anger or hostility at her loss, but the connection between rage and abandonment is there. In "The Lifeguard," in the same collection, the angry, destructive act, as in *Falling in Place*, is executed by a child. A twelve-year-old boy takes two other children out in a boat and, again inexplicably, sets fire to it. The fact that the aggressive acts in Beattie's work are often performed by children is appropriate, for the narcissistic rage infusing her world belongs to the powerful, primitive emotions of infancy and early childhood. Spangle's nightmare of the fireball expresses the same rage, yet he too does not consciously experience anger—Spangle only feels, as do the other characters, afraid.

The insecurity and untrustworthiness of the world the Beattie characters inhabit have grounds in the objective conditions, the economic and social instability of the times. In *Falling in Place* it is 1979 and in the novel, as in fact, Skylab is falling and terrifying everyone. *Love Always* makes frequent references to the McDonald's massacre. As Lasch has argued, the external social conditions serve to reinforce an internal psychic condition. Beattie's world is both a reflection of real instability and violence in the culture and a projection of inner psychic anxieties—anxieties rooted in the subjective experience of emptiness and isolation, and in the threatening rage, terror, and aggression at its core.

Detachment, then, both from others and from one's own affective or emotional life, provides the main defense against these dangerous feelings for Beattie's characters; it also characterizes Beattie's ironically detached narrative style. *Falling in Place* offers a metaphorical representation of her characters' lives in the Segal exhibit John Joel visits at the museum: "All these plaster people sitting around on subways or sprawled in bed." He reads the artist's description of one of the scenes: "Though the figures are cast from friends, by adding color to them, I touched on terror, hallucination, nightmare" (120). Beneath the mundane settings, the bored poses, and the featureless faces of these plaster people, the artist expresses the same rage and aggression, the same violence, that Beattie's characters secretly harbor. John Joel stares at one sculpture of a woman breaking through a tile wall, "her left breast showing, her left leg and pubic hair, some monster of the shower, with eyes that you couldn't really look into because they were looking down, just indentations, or because of the way the light was. To the side of the woman breaking through the tiles were four other women, or fragments of women's bodies" (121).

The angry violence toward women that this sculpture displays is related to the fact that it has no eyes, or "eyes that you couldn't really look into": the rage in Beattie's work stems from a child's rage at being "unseen," unrecognized or unaffirmed by its mother or the environment (much as Charles's despair in *Chilly Scenes* is elicited by his daily encounter with a blind man). The sculpture provokes John Joel to angry, destructive thoughts about his sister: "He would like to be able to push her from behind so that she would go through a wall like Superman, though hopefully with more pain" (121). The aggressive violence, in the sculptures as well as in the characters' lives, is also linked to an inhuman, deathlike isolation. Later in the novel, John Joel associates the exhibit with his desire to escape from an afternoon picnic with his mother.

Imagining the sculptures, he thinks "that it would be wonderful to be so white and still" (149).

A more recent story, "Windy Day at the Reservoir" (*What Was Mine*), reveals these same dynamics still at play. The story begins by focusing on two married couples, close friends, who are characteristically harboring secrets from each other. Fran and Chap are house sitting in Pia and Lou Brunetti's Vermont summer home. While occupying the Brunetti house, Fran and Chap come to realize how little they know their friends; as usual in a Beattie story, the facade of human relationships collapses to expose the reality of distance and isolation underneath. Fran and Chap also come to understand the distance that exists within the Brunetti marriage, as well as the chasm yawning beneath the surface of their own. By the end of the story, both couples have separated. We learn, furthermore, that the two wives idealize and worship one another, and their identities are, to some extent, merged: Fran tries on Pia's stylish clothes, for instance, and is delighted at how perfectly they fit. Pia, however, has kept from Fran the fact that she has recently had a breast removed. Chap, who is in on the secret, believes Pia was "worried that with her breast gone, she'd . . . lose stature in [his] wife's eyes" and that it would "distance them" (196). Beneath the merged and idealized relationship is, once again, the threat of bodily disintegration and loss, exposing the familiar narcissistic scenario.

The story also includes two other significant characters—the Brunetti's neighbor, Mrs. Brikel, and her 26-year-old retarded son, Royce. The mother-child relationship enacted here provides the underlying psychological context for the story's predominant theme of distance and isolation; it reveals again the primary relational dynamic at the heart of Beattie's vision. The description of Royce's early childhood features a mother-child dyad defined by mutual rage:

Though he had no memory of it, his screaming when he was two years old had brought his mother to tears, daily. She had taken tranquilizers and considered institutionalizing him. His father had stopped coming, because his mother would no longer speak to him. Sometimes, for as much as a week, he and his mother would stay inside the house. In the house, she could run away from him and lock herself behind a door. . . . When he reached for her glasses, she stopped wearing them and functioned in a fog. . . . She would smash delicate things that fascinated him before he had a chance. (229)

The mother's rage mirrors the child's and leads to her isolation and despair. Both mother and child embody an isolated, enfeebled state fueled by narcissistic rage. The child's rage is again connected to a voracious and frightening appetite. Royce is portrayed as greedy; he covets his mother's pies (Mrs. Brikel bakes a pie for Fran and Chap but can only give them half since it would "upset" Royce). His greed is also tied up with his fear of choking: when eating fish "he chewed and chewed so carefully to make sure there were no bones" (226), and he practices the Heimlich maneuver on imaginary victims. Royce's appetite, like John Joel's fat, is also a form of aggression. He enjoys sitting on the most sloping part of the living room floor, a copy of *The Cat in the Hat* propping up one side of his recliner chair to make "the tilt better": "He teased his mother by leaning way over the side of the chair and waving his arms, saying 'Whooooooo' sometimes, pretending he was falling off the side of a ship. He could always make her ask why he didn't sit elsewhere" (227). *The Cat in the Hat*, that story of childhood's secret anarchy, reflects Royce's own riotous appetite in relation to his mother. Though it threatens to go out of control, Royce enjoys teetering on the edge, taunting his mother with that very threat. By the end of the story, however, the taunting threat becomes a reality: he loses control, slips over the edge, and drowns.

While his mother is out one afternoon, Royce puts on his father's old top hat in an attempt to imitate a man he saw in a movie, an Englishman who "reached for some princess's hand" (228). The top hat, of course, also recalls that of the Seuss character. He walks off by himself to the reservoir. A girl later reports that she thinks she saw his hat blow in the water. Royce's descent into the lake is described as follows:

Maybe the fish said *glug-glug*. Maybe they talked the way fish did in fairy tales, and said something like: Come into the kingdom of the deep. Or maybe the hat itself started to talk, and that was what made Royce edge into the water, looking back as if taunting someone behind him as he advanced. (231)

As in Charles's Bermuda dream of Laura and the fat man, love and fulfillment—the fairy tale kingdom in which the princess's hand is finally grasped—is associated with drowning and death. The hat, symbolic of the love-hunger, the unruly appetite with which he taunts his mother, ultimately calls him to his death.

With Royce gone, Mrs. Brikel fixes the sloping floor and insulates the house, which she couldn't do before because Royce "was never cold" and didn't like the heat. At the end of the story, she sits in the newly upholstered recliner chair and admires the freshly laid floor: "The high polyurethane gloss made the floorboards glisten like water. It looked like a large, calm lake that she could imagine gliding swiftly over. Just looking at it, she could feel the buoyance of her heart" (237). At last fully insulated from her child's narcissistic rage, and her own, her life has become a calm surface that she can glide "swiftly over." The placid surface life is achieved at the expense of the angry child-self. This brings us back to the detached lives of the story's drifting couples, indeed to the numbed and shallow lives of so many Beattie characters.

Finally, the 1989 novel *Picturing Will* was greeted by several reviewers as a breakthrough for Beattie, as a work in which she sheds some of her ironic detachment and displays a firmer sense of direction. I agree that there is an effort to assert something beyond the usual drift and despair here, though whether it succeeds is open to question. The parent-child relationship is the focal theme of this novel and even determines its structure: the book is divided into three parts, titled "Mother," "Father," and "Child." The child, Will, is a product of an accidental birth from an equally accidental, arbitrary marriage: his mother, Jody, met his father, Wayne, when the heel of her shoe snapped as she passed him on a crowded street; she passively moved into marriage "without knowing much about him" (5). Soon after Will is born, the restless Wayne disappears. Jody, a photographer, struggles with motherhood while supporting herself by taking wedding pictures. The novel opens when Will is five years old and Jody is debating whether to commit herself to Mel, the manager of a New York art gallery, who is devotedly attached to her as well as to Will. Mel talks the gallery owner, Haverford (Jody refers to him jokingly as Haveabud), into showing Jody's photographs and becoming her manager.

As Jody's career takes off, Mel assumes the more maternal, nurturing role in relation to Will. Interspersed throughout the book are italicized passages that recount the worries and trials of raising a child. At the end of the novel, we learn that the passages are entries from Mel's journal.

The lyrical nature of these sections represents a stylistic change for Beattie, though the content reveals the familiar anxieties. All of the passages essentially deal with a child's fragility in relation to a perilous and unstable world. The following passage about cartoons is typical:

Cartoons aren't satirical exaggerations but normative presentations of everyday situations. The child also will suddenly crash into a wall, unable to correctly judge speed versus distance.

In cartoons, people drop off cliffs.

The child wakes up on the floor, tangled in covers, having toppled—who knows how?—from the bed.

In cartoons, beasts roar and devour people.

Turn a corner in a city, and a gang of pink-haired punks hurtles in front of the child.

In cartoons, buildings suddenly explode.

Remember that the child also sees TV news. (91)

The novel indeed validates Mel's view of a shockingly unreliable world. Haveabud accompanies Mel and Will on a trip to Florida to visit Will's father. Haveabud brings along a young boy, Spencer, and in a motel room one evening, Will is forced to witness a lurid sexual encounter between the two. As Hulbert notes in her review of the novel, "It seems not just that adults can't protect Will, but that they are all unwittingly complicit in his corruption" (34). In the brief part 3 "Child" section that concludes the book, we learn that "years ago Will had started to tell Jody about Haveabud, and she ad shushed him. Nothing negative could be said about her manic mentor" (228). Will, grown up with a child of his own now, wonders why he had never told Mel about the incident. Perhaps, he thinks, "Mel had been so shaky when he arrived back in Florida that Will realized he should not bring up anything that might cause further trouble" (228). The caretaker's fragility matches the child's: neither Will's mother nor the maternal Mel could be trusted to support him.

Nevertheless, the novel seems to be wanting to assert some form of trust. Mel's final journal entry reads:

Who was the real child? Who was naive? Let the current rush around us, I thought, heady, as I often was, with my certainty that we'd stand firm. That we'd make it. Always. Every time we tempted fate. (221)

The novel ends with Will urging his son to "throw the ball. . . . Come on. You have to let go of it sometime. Come on, baby, throw me the ball" (230). The parent is encouraging the child, in other words, to "let go"—an encouragement that implies trust. Usually in Beattie's fiction, relaxing one's defenses and "letting go" means, as it does for Royce or Charles, disaster. The image that immediately precedes Will's soothing encouragement, however, suggests that the trust here too may be suspect. Will observes that his child, as he holds his arms stiffly and jumps, looks "something the way penguins did before they became extinct" and that word "extinct" inserts the ominous note. It recalls the obsessive interest in dinosaurs and the fact of their extinction exhibited by the sexually abused boy, Spencer. "How, in short, could anything be trusted when something as calamitous as the mass extinction of dinosaurs had transpired?" Spencer wonders (108).

As Hulbert notes, this novel "aims at greater certainty" (35). Not all of the characters are drifting or directionless—they have made commitments and formed attachments. The reader is still left wondering, however, how deep those commitments and attachments are and whether the certainty or trust is real—so little in the novel seems to confirm it. Are the characters, in effect, simply holding hands, like Spangle's girlfriend in *Falling in Place*, saying that "there was no fireball when there was"? Hulbert claims that the characters' efforts "to break out of their barren worlds" ultimately "come to seem acts more of duty than of discovery" (35). I agree. The sad fact about this novel is that the certainty—the trust in self and other—that it appears to assert finally seems more *willed* than genuinely found.

Chapter 9

Desire and the Uses of Illusion: Alice Hoffman's *Seventh Heaven*

Alice Hoffman's novel *Seventh Heaven* is, above all, about desire. By desire I mean not only the erotic but also a more general condition of being and feeling. The condition is generated by absence; loss or lack is the seed of desire. I am associating desire, therefore, with a yearning or striving for *presence*—presence as an experiential state that involves both self and other. The yearning for the presence of an other also contains the wish to recapture one's own existential presence or fullness of being. Desire seeks to restore what has been lost, denied, or split off from one's being so that one may be more fully present, more fully alive.

Hoffman's novel is specifically about the pain, as well as the potential joys, bound up with the condition of desire, and the difficulty of awakening to it. Desire is painful because it involves recognition, or at least an unconscious connection, with the absence or loss—and the accompanying fear and anger—at its source. *Seventh Heaven* depicts a whole community—a fictitious suburb of Long Island in 1959—that has insulated itself from desire. Into this community moves a young divorced mother—Nora Silk—who disrupts its surface order and calm but ultimately revives its inner life. Nora becomes the agent of desire, and the fact that she is a mother is, as I will discuss, psychologically significant. Nora is also associated with witchcraft and voodoo. The house she moves into is said to be haunted, and running throughout this novel, as in many of Hoffman's other works, is a magical, mystical element. A child reads minds, a ghost appears, and inner wishes have external, material effects. In the middle of the novel, when the inhabitants of the community find themselves "overcome with desire, a desire that made everything ache, fingers and elbows and toes" (151), that desire is accompanied by an atmosphere of fog, disorientation, and the presence of ghosts: "People stared at each other from their driveways and wondered what they were doing on this street, and the ghosts whispered in their ears, egging them on, and things began to happen for no reason at all" (152).

Our earliest experience of desire originates in an irrational or prerational realm. Desire also generates creative activity, particularly the creation of illusions. Thus the irrational and the illusory, as Hoffman's work imaginatively conveys, are indeed entangled with desire. Her novel playfully taps a deep level of psychodynamic functioning. Illusions are created out of desire and can provide a route back to it. If desire comprehends the intense and painful truth of inner experience, then one can, paradoxically, access truth via illusion. *Seventh Heaven* shows how illusions can actually promote honest, creative, and healthy living.

The positive role of illusion in psychic life is also a central concern of D. W. Winnicott's theoretical writing. Winnicott uses the term "illusion" at various times, as Thomas Ogden has noted, to refer to two quite different phenomena: "The first is the illusion of the subjective object (more accurately described as the illusion of the invisible subject and object), where the mother's empathic responsiveness protects the infant from premature awareness of the self and of the other" (210). This is the illusion of oneness and omnipotence or, in Winnicott's words, the illusion that mother's "breast is part of the infant. It is, as it were, under the baby's magical control" (PR 11). The mother's task is gradually to disillusion the infant, making possible the second, more developmentally advanced form of illusion—the illusion found in playing, in the making of transitional objects or symbols. Transitional objects such as teddy bears occupy an intermediate, illusory, or "potential" space between internal fantasy and external reality. They represent a form of illusion, as Ogden explains, in which "the experience of oneness with the mother and separateness from her coexist in a dialectical opposition" (210). This form of illusion is created out of desire: it arises out of necessary frustration, out of imperfect or incomplete maternal adaptation to infantile need.

Thus desire generates creative illusion or symbol making. As Ogden states, "Symbols are required only when there is desire" (211). Lacan's ideas about the relationship of desire to the creation of the symbolic realm are quite similar to Winnicott's here. The crucial difference between the two theorists, however, is that for Lacan, the symbolic alienates us from the intensity of inner experience, while for Winnicott, the symbolic provides the very route back to that intensity. Creative illusions keep us in touch with a passionate inner reality. The potential space of symbolic play, Winnicott argues, "constitutes the greater part of the infant's experience, and throughout life is retained in the intense experiencing that belongs to the arts and to religion and to imaginative living, and to creative scientific work" (PR 14). Winnicott also emphasizes the paradoxical reality, or, in Ogden's terms, the "dialectical opposition," of the transitional realm of illusion. The inability to maintain this paradoxical state of illusion can in fact have pathological results: "What emerges from these considerations is the further idea that paradox accepted can have positive value. The resolution of paradox leads to a defence organization which in the adult one can encounter as true and false self organization" (PR 14).

The suburban community as a whole in *Seventh Heaven* can be understood metaphorically as an expression of Winnicott's "false" self. The false self is a compliant, social self that protects—or in pathology, engulfs—an underlying "true" self. The true self refers to a basic "sensorimotor aliveness" (Winnicott, *Maturational Processes* 149), to a spontaneous, authentic expression of core being. The false self can defend against the helpless dependency, the neediness and frustrations, of early emotional life. It is an ideal, "good" self that denies the painful, "bad" feelings of separation, anger, and hostility. Hoffman's depiction of American suburbia in the fifties reflects this type of defensive structure: built on the principles of compliance and conformity, suburbia projects an ideal of the good life that denies the existence of separateness and difference, of loss and pain—indeed, of any passion at all. The following description of the subdivision also typifies Hoffman's playful "transitional" style: it is at once fantastic and naturalistic, exaggerated beyond our sense of ordinary reality, yet plainly and factually asserted.

Each house in the subdivision was the same, and for the longest time husbands pulled into the wrong driveways after work; children wandered into the wrong houses for cookies and milk; young mothers who took their babies out for walks in their new carriages found themselves wandering past identical houses, on identical streets, lost until twilight, when the ice-cream man's truck appeared, and they could follow the sound of his bell, which traced his reliable route past their doorsteps. (14)

Hoffman makes the falseness, the flimsiness of the suburban facade quite obvious. Compliance, conformity, and a neatly kept lawn cannot, of course, stave off the reality of loss—of death—or of "bad," dangerous, and violent passions. The main street in the subdivision is significantly named Hemlock Street, and on the other side of the parkway intersecting the area protrudes Dead Man's Hill. Though the children are told "Good night, sleep tight," they are aware of monsters in closets and under trees. "They never told their parents or whispered to each other. Sometimes the monsters reappeared on paper in school, drawn with crayons and colored pencils; they had purple hair and large yellow eyes, and you could tell they didn't believe in good nights or sleeping tight" (23). The novel is also framed by two incidental accounts of abusive families. In an early chapter entitled "Sleep Tight," the detective Joe Hennessy is called to a house where neighbors had made anonymous complaints. He discovers a battered wife—her "legs were purple with bruises"—and a little girl who kept her room perfectly neat and "was doing a good job of faking sleep" (47–48). The wife refuses to make a complaint, and a few weeks later Hennessy discovers that the family has silently left town. Toward the end of the novel, Hennessy is called to a home where a boy has stabbed his father to death. He learns that the father had consistently beaten the boy, but neither the neighbors nor his fellow policemen want to hear the story. The boy is dismissed as crazy, "off his rocker," and quickly carted off to the state mental hospital.

Though the hollow, fraudulent nature of fifties suburban life is hardly an original theme in contemporary art and literature, Hoffman's perspective is distinguished by its affectionate attitude. Her portrayal of suburbia's deceptive facade is suffused with compassion for the vulnerabilities and fears that prompted its construction. Her perspective does not project the same sense of impending disintegration, the sort of explosive violence, that lurks beneath the placid surface lives of, for instance, Ann Beattie's aging fifties children. Nor does it convey the menace and malignancy harbored within a David Lynch vision of suburban life. The type of death or loss that most haunts Hoffman's suburban characters is a deadness within, a loss of inner vitality, expressed through images of ice, entrapment, and constriction. The novel is dedicated to the memory of Houdini, the escape artist whose magical feats of release dominate the imagination of Nora Silk's son Billy. The deadliness of Dead Man's Hill is specifically associated with that of frozen entrapment: "The sunlight reflecting off the ice would make you so dizzy you'd just lie there after your sled overturned, and then in a panic you'd get up as quickly as you could, terrified, convinced that if you didn't move soon the ice would freeze you into place, and that's the way they'd find you, sometime in the spring, deep within the thaw of Dead Man's Hill" (91–92).

Only through a painful reawakening to desire, the novel suggests, can one escape this frozen, deathlike state that constricts and isolates the self. In the middle of the novel, Joe Hennessy's wife, Ellen, feels "something she didn't want and didn't understand surface within her. It was the desire, and it hit her hard, and she was so furious about all those years when she had never wanted anything that she grew colder each day, until she was a perfect piece of ice and Joe Hennessy couldn't touch her, he couldn't even be in the same room with her" (154). The agent of desire in this suburban community, as stated before, is Nora Silk. Though she is represented as possessing a vivacious, irrepressible spirit, she also comes significantly weighted with associations of loss, death, and abandonment. She is, first of all, divorced, a word so threatening to the wives of the neighborhood that "no one had to say it, but the word was there, it had entered their vocabularies and now hung above them, a cloud over their coffee cups" (62). She moves into the house of Mr. Olivera, the first person in the neighborhood to have died and therefore "violated the pact" (15), the unspoken agreement to keep up appearances. Furthermore, we learn that Nora is parentless and was raised in an isolated, run-down house by a misanthropic grandfather who practiced voodoo. The spirit of desire she embodies, in other words, is directly related to her history of ruptured human connections, of absence and loss.

Nora is a threat to the community because of these associations with violated trust or connection, and because the desire she emanates has the power to expose these possibilities beneath the suburban facade—the false self-defense—erected to protect against them. Desire rises from the true self, from the passionate and bodily claims of one's unique subjectivity. It is precisely Nora's passion, sensuality, and uniqueness as she attempts to function as a suburban mother that so disrupts the community. The sensuality implied in her name is expressed in her fantasies—she looks at Hennessy's hands, for instance, and "wondered what his touch would feel like on her shoulders, on her thigh" (65)—and enacted in her affair with a seventeen-year-old boy in the neighborhood, Ace McCarthy. Though she does try to fit in and accommodate herself to the suburban conventions—"she would try to remember to fix Bosco and milk every day at three" (37)—she is unable to suppress her difference and vitality. " 'Get a load of that,' " one of the husbands remarks on seeing her at the hardware store: "Instead of wearing a skirt, as their wives would have, Nora had on black pants and black leather boots; her hair was pulled back into a ponytail and she wore silver earrings shaped like stars" (84).

Although Ace McCarthy comments to Billy that his mom "doesn't look like someone's mother" (55), the point is that she *is* a mother. Most importantly, she is a loving, though imperfect and flawed mother. Unlike the other mothers of the neighborhood, Nora has not forfeited her being in assuming the part of the perfect, conventional mother; her subjectivity has not been sacrificed to the maternal role prescribed by the suburban community. Nora Silk represents a maternal subject of desire, and as such, she has a liberating effect on the community. The issue of maternal subjectivity has become a major topic in recent feminist psychoanalytic theory (see the introduction to this volume). Jessica Benjamin (*The Bonds of Love*), in particular, has discussed the importance of recognizing the mother as a subject of desire. Healthy development involves mother and child's mutual recognition of the other as an individual subject, as an agent of desire. Only a mother with her own selfhood intact can make selfhood fully possible for her child. Hoffman's novel plays out a similar dynamic: Nora's very inability to suppress her individual subjectivity, her passion and sexuality, in her role as suburban mother is what frees the others to discover themselves as subjects of desire as well.

Nora's imperfections as a mother are part of the novel's affirmation of her as a fully human (therefore imperfect) maternal subject. That she genuinely loves both her sons, Billy and James, is never questioned. Her mothering of Billy, however, is obviously flawed; in regard to her eldest son, Hoffman presents Nora as insufficiently empathic. Eight-year-old Billy is the sort of hurt, troubled child who appears frequently in Hoffman's fiction, from four-year-old Simon, who has stopped growing, in *Illumination Night*, to the angry, juvenile delinquent Keith in *Turtle*

Moon. Billy suffers from the loss of his father (after his father left, we are told, he developed the habit of twirling his hair so hard he'd pulled it out in large patches) as well as from an acute awareness of his own, and his mother's, difference and alienation from the suburban community: "By the end of October, every mother of every child in his class knew that Nora was divorced; . . . and that was the end of Billy's chance for any sort of social alliances" (74). Nora only exacerbates his social problems in her attempts to help him make friends: "Already, she had completely humiliated him by inviting three kids he hated over to their house, one per week" (74). Nora fails to recognize that her efforts are intrusive and counterproductive until Hennessy gently chides, " 'They have to make their own friendships. You've got to let it happen naturally' " (86).

Nora's empathic flaws are related to Billy's particular defenses—his obsessions with fire, magic, and Houdini. He practices making himself invisible: "He could almost believe he was becoming invisible; he could feel something curling up inside himself" (54). In keeping with Hoffman's magical, transitional vision, the psychological or internal is also given external validation. At one point, "Hennessy noticed that Billy was growing fainter. It was as if he were retreating inside his clothes or as if—and this was probably just a trick of the fluorescent lighting above them—he were disappearing" (85). After Hennessy tells Nora that she should let Billy make his own friends, however, "He swore that Billy was getting visibly more solid" (86). Billy needs to discover his own selfhood and agency, his own desire—a process that his mother's intrusive efforts were only impeding. He is fascinated with fire perhaps because it is both a potent, effectual force that he longs to possess and a source of destructive energy, symbolic of inner rage in need of release. Houdini, who Billy believes "could shine like a lamp lit from within and pass right through the hemp, the metal, the tides" (76), through all external constraints, also represents a liberating expression of subjective agency.

Despite his withdrawn and reticent nature, Billy does possess a curious power—he can read people's minds. Nora "was never quite certain if she had said something out loud or if Billy's antennae had picked up what she'd been thinking in spite of any silence" (32). Billy does not perceive this ability, however, as power: "Clairvoyance," he thinks, "was a burden" (76). Billy's mind reading is not a true power because it reflects a regressive, undifferentiated state—a lack of boundaries between self and other. Billy stresses how Houdini's "talent was pure and true" precisely because "he could fight against real boundaries" (76). Clairvoyance exemplifies the sort of "bad" or malignant narcissistic illusion that Emmanuel Ghent has discussed, a defensive rather than creative illusion. Defensive illusions, Ghent believes, arise out of a breakdown or "failure of the normal processes of creative illusion and play" (147). Billy's clairvoyance protects against separateness and loss, but in so doing, prevents the recognition of both self and other as individual subjects. In its suggestion of narcissistic oneness and omnipotence, clairvoyance represents a defense that only enforces Billy's insularity and isolation. Thus his loss of this ability at the end of the novel is characterized by a Houdinilike unshackling or release: "The constant hum he heard was gone and with it the headache he always had when he picked up anyone's thoughts" (240).

In the process of achieving his freedom, Billy is assisted not by his mother but by his mother's teenage lover, Ace McCarthy. Ace befriends him and teaches him to play baseball. The novel concludes with Billy making the Little League team, thereby breaking out of his isolation. By internalizing Ace's care and confidence in him—"He kept thinking about what Ace had said to him until he believed it" (239)—Billy is able to play out his potential and discover the true power of his singular mind, his own subjectivity. A Lacanian critic might interpret Ace's role in Billy's emancipation as that of a necessary third force—representative of the father or phallus—that breaks up the narcissistic mother-child dyad. A more plausible interpretation, to my mind, is that Ace provides an empathic, nurturing function that was deficient in the original relationship. Ace's empathic and caretaking abilities, as I will discuss later, are indeed highlighted throughout the novel. Indirectly, however, Billy is also freed by his mother as a subject of desire. Had Nora not acted on her desire and violated the social norm by having an affair with this teenager, Ace would never have entered Billy's life.

Nora's liberating effect on other characters in the novel is more direct. In Joe Hennessy she triggers an almost unbearable desire: "After a dinner of fish sticks and beans and twelve hours of black coffee, he'd be so stricken with desire that he would have given it all away, his house, his family, his job, for one night with Nora Silk" (155). Nursing fantasies of divorce and escape, Hennessy opens up a secret savings account and hangs around the courthouse to hear the lawyers discuss their divorce cases: "Each story gave him hope and fueled his desire" (156). While lying in bed, he fantasizes making love to Nora and the illusion feels so real, so palpable, he wonders how his wife cannot hear them: "How could she not see the shape of Hennessy's mouth on Nora's skin?" (88). Nevertheless, Hennessy is forced to face the illusory nature of his desire. One night he discovers Nora's affair with Ace McCarthy. He immediately goes home, sleeps "a long dreamless sleep," and the next morning withdraws all the savings from his account.

It is not the reality, however, but the dream of his affair with Nora that constitutes Hennessy's real awakening. Loss and illusion are built into desire, and Hennessy, like many of the other characters in the novel, desperately needed to open himself to the full experience. We learn that "he had always wanted to be a cop . . . because he was addicted to order. He liked to know his shirts would be hanging on the left side of the closet; he liked to know he'd be having tunafish casserole and rice every Friday night, although he preferred steak" (43). His addiction to order mirrors that of the suburban community as a whole, but unlike the other residents, Hennessy is unable to suppress an awareness of the false security that order provides. His promotion at the beginning of the novel from uniformed cop to plainclothes detective suggests a metaphoric dismantling of the false self that prefigures the main theme and movement of the novel. The loss of his uniform is accompanied by a dizzying sense of disorientation:

He had been trying to make plainclothes for two years, but as soon as he gave up his uniform something had gone wrong. In the past few days he had completely lost his sense of taste; he'd stood at the refrigerator and guzzled half a jar of black-olive water, thinking it was grape juice, until an olive slid down his throat. . . . The telephone would ring and he'd go to open the front door. (42–43)

As a detective, Hennessy is now "privy to things he never knew about before," things that he could have known while in uniform, "but he realized he had never wanted to hear about certain cases. It wasn't ten-dollar speeding tickets and school assemblies now, it was dirtier business" (45). As he enters the home of the abused wife, he is forced to confront the pain and violence beneath the false self-construct of both the community and the self. That confrontation, however abhorrent and frightening, is nevertheless a vital part of his desire—this is a job he had been wanting for years. Hennessy's desire for Nora is an extension of a process of desire that had begun with his promotion—a process of releasing a defensive rational control and surrendering to the full ambivalence of passionate existence. After leaving the battered woman's home, he sees Nora for the first time:

He should have turned around and walked up the path to his house, but instead he looked up at the last few stars, and they filled him with yearning the way diamonds did other men. He turned his gaze east, to see if the sun was rising, and that was when he saw the woman up on Olivera's roof, cleaning out the rain gutters, oblivious to anything else on the street, and Hennessy realized that it was too late to make any deals. He had already asked for things, and what happened was what always happened whenever a desire was granted. He wanted more. (52)

While Nora extends and accelerates the process of desire in Hennessy, she initiates that process for several of the other characters. Hennessy sees Nora and "wanted more," but many of the characters come to realize, like the teenage Rickie Shapiro, that they "had never truly wanted anything before" (111). Rickie "had always done exactly what she was supposed to" and had "thought everyone was doing what she was doing, being a good girl" (203). Under Nora's influence (she babysits for Nora), Rickie tentatively begins to loosen her false self-defense, letting her hair go natural—"it was thicker and somehow wild, as if she had given up trying to control it" (97)—and submitting to her "bad girl" desire for Ace McCarthy. After arranging a secret rendezvous with Ace, however, Rickie suddenly closes up in fear and rejects him. For a while she retreats to a safer choice, the captain of the football team, who whispers to her lovingly, " 'God, you're perfect' " (202). By the end of the novel, though, Rickie realizes that the facade of perfection is actually the more dangerous choice. Her "perfect" family has begun to unravel: her parents separate and her brilliant brother Danny has become withdrawn and reclusive. "Nothing was perfect, Rickie Shapiro could see that now. . . . Everything seemed to be on shaky ground now, silt really, that gave way when you touched it with your toe. Rickie had been taught to respect and follow all the rules, at any cost, even losing her chance with Ace, and now it seemed there was a possibility that she'd been tricked" (202–3).

Rickie's realization—her ability to tolerate the loss, hurt, and anger of an imperfect reality and an imperfect self—is also her release: it frees her from the bondage, the deathliness, of a false self existence. Similarly, her brother Danny, a high school baseball star and class valedictorian, had always been a good boy—"He was trustworthy, everyone knew that" (139). His liberation, like Hennessy's, finally comes in the pursuit of illusion and the very disillusionment bound up with the experience of desire. Toward the end of the novel, Danny runs away to Florida, pursuing the fantasy of trying out for the Yankees at their spring training camp. On the bus south, "Danny felt dizzy with joy. He had almost been swallowed up by his hometown and now he was ready for the world, not some safe, constricted suburb, or even a protected campus, like Cornell" (218). Once at the camp, he talks his way past the guard, and a bemused coach lets him take a turn at bat.

Danny actually hits the ball hard, several times, and on the last pitch even knocks a sparrow out of the sky. The coach tells him that he's good, " 'But I see a dozen boys as good as you every week' " (221). Danny then watches a rookie hit the ball farther than he "could have if he had hit balls for the rest of his life. The rookie batter was a nothing, a nobody, he probably wouldn't even make the final cut, but as soon as he hit the curveball Danny knew he didn't have a chance. Not now. Not ever" (222). Danny buys a box of oranges for his mother, returns home, and sends in his acceptance to Cornell. Danny's return home, however, is not a defeat; rather, it represents a return to himself, a sober but liberating self-acceptance. Danny's freedom, like Billy's loss of clairvoyance, lies paradoxically in the discovery of his own limits. Only by pursuing the illusion of his desire could he both extend and find his limits, a process of self-discovery. Desire in Hoffman's world does not lead to ecstasy; the release it provides is not an escape but a return—a return to a deeper and more authentic experience of self.

The novel features other characters like Hennessy and the Shapiro children who are "good," trustworthy caretakers. With the advent of Nora Silk into the community, however, they experience a crisis that threatens to shatter that role. Donna Durgin, for example, had always been a model wife and mother. Since her first pregnancy, however, she had also been fat, and it is clear that the fat represents a loss of self-contact or centeredness: "Most of the time she didn't look at herself, she didn't even think about herself, or, if she did, she imagined herself as a cloud, as if the center of herself had drifted away in strands of cotton netting" (119). While having her washing machine repaired one day,

Donna is suddenly jolted back to herself by a casual compliment the serviceman pays her:

"I can tell you work hard," the serviceman said. "You wouldn't believe some of the laundry rooms I've seen. You're somebody who really cares."
The serviceman turned and went back to the washing machine, but Donna Durgin didn't move. She'd been wounded by his kindness; all it took was a few words from a stranger and something inside her snapped. (121)

The serviceman's kindness, his recognition of her "caring," is painful because it makes her aware of what she has been missing. The maternal caretaker has herself been deprived of care and recognition: "Who had smiled at Donna in the past few months? Who had asked her what she thought or what was inside her or noticed that the cuffs of Robert's inky shirts were always white after Donna had washed them and ironed them and folded them into the bureau drawer?" (123). Donna begins to diet, to dream about fancy clothes, and to watch Nora with increasing fascination. She sees Nora playing in the snow with her children and notices the baby stuffing snow in his mouth: "Donna stood there staring, even though any other mother on the block would have looked away" (126). Nora's spontaneity, her natural exuberance, has not been squelched by her role as caretaker or by maternal overconcern. Donna, however, feels she must shed the maternal caretaking role completely in order to free herself, much like the Nora of Ibsen's *A Doll's House*. Without giving notice, Donna runs off, leaving her family and the community stunned. When Hennessy finally locates her, she is working in the lingerie department of Lord & Taylor and is so slim and fashionable he barely recognizes her. Donna explains, " 'I was dead. . . . I was disappearing more each day. Is that what life is supposed to be?' " (193). When Hennessy asks about her kids, Donna responds, again echoing Ibsen's Nora, " 'What good was I to them?' "
The novel nevertheless enforces Donna's deep love for her children. The clairvoyant Billy is able to hear her inner pain as she secretly stands outside her house one night: "The cry was so awful, in a wordless way, that Billy got out of bed and pulled the blinds up and he heard much more than he'd ever heard from anyone's silence before" (185–86). The intensity, and the painful fragility, of the mother-child bond is indeed central to Hoffman's vision, a point that I will come back to later. By

the end of the novel, Donna has begun divorce proceedings, and she tells Nora, " 'I'm going to get my children, too, you know' " (254). Donna's desire, like Hennessy's and Danny's, finally leads to a return that is also a renewal and reaffirmation of self. Donna returns to mothering, and thus her model is ultimately Nora Silk, not Nora Helmer. Nora Silk is perhaps Hoffman's deliberate reworking of Ibsen's Nora into a female subject of desire who can also mother.

Ace McCarthy is another trustworthy caretaker, constricted by his role in his family and community and finally freed by his surrender to desire. Ace not only nurtures Billy, patiently teaching him to play ball, but he was also the one who had taught Danny Shapiro how to hit: "He didn't mind spending hours in the deserted athletic field when the temperature hit ninety-five degrees in the shade. He was the only one willing to pitch balls to Danny until dark, or until one of their mothers came looking for them" (138). In his role as selfless nurturer, Ace takes after his father, who is so good and caring, so perfect, his children refer to him as "the Saint." As with Rickie Shapiro and Donna Durgin, however, the novel exposes the defensiveness of the saintly, all-good role that denies anger and pain; it reveals the dangers of too successfully repudiating the full reality of inner experience.

Ace and his brother Jackie struggle with the inner badness that their father seems unable to acknowledge or tolerate. Unlike Ace, Jackie acts out his anger; he is the quintessential rebellious "bad boy" who even steals cars from the garage of his father's gas station. While Jackie waits for his father to discover a missing Cadillac, we are told that he "was looking forward to seeing the Saint blow up. . . . This is when the Saint goes nuts, when he raises his voice, maybe even smacks me" (92). This is the response Jackie wants—it would be a profound relief to see his father express, admit, and survive rage. The Saint, however, only collapses against the wall "as if someone had hit him hard" (93). Jackie provokes him further by making an anti-Semitic remark about Mr. Shapiro, the Cadillac's owner. The Saint grabs him and pushes him up against the wall:

This was it, this was the explosion Jackie had thought he wanted; finally he'd see the Saint act like a human being. But it wasn't the way Jackie had expected, and it brought him no satisfaction when the Saint let go of him. As the Saint backed off he looked smaller than ever; you could snap him in two with one strong hand. (93–94)

The Saint's fragility prevents him from fully recognizing the "bad" Jackie and thus giving him the support he needs. Jackie is finally punished in the novel's most tragic incident, when he picks up the high school fast girl, Cathy Corrigan. The narrator tells us that you went to Cathy "when you wanted a girl to do things no one in her right mind would do" (102). Hoffman presents her as an awkward, pathetically needy child who uses sex in a desperate bid for acceptance and love. Cathy has a crush on Jackie, but because of Jackie's own sense of worthlessness, her feelings only make him more contemptuous and cruel. Once in the car, Cathy finds herself pressured into having sex not only with Jackie but with all of his friends as well. After the others have left, Cathy asks Jackie if he would kiss her. Though he knows the kiss would be a gesture of affection, not merely sex, he relents. Jackie is surprised to find himself enjoying the kiss when the car containing his pals pulls up: "He didn't want anyone to see them together; it was death to be caught kissing her" (106). Jackie shoves her over the front seat and floors the gas pedal; the car hits a patch of ice and Cathy is killed in the wreck.

The accident is less a result of Jackie's cruel, aggressive side than of his fear of exposing his caring side—a tenderness that kissing Cathy Corrigan betrayed. Jackie emerges from the experience shattered but transformed. He becomes a good boy, marries a girl he meets at church, and is made a partner of his father's gas station, a position Ace had always assumed would be his. Nevertheless, Jackie is haunted, literally, by Cathy's ghost, and develops a terrifying phobia of the dark. While most of the other characters experience a liberating return to self in the process of yielding to desire, Jackie, by defending against desire and the vulnerability of caring, undergoes a retreat. Unable to tolerate darkness and loss, he seeks refuge in the suburban conventions he had originally rebelled against.

With the help of Nora Silk, Ace is more successful than his brother in struggling with his own inner darkness and pain. Unlike his father, Ace recognizes Jackie's "badness" and indeed identifies with it. As Jackie hands him some money from the stolen Cadillac, "Ace felt a new kind of badness inside his chest, and it was cracking him apart trying to get out. Bad blood moved down his arms and legs. It was the beginning of the end of something" (41). Ace's initiation into badness here echoes Hennessy's entrance into the dark interior of suburban life that first accompanied his promotion, his initial descent into desire. Ace is not as adept as his brother, however, at denying his inner pain or that of others: he cannot help feeling sorry for Cathy Corrigan as she sits in front of him in class, and after the accident, he cannot forgive Jackie or himself. He adopts Cathy's abandoned puppy and forms a fierce bond with it. He also witnesses Cathy's ghost, but rather than fleeing from it, he reaches out in an attempt to make contact. He knows it is her ghost "because no other ghost could fill him with such despair or make him bleed from a wound that wasn't even there." After the ghost disappears, Ace "lowered his head and wept; not knowing if he'd been blessed or cursed, he was completely lost" (147). It is at this point that he "found himself in Nora Silk's arms, where he cried for as long as he needed, before she took him home" (148).

This is also the point at which the novel marks a transition from 1959 to 1960. The unrest and vitality of the coming decade corresponds with the increasing disturbance and revival of Hoffman's suburban characters. Like Ace, they are lost, aching, and "overcome with desire" (151), a condition that entails, however, the recovery of passionate, authentic living. Hennessy and his wife come to rediscover their sexual relationship, several of the wives venture into jobs outside the home, and Ace finds that his ruptured relationship with his father and brother, though painful, is also a release: he will not be pumping gas for the rest of his life as he had always assumed. Fortified by Nora's love, Ace dares to expand the limits of his imagination and act on his own desire. At the end of the novel, he accepts his father's gesture of love—the gift of a new car—and leaves town with Cathy's dog in tow.

Though most of the characters, like Ace, move toward a positive, "happy" ending, Hoffman's vision is not wholly, or naively, rosy. Cathy's dog, Rudy, who accompanies Ace, is a reminder of loss, abandonment, and sorrow—of the dangers of human attachment at the root of desire. The dog, moreover, is particularly associated with that most primal human attachment—the mother-child bond. The dog is significantly a puppy, "not more than six months old," when Cathy dies and he is left outside in the cold. He immediately bonds to Ace and won't let him out of his sight. When Ace picks the dog up for the first time,

"He could feel a second heartbeat against his own; he could feel his chest go tight with cold and an agony that had no name" (117). The second heartbeat suggests that of a baby and its excruciating vulnerability. Ace's agony recalls Donna Durgin's silent pain as she stands outside her house after having abandoned her children. In an extraordinary scene toward the end of the novel, the narrative voice enters the dog's head and we hear an expression of the same anguish, the same desire. The abandoned puppy, in a reversal of the dynamic now, assumes the maternal, caretaking role. Rudy hears Nora's baby banging on his crib, clamoring for attention; he pushes open the bedroom door with his nose and enters James's room: "Rudy sat by the crib until the baby moved his thumb into his mouth and closed his eyes. . . . He kept his eyes open and listened to the sound of human breathing, a sound so helpless it could make even a dog shed tears" (249). As the scene continues, Rudy imagines running free, "But the sound of human breathing made him stay on the red-and-white rag rug." True freedom for the dog lies in the attachment, the human bond, that is the essence of his desire:

It didn't matter that he could run faster than any man, or if somewhere there were still rabbits who put down their ears and trembled in the dark. Even when he was asleep he was ready for the whistle or the clap of human hands that might wake him. He longed for the call; in his dreams when he was running only inches away from the moon, a full moon, white enough to blind a man in seconds, he was ready to be claimed by the person he belonged to. (249)

The portrayal of human attachment, particularly the original infant-mother attachment, as both powerful and terrifyingly frail, is a theme that runs throughout Hoffman's fiction. *Fortune's Daughter* traces the lifelong agony of a woman who, as a teenager, was forced to give up her baby. In *Turtle Moon* the bad boy Keith, who like Billy is a product of divorce, comes to deal with his loss and pain through the experience of two intense attachments: one with an abandoned baby whose mother was murdered, and the other, again, with a dog. *Seventh Heaven* reinforces the mother-child attachment theme through a variety of other images as well. Toward the end of the novel, Nora tries to get rid of the ants in her kitchen by putting out poison. As she watches the ants race back and forth "trying desperately to save their eggs," she breaks down and weeps: she "wept as the ants dragged more and more unsalvageable eggs out from their nest. She wept as she brushed the eggs into a paper plate and took them out to the backyard" (252). At the beginning of the novel, Nora uses salt to get rid of the crows in her chimney, "knowing as she did that if those crows had had eggs in their nest, she would never have been able to chase them off with salt" (36).

A baby's helplessness, the vulnerability of its trust, is also highlighted in an incident in which Hennessy watches a baby carriage roll off a curb into a parking lot: "A car pulling out had just missed the damned thing as Hennessy leapt out of the patrol car so he could grab the baby, who had been sound asleep. Hennessy stood there sweating as the baby opened its eyes and stared hard into his face with complete trust" (44). Similarly, we are told that Billy would sometimes forget about his baby brother when he was supposed to be taking care of him. He would run back up the street to find James "hysterical, his face snotty and streaked with tears." James would then grab onto Billy and not let go; he would "put his face against Billy's chest to listen for his heartbeat," and Nora would find them "glued together" (82)—a dynamic repeated in Ace's relationship with the abandoned puppy. At such times, the narrator tells us, Billy would think about Houdini. The association here links the escape artist with release from the frighteningly intense, symbiotic bond of infantile attachment.

The novel as a whole, however, ultimately confirms infantile trust by asserting an overriding faith in maternal presence. This brings us back to Nora Silk and her associations with magic and illusion. Like many of the other characters, Nora too pursues an illusion—the illusion of the suburban community as good and safe, as the perfect protective environment for her children. She also is forced to confront a dark, disorderly, and imperfect reality. Her house, in perpetual disarray, is falling apart; she is shunned by the other mothers in the neighborhood; and her son is being teased and attacked by the other children at school. Though Nora comes to recognize fully the imperfect reality, she nevertheless maintains her faith in the essential goodness of the community. She stands outside her house on New Year's Eve, listening to the sounds of a neighbor's party, and thinks,

Who were these people who danced in the dark, whose children taunted Billy and threw rocks? Good people, she had to believe that, people who tucked their children in at night, who packed school lunches with tender care, who made the same sacrifices she did, maybe even more, so that their children could play in the grass and sleep tight and walk to school holding hands, safe on the sidewalk, safe in the streets, safe the whole night through. And it was not their fault, or anyone else's, that tonight Nora felt as if she were the only person on the planet who was all alone. (144)

Nora accepts the darkness—the cruelty in life, the pain of her separateness and aloneness—but maintains her faith nonetheless. Her ability to forgive imperfection both in the protective environment and in herself—"So Nora was wrong, she'd been wrong about other things before, she wasn't perfect" (59)—makes this same process possible for the community as a whole. The dynamic is similarly reflected in the novel's forgiveness of Nora's imperfectly empathic mothering. The narcissistic ideal of oneness and perfection, rigidly upheld in the defensive suburban facade, is loosened and released. The protective environment—the mother—is imperfect and separate, and that recognition is finally liberating.

Nora's faith in goodness may be based in illusion, but it ultimately has a real, transformative power: her presence allows the community to shed its false self defense, and her enduring faith makes genuine goodness possible. In order to surrender to desire—to a passionate reality outside or beyond rational control—one needs to have faith. In psychodynamic terms, the baby needs to believe that neither self nor mother will be destroyed by the angry, "bad" passions released in the process of "letting go." One needs faith in the durability of maternal presence, faith that goodness will survive. Nora's associations with magic and witchcraft (her voodoo literally shrinks the class bully who had been tormenting Billy) connect her with the earliest infantile illusion of magical control; at the same time, however, she is figured as a limited and imperfect maternal subject. Her character again maintains the paradoxical tension typical of Hoffman's vision. As Winnicott has argued, some experience of magical or omnipotent illusion is necessary in order for the illusion to be shed; the illusion engenders the faith that makes surrendering the illusion possible.

Interestingly, Nora's ex-husband, Roger, is also a magician, but he is a bad magician—"His heart wasn't in it. . . . children could see right through him" (29). He is bad because he is cynical about the world and his magic: "He was a putdown artist" with "a particular knack for killing his audience with cynical one-liners" (30). His lack of faith connects, moreover, with his curious lack of presence or reality. Children could indeed "see right through him" because "his heart wasn't in it." Even when their marriage was good, Nora "had sensed something false about Roger. She wanted to believe in him, but there seemed to be less and less of him to believe in every day" (29). Billy, too, whenever he "tried to conjure up his father he got nothing more than an image of Roger during his blackout trick, an illusion in which Roger was a man in top hat and tails with no body, no face, and no hands" (30).

In contrast, Nora's magical quality is associated with faith and presence, a quality that is also related to the novel's narrative perspective. The omniscient narrative voice that enters the minds of all of the characters, including the dog's, creates the sense of an abiding presence—a presence that transcends and connects the separate subjectivities of the individual characters. Although we hear the first-person voice of each character in the novel's dialogue, the inner voices of the characters are never heard directly from the subjective "I" perspective. The characters are consistently referred to in the third person—"Hennessy realized," "Danny felt," "Nora believed"—as we hear their innermost thoughts and feelings. The rendering of inner subjective reality from this outside perspective enforces the sense of an objective presence that encompasses even the most intimate, solitary self. The magical, omnipresent narrative voice thus stands in dialectical opposition to the novel's central theme of confrontation with limits, separateness, and loss. The dialectic again reflects the transitional nature of Hoffman's vision, its ability to sustain, rather than resolve, the paradoxical tension at the heart of creative, imaginative living.

The concluding scene, as it captures a suspended moment in time, contains the same tension. With her baby in her lap, Nora sits in the bleachers, watching Billy's Little League game. She is now a valued friend of the other mothers; Nora and the community have formed a genuine bond. Her illusion of the suburban neighborhood as a good place to live has in fact become a reality. Nevertheless, the possibility of broken bonds—particularly the mother-child bond that the image of Nora holding James evokes—and the potential of loss and absence, of death, still figures in the picture. The fulfillment or flowering of desire, like the "wild roses that bloomed for only one week out of the year" on Dead Man's Hill (253), is at best, temporary.

The novel ends with an image of the moon: Nora "leaned against the bleachers and pointed upward so that the baby could see the first ball rise into the outfield, far above them, where the moon hung suspended, white and full, appearing in the sky hours before dark" (256). The moon, that long-held symbol of romantic desire, recalls the full moon of the dog's dream—the blindingly intense, white moon that urges him to freedom at the same time that it tugs him back to human attachment, making him long for the human call and its promise of reunion. The final vision both acknowledges the coming dark and celebrates the suspended light of the full, white moon—the momentary fullness and wholeness that is the dream, the seventh heaven, of the heart's desire.

Chapter 10

Afterword

The essays in this volume reveal certain recurring relational themes. While those themes obviously reflect my own psychological issues and interests, I hope I have also proved their significant, shaping role in the texts themselves. The first and perhaps most fundamental theme concerns the paradoxical tension inherent in human relational life. From the moment of birth, we need and are dependent on other human beings, and that dependency makes for inevitable ambivalence. We love and hate the same person; we need the other's recognition and care, but the helplessness bound up with that need incites anger and fear. The key developmental task, as Winnicott and other object relations theorists have argued, is to tolerate the tension of ambivalence and accept the paradoxical nature of passionate life. Our need for deep contact and connection with an other also competes with the need to keep intact an inviolate core self, and thus the dialectical tension between I-ness and we-ness, separateness and one-ness, plays beneath the surface of every significant relationship through-out our lives.

The two writers who frame this collection, Wordsworth and Hoffman, both celebrate a liberating vision that is achieved precisely through the struggle to tolerate ambivalence and sustain paradox. The tension between oneness and separateness is not resolved in favor of either pole in their work; their imaginative worlds share an enjoyment of the intermediary, suspended state of transitional, illusory play. For both writers, freedom is found not in an escape from bonds and limits, but in the very discovery of limits and in the revitalized trust in human bonds. In the works of several of the other writers, we see the tension often resolving in favor of one or the other pole. Merging and drowning fantasies figure consistently throughout these works, though they are accompanied by differing defensive responses. The Rhys novel yields to despair and death; Beattie's work defends with ironic detachment; and the two other male writers, Lawrence and Updike, display the characteristically male defensive strategies of domination and control. Morrison's novel shows how the ability to sustain the dialectical tension is deeply affected by the larger cultural context. If subjectivity or I-ness has been denied on the cultural as well as the immediate baby-caretaker level, then the establishment of boundaries and the maintenance of tension, as *Beloved*'s characters so movingly reveal, become all the more difficult. Several of the works, furthermore, depict narcissistic mothers with impaired boundaries, a phenomenon that must be understood, again, as part of the larger cultural denial of female/ maternal subjectivity.

Another interesting pattern that emerges in the works of the women writers is the important role played by a nurturing, maternal male figure. Edgar in *Wuthering Heights*, Paul D in *Beloved*, Mel in *Picturing Will*, and Ace in *Seventh Heaven* are all tender caretakers who provide critical psychological support for other characters. The pattern suggests that the nurturing care of a child is not restricted by gender, and that a male's involvement can be as profound as a female's. I do not interpret the liberating role that these male characters play as evidence that a male figure is necessary to rescue the child from the maternal dyad. Rather, these works all convey the clamorous need for a nurturing other; if the experience with the original female other has been particularly frustrating and thus ambivalence remains severe, the turn to a nurturing male represents a safer choice than another female.

Real liberation comes, however, not only with the alternative male mothering, but also, as in the Hoffman novel, with forgiveness of the female mother's imperfection. If the child, like Wordsworth, can come to feel that the mother "never did betray the heart that loved her," then the stage is set for trust—trust in women as well as men. As long as women remain the primary caretakers in our society, then trusting women will continue to be more problematic than trusting men. And trust, finally, is perhaps the most pivotal theme of this study. If selfhood is relationally constructed, then trust is the glue. Much in the world conspires against trust; numerous forms of social oppression and injustice create real and present obstacles to the formation of trust. Nevertheless, without it—without faith in the potential goodness in both self and other—we remain imprisoned, personally as well as politically, by apathy and despair. Even the bleakest of the literary works in this study, however, still represent testaments of faith. Trust is implicit in the creative, artistic act itself, in the conversion of private suffering into communicable form, and in the assumption that inner experience, no matter how dark or painful, can indeed be shared.

Notes

1. Introduction

1. Jane Flax, in *Thinking Fragments: Psychoanalysis, Feminism, and Postmodernism in the Contemporary West,* makes the point that postmodernists "seem to confuse two different and logically distinct concepts of the self: a 'unitary' and a 'core' one," and she argues that "those who celebrate or call for a 'decentered' self seem self-deceptively naive and unaware of the basic cohesion within themselves that makes the fragmentation of experiences something other than a terrifying slide into psychosis" (218–19).

2. The best summary of Klein's work can be found in Hanna Segal, *Introduction to the Work of Melanie Klein.* An in-depth account of the various object relations theories presented here is beyond the intent and scope of this introduction. I refer the interested reader to Greenberg and Mitchell for by far the most comprehensive synthesis and incisive analyses of object relations theories within the psychoanalytic tradition. For brief synopses of several of these preoedipal theories as they bear on the concept of narcissism, see also Lynne Layton and Barbara Schapiro, 1–19.

3. John Bowlby's work also focuses on infantile dependence, specifically on attachment and loss as the most powerful determinants in psychological development. Unlike the other British object relations theorists, however, Bowlby grounds his theory in ethology and in the Darwinian theory of natural selection. He postulates "attachment" as a form of instinct (*Attachment and Loss,* 2 vols.). Bowlby's work, with its heavy biological emphasis, does not delve into the emotional and relational vicissitudes or the various symbolic manifestations of unconscious mental life.

4. Alice Miller's *The Drama of the Gifted Child*, and James Masterson's *The Real Self* and *The Search for the Real Self*, also present extensive discussions of the "false self"—its strategies, behavioral traits, and consequences on the emotional life of the individual.

5. The "isomorphism" of the child/mother experience in psychoanalytic theory is also raised as a critical issue in the introduction to *The (M)other Tongue: Essays in Feminist Psychoanalytic Interpretation*, ed. Shirley Nelson Garner, Claire Kahane, and Madelon Sprengnether, e.g., 25; by Susan Suleiman in "Writing and Motherhood," in that volume (352–77); in the introduction to *Narrating Mothers*, ed. Brenda O. Daly and Maureen T. Reddy, 1–18; and by Madelon Sprengnether in *The Spectral Mother*. Sprengnether tries to bridge French and Anglo-American psychoanalytic theories by reorienting the mother's position as both present (as she is in object relations theory) *and* absent (her role in the Lacanian formulation). She conceptualizes subjectivity as based on an "elegiac construct"—understanding the ego, in Freud's terms, as " 'the precipitate of abandoned object-cathexes' "—and thus she sees the organization of the self as always precipitated by the loss of the mother. For Sprengnether, this loss is originary, not secondary to symbiosis or, in Lacanian terms, the Imaginary. The mother's body is "both origin and Other" (9), representative of both home and not home, the site of Freud's uncanny. If such separation is originary, then there is no need for the father or phallus to instigate difference and the process of signification. Thus "the body of the (m)other may actually provide a new, and material, ground for understanding the play of language and desire" (10).

    While Sprengnether presents a fascinating critique of both Freud and Lacan, in her own theorizing she both normalizes and universalizes a condition of radical self-estrangement. The assumption of such deep self-alienation or "internal splitting" (234), which Sprengnether sees as fundamentally characteristic of the maternal experience and of the human condition in general, is open to question from other psychoanalytic and clinical perspectives.

6. See Alfred Flarsheim (508) for a discussion of Winnicott's concept of illusion and the specific ways in which Winnicott's "illusion" differs from the term "delusion."

7. Arnold Modell also discusses the transitional object as the basis for a psychology of creativity in art and life. See *Object Love and Reality*, e.g., 28–42, and *Psychoanalysis in a New Context*, e.g., 187–98.

8. Jones draws on Christopher Bollas's conception of the mother as a "transformational object." As Bollas explains in *The Shadow of the Object*, "the mother helps to integrate the infant's being (instinctual, cognitive, affective, environmental) . . . the mother is experienced as a process of transformation" (14).

9. Rogers's most recent book, *Self and Other*, argues not only for a reorienting of psychoanalytic theory from drive-centered to person-centered, but also for a reorienting of object relations theory such that it will have completely

"dispensed with the assumptions of libido theory and the metapsychological trappings of ego psychology" (44). Rogers would like to see an object relations theory grounded in Bowlby's biological attachment theory and developed in terms similar to the systemic model of cybernetics.

10. See in particular Holland's *Critical I*, in which he argues against Lacan and postmodern critical theories for an acknowledgment of author and reader as individual persons.

11. For an interesting discussion of "empathic reading" from a Kohutian perspective, see J. Brooks Bouson, e.g., 169–72.

12. For a brief summary of recent psychoanalytic ideas about the relationship of narcissistic injury to artistic creativity, see also Layton and Schapiro, 19–27.

4. Gender, Self, and the Relational Matrix: D. H. Lawrence and Virginia Woolf

1. John Clayton's recent book *Gestures of Healing: Anxiety and the Modern Novel* uses an object relations framework to make a compelling argument about modernism in general. Clayton looks at modernism as "a condition of feeling shaped by particular kinds of childhood experience during the unfolding of a particular historical moment" (viii). That condition of feeling is primarily anxiety—"the experience of being a fragile or empty self in an empty world" (6)—and it is shaped, Clayton believes, by a specific familial configuration in which the mother is narcissistic and controlling and the father weak and ineffectual: "Controlling mother, weak father who has fallen: This description is a kind of cultural metaphor for altered relations in the modern nuclear family; it is also a description of the actual families of British and American early modernist novelists" (33). Clayton is not arguing for the resurrection of the patriarchal family, but he is analyzing the anxiety aroused when "traditional grounds of support have been lost" (31). He concludes that modernist literature and art offer "an orientation to a disorienting reality" (140); they reflect reparative acts—gestures of healing—in response to, and in a struggle against, anxiety, emptiness, and alienation.

2. Heinz Kohut discusses the particularly fluid self-structure of creative artists in "Childhood Experience and the Creative Imagination," in Ornstein 1:271–74.

3. The first extensive Freudian study of Lawrence is Daniel Weiss's *Oedipus in Nottingham*. Other psychological studies focusing on Lawrence's relationship with his mother and his attitude toward women have employed a variety of approaches, including Jungian, Eriksonian, and Laingian. See, for instance, Marguerite Beede Howe, Gavriel Ben-Ephraim, and Judith Ruderman. Jeffrey Berman analyzes Paul Morel as a "troubled Narcissus" and illuminates the preoedipal ambivalence that informs all of the characters' relationships in *Sons and Lovers*. Daniel Dervin and Margaret Storch also

highlight preoedipal dynamics in Lawrence's texts. Dervin's is a more general, theoretical examination of Lawrence's work, applying Winnicott's ideas in particular to an analysis of Lawrence's creative process and development as a writer. Storch relies almost exclusively on Melanie Klein's theories to illuminate the deep ambivalence and splitting of mother/woman that she finds in Lawrence's fiction.

4. See Kohut; Stern; and Benjamin. For brief summaries of their ideas, see also the introduction to this volume.

5. Woolf's work has attracted a voluminous amount of attention by both psychoanalytic and feminist literary critics in recent years. Some notable psychological studies include those by Jean O. Love, Roger Poole, and Louise DeSalvo. These critics view Woolf's fiction as a therapeutic working through of trauma; Love and Poole concentrate on Woolf's mental illness and breakdowns in relation to her art, while DeSalvo focuses on the childhood sexual abuse Woolf suffered at the hands of her half-brothers. Mark Spilka stresses Woolf's inability to mourn her mother's death and sees her incomplete grieving as central to her writing. Phyllis Rose and James Naremore discuss Woolf from the Laingian perspective of "the divided self," while Makiko Minow-Pinkney uses Lacanian concepts in her feminist argument.

   Shirley Panken's study offers a balanced psychoanalytic view of the intersections of Woolf's life and art. She views Woolf's fiction "as a means of gaining the love of exalted, maternal figures, of mourning her losses, of grappling with her emotional dilemmas" and sees evidence in both the work and the life as pointing toward an overriding "need for rescue" (7). Because Woolf was unable to internalize "a consistently nurturing and sustaining relationship with her mother or father," Panken concludes that "Woolf's ability to heal early emotional wounds, her capacity to separate, individuate and create an integrated identity, remained unresolved" (13). Despite the conflicts revealed in the fiction, however, Panken stresses Woolf's creative "power to impose form over chaos" (12).

   Elizabeth Abel, Ellen Bayuk Rosenman, and Jane Lillenfeld also focus on the centrality of the relationship with the mother in Woolf's novels. Abel examines what she sees as both Freudian "patricentric" and Kleinian "matricentric" narratives in Woolf's fiction, outlining "the forces guiding Woolf's trajectory from matrilinear to patrilinear definitions of the daughter" (*Virginia Woolf* 85). She ties Woolf's work to the social history of gender within psychoanalysis. Rosenman and Lillenfeld focus on the desire for fusion or symbiotic oneness with the mother. Lillenfeld works with the archetype of the Great Mother. Rosenman emphasizes Woolf's desire to recover her dead mother (who died when Virginia was thirteen). Rosenman's critical analysis, though it mentions Chodorow a couple of times, does not really employ a depth-psychological perspective.

   Ernest and Ina Wolf, J. Brooks Bouson, and Jeffrey Berman all analyze Woolf's characters in terms of underlying and pervasive narcissistic disturbance. Berman sees the repeated references in *Mrs. Dalloway* to a wounded or diseased heart as highlighting the injured narcissism that is the novel's prime subject. The Wolfs and Bouson examine Woolf's work within a specifically Kohutian framework. The Wolfs analyze the fragile, narcissistic self-structure of Mrs. Ramsay and relate it to Woolf's own family history. Bouson emphasizes the defensive strategies in *Mrs. Dalloway* that serve to protect against a narcissistic disintegration of self, and she shows how critics collude in upholding these defenses in their readings of the text.

6. Panken analyzes the difficulties Woolf herself faced in establishing a firm feminine identification with her mother: "Julia Stephen's depression, excessive involvement with her family of origin, preoccupation with her dead husband, favoritism of son, distancing of Leslie, at the same time envisioning him a father-figure, did not provide a consistent or firm feminine model for Virginia. Following the mother's death, Woolf's inability to mourn, to resolve her submerged anger regarding her mother, interfered with the evolution of her feminine and heterosexual identification" (15–16).

7. Panken also discusses the importance of the oral and incorporative imagery in Woolf's work and its roots in Woolf's own developmental history (e.g., 134–35).

8. John Clayton believes that beneath the separate voices and multiple points of view in Woolf's work, there is an assurance of unity in the underlying voice: the omniscient narrative voice offers "loving reassurance of wholeness and continuity even as the world represented is one of fragmentation and evanescence" (118). For him, Woolf's aesthetics manifest a "healing fusion" (176), and he claims to leave her texts with an "assurance of wholeness" (180). I don't share this response; rather, I am moved more by the sense of heroic effort (epitomized by the final image of Bernard) that her work evokes, by the struggle *not* to succumb to a deathlike fusion or dedifferentiated state.

9. Some feminist critics complain that psychoanalytic object relations theories contribute to "mother bashing"—blaming the mother for all psychological ills. This is a simplistic notion that should not be inferred from my arguments about the narcissistic problems of mothers in the texts I analyze. The relational perspective allows us to understand *all* psychological problems as contextual, as belonging to a larger systemic network of relationships. If the mothers are represented as lacking full subjectivity, as being without a sense of their own agency and authentic selfhood, this must be understood as part of a larger cultural deprivation and negation of women's narcissistic needs. The culture's denial of women's authority and freedom enforces and exacerbates women's narcissistic wounds; such narcissistic problems then necessarily complicate women's mothering. This general assumption underlies my perspective here but is outside the scope of my critical analysis, which focuses specifically on the interpersonal and intrapsychic dynamics of the texts.

5. *Boundaries and Betrayal in Jean Rhys's* Wide Sargasso Sea

1. See, for instance, Deborah Kelly Kloepfer, Kathy Mezei, and Nancy R. Harrison. Most recent psychoanalytic studies of Rhys have employed a Lacanian perspective. These studies tie the novel's portrayal of female subjectivity as alienated and illusory to Lacan's ideas about the maternal/female position in language and culture.

2. See, in particular, Gilbert Rose's *Trauma and Mastery in Life and Art* and David Aberbach's *Surviving Trauma*.

3. It is interesting to note how the theme of corruption/contamination by the other gets played out in the white and black imagery here (her white dress, his face "black with hatred," etc.). The imagery has racial implications and is indeed tied in with Antoinette's complicated and ambivalent relationships with the black characters in the novel. Toni Morrison, in her recent study *Playing in the Dark*, explores the political dimension of such imagery as it figures throughout American literature.

7. *Internal World and the Social Environment:* Toni Morrison's Beloved

1. Madonne Miner sees Cholly's rape of Pecola as arising out of his desperate desire for recognition, for "confirmation of his presence" (179). This reading again supports Benjamin's thesis about the deep intertwining of love, recognition, and domination. Miner also discusses identity issues in *The Bluest Eye* in terms of a "constantly shifting balance between seeing and being seen" and the "distortion of this visual balance" (184) that sexism and racism create.

2. The emphasis here on Paul D's "holding" quality calls to mind Winnicott's argument about the need for the mother to provide a reliable and protective "holding environment" for the infant. Such "holding" forms the basis for trust in both self and world (see Winnicott, *Maturational Processes*, e.g., 43–44).

3. Stories and storytelling figure prominently in the fiction of many black women writers, and their significance is rooted historically in the slave narrative and in the rich folk tradition of black culture. See Willis for a historically informed rhetorical analysis of how black oral tradition shapes narrative form in black women's fiction; see Skerrett for a discussion of storytelling in *Song of Solomon*. My depth-psychological analysis of the function of stories in *Beloved* is compatible with and can complement historical, sociological, and rhetorical perspectives.

Works Cited

Abel, Elizabeth. *Virginia Woolf and the Fictions of Psychoanalysis*. Chicago: U of Chicago P, 1989.

———. "Women and Schizophrenia: The Fiction of Jean Rhys." *Contemporary Literature* 20 (1979): 155–77.

Aberbach, David. *Surviving Trauma: Loss, Literature, and Psychoanalysis*. New Haven: Yale UP, 1989.

Aldridge, John. "The Private Vice of John Updike." *John Updike*. Ed. Harold Bloom. New York: Chelsea House, 1987.

Allen, Mary. *The Necessary Blankness: Women in Major American Fiction of the Sixties*. Urbana: U of Illinois P, 1976.

Angier, Carole. *Jean Rhys: Life and Work*. Boston: Little, Brown, 1990.

Atwood, George, and Robert Stolorow. *Structures of Subjectivity: Explorations in Psychoanalytic Phenomenology*. Hillsdale, NJ: Analytic Press, 1984.

Beattie, Ann. *Chilly Scenes of Winter*. New York: Popular Library, 1976.

———. *Falling in Place*. New York: Random House, 1980.

———. *Love Always*. New York: Random House, 1985.

———. *Picturing Will*. New York: Vintage, 1989.

———. *Secrets and Surprises*. New York: Random House, 1978.

———. *What Was Mine*. New York: Vintage, 1991.

Ben-Ephraim, Gavriel. *The Moon's Dominion: Narrative Dichotomy and Female Dominance in Lawrence's Early Novels*. East Brunswick, NJ: Associated UP, 1981.

Benjamin, Jessica. *The Bonds of Love: Psychoanalysis, Feminism, and the Problem of Domination*. New York: Pantheon, 1988.

Berman, Jeffrey. *Narcissism and the Novel*. New York: New York UP, 1990.

Bloom, Harold. Introduction. *John Updike*. 4–8.

189

Bollas, Christopher. *The Shadow of the Object: Psychoanalysis of the Unthought Known.* New York: Columbia UP, 1987.

Bouson, J. Brooks. *The Empathic Reader: A Study of the Narcissistic Character and the Drama of the Self.* Amherst: U of Massachusetts P, 1989.

Bowlby, John. *Attachment and Loss.* 2 vols. New York: Basic, 1969–1973.

Brontë, Charlotte. *Jane Eyre* [1847]. New York: Dell, 1961.

Brontë, Emily. *Wuthering Heights* [1847]. Ed. William R. Sale, Jr. New York: Norton, 1972.

Burgin, Richard. "A Conversation with John Updike." *John Updike Newsletter* 21 (1979): 1–10.

Chase, Richard. "The Brontës, or Myth Domesticated." *Forms of Modern Fiction.* Ed. William Van O'Connors. Bloomington: Indiana UP, 1954. 102–19.

Chodorow, Nancy. *The Reproduction of Mothering: Psychoanalysis and the Sociology of Gender.* Berkeley: U of California P, 1978.

Clayton, John J. *Gestures of Healing: Anxiety and the Modern Novel.* Amherst: U of Massachusetts P, 1991.

Crews, Frederick. "Mr. Updike's Planet." *New York Review of Books* 4 Dec. 1986: 7–14.

Curtis, Jan. "The Secret of *Wide Sargasso Sea.*" *Critique* 31 (1990): 185–97.

Daly, Brenda O., and Maureen T. Reddy, eds. *Narrating Mothers: Theorizing Maternal Subjectivities.* Knoxville: U of Tennessee P, 1991.

Deri, Susan. "Transitional Phenomena: Vicissitudes of Symbolization and Creativity." *Between Reality and Fantasy: Transitional Objects and Phenomena.* Ed. Simon A. Grolnick and Leonard Barkin. New York: Aronson, 1978. 45–60.

Dervin, Daniel. "Play, Creativity, and Matricide: The Implications of Lawrence's 'Smashed Doll' Episode." *Mosaic* 14 (1981): 81–94.

———. *A "Strange Sapience": The Creative Imagination of D. H. Lawrence.* Amherst: U of Massachusetts P, 1984.

DeSalvo, Louise. *Virginia Woolf: The Impact of Childhood Sexual Abuse on Her Life and Work.* Boston: Beacon, 1989.

Dinnage, Rosemary. "A Bit of Light." *Between Reality and Fantasy: Transitional Objects and Phenomena.* Ed. Simon A. Grolnick and Leonard Barkin. New York: Aronson, 1978. 365–77.

Dinnerstein, Dorothy. *The Mermaid and the Minotaur: Sexual Arrangements and the Human Malaise.* New York: Harper & Row, 1976.

Ellis, David. *Wordsworth, Freud, and the Spots of Time.* Cambridge: Cambridge UP, 1985.

Erikson, Erik. *Childhood and Society.* New York: Norton, 1950.

———. *Identity, Youth, and Crisis.* New York: Norton, 1968.

Fairbairn, W. R. D. *An Object Relations Theory of the Personality.* New York: Basic, 1952.

Fine, Ronald E. "Lockwood's Dreams and the Key to *Wuthering Heights.*" *Nineteenth-Century Fiction* 24 (1969): 16–30.

Flarsheim, Alfred. "Discussion of Anthony Flew." *Between Reality and Fantasy.* 505–10.

Flax, Jane. *Thinking Fragments: Psychoanalysis, Feminism, and Postmodernism in the Contemporary West.* Berkeley: U of California P, 1990.

Freud, Sigmund. "Mourning and Melancholia." *The Standard Edition of the Complete Works of Sigmund Freud.* Trans. and ed. James Strachey. Vol. 14. London: Hogarth, 1953–1974.

Friedman, Michael. *The Making of a Tory Humanist: Wordsworth and the Idea of Community.* New York: Columbia UP, 1979.

Frosh, Stephen. *The Politics of Psychoanalysis: An Introduction to Freudian and Post-Freudian Theory.* New Haven: Yale UP, 1987.

Gardiner, Judith Kegan. *Rhys, Stead, Lessing, and the Politics of Empathy.* Bloomington: Indiana UP, 1989.

Garner, Shirley Nelson, Claire Kahane, and Madelon Sprengnether, eds. *The (M)other Tongue: Essays in Feminist Psychoanalytic Interpretation.* Ithaca: Cornell UP, 1985.

Ghent, Emmanuel. "Paradox and Process." *Psychoanalytic Dialogues* 2 (1992): 135–59.

Gilbert, Sandra M., and Susan Gubar. *The Madwoman in the Attic: The Woman Writer and the Nineteenth-Century Literary Imagination.* New Haven: Yale UP, 1979.

Gilligan, Carol. *In a Different Voice: Psychological Theory and Women's Development.* Cambridge, MA: Harvard UP, 1982.

Gleick, James. *Chaos: Making a New Science.* New York: Viking, 1987.

Greenberg, Jay R., and Stephen Mitchell. *Object Relations in Psychoanalytic Theory.* Cambridge, MA: Harvard UP, 1983.

Greiner, Donald. *The Other John Updike.* Athens: Ohio UP, 1981.

Gross, Terry. "Fresh Air: Interview with John Updike." National Public Radio. WBUR, Boston. 18 October 1990.

Guntrip, Harry. *Personality Structure and Human Interaction: The Developing Synthesis of Psychodynamic Theory.* New York: International UP, 1961.

———. *Schizoid Phenomena, Object Relations, and the Self.* New York: International P, 1969.

Hafley, James. "The Villain in *Wuthering Heights.*" *Nineteenth-Century Fiction* 13 (1958): 199–215.

Harrison, Nancy R. *Jean Rhys and the Novel as Women's Text.* Chapel Hill: U of North Carolina P, 1988.

Hartman, Geoffrey. *Wordsworth's Poetry, 1787–1814.* New Haven: Yale UP, 1971.

Heffernan, James. "The Presence of the Absent Mother in Wordsworth's *Prelude.*" *Studies in Romanticism* 27 (1988): 253–72.

Heisenberg, Werner. *Physics and Philosophy: The Revolution in Modern Science.* New York: Harper & Row, 1958.

Hoffman, Alice. *Fortune's Daughter.* New York: Putnam's, 1985.

———. *Illumination Night*. New York: Putnam's, 1987.

———. *Seventh Heaven*. New York: Putnam's, 1990.

———. *Turtle Moon*. New York: Putnam's, 1992.

Holland, Norman. *The Critical I*. New York: Columbia UP, 1991.

———. *The Dynamics of Literary Response*. New York: Oxford UP, 1968.

Horvath, Brooke. "The Failure of Erotic Questing in John Updike's Rabbit Novels." *Denver Quarterly* 23 (1988): 70–89.

Howard, Jane. "Can a Nice Novelist Finish First?" *Life* 4 Nov. 1966: 74–74A +.

Howe, Marguerite Beede. *The Art of the Self in D. H. Lawrence*. Athens: Ohio UP, 1977.

Hulbert, Ann. "Only Disconnect." *New York Review of Books* 31 May 1990: 33–35.

Jones, James. *Contemporary Psychoanalysis and Religion: Transference and Transcendence*. New Haven: Yale UP, 1991.

Jordan, Judith V., Alexandra G. Kaplan, Jean Baker Miller, Irene P. Stiver, and Janet L. Surrey. *Women's Growth in Connection: Writings from the Stone Center*. New York: Guildford, 1991.

Kernberg, Otto. *Borderline Conditions and Pathological Narcissism*. New York: Aronson, 1975.

———. *Internal World and External Reality*. New York: Aronson, 1980.

Klein, Melanie. *Envy and Gratitude and Other Works, 1946–1963*. New York: Dell, 1975.

Klein, Melanie, and Joan Riviere. *Love, Hate, and Reparation* [1937]. New York: Norton, 1964.

Kloepfer, Deborah Kelly. *The Unspeakable Mother: Forbidden Discourse in Jean Rhys and H. D.* Ithaca: Cornell UP, 1989.

Kohut, Heinz. *The Analysis of the Self*. New York: International UP, 1971.

Kuhn, Thomas. *The Structure of Scientific Revolutions*. Chicago: Chicago UP, 1962.

Langer, Suzanne. *Philosophy in a New Key*. Cambridge, MA: Harvard UP, 1942.

Lasch, Christopher. *The Culture of Narcissism: American Life in an Age of Diminishing Expectations*. New York: Norton, 1978.

Lawrence, D. H. *The Complete Short Stories* [1922]. Vol. 2. New York: Viking, 1961.

———. *The Rainbow* [1915]. New York: Viking, 1972.

———. *Sons and Lovers* [1913]. New York: Viking, 1974.

———. *Women in Love* [1921]. Harmondsworth, England: Penguin, 1987.

Layton, Lynne. "A Deconstruction of Kohut's Concept of the Self." *Contemporary Psychoanalysis* 26 (1990): 420–28.

Layton, Lynne, and Barbara Schapiro, eds. *Narcissism and the Text: Studies in Literature and the Psychology of Self*. New York: New York UP, 1986.

Lillenfeld, Jane. " 'The Deceptiveness of Beauty': Mother Love and Mother Hate in *To the Lighthouse*." *Virginia Woolf: Modern Critical Views*. Ed. Harold Bloom. New York: Chelsea House, 1986.

Loewald, Hans. *Papers on Psychoanalysis*. New Haven: Yale UP, 1980.

————. *Sublimation: Inquiries into Theoretical Psychoanalysis.* New Haven: Yale UP, 1988.

Love, Jean O. *Virginia Woolf: Sources of Madness and Art.* Berkeley: U of California P, 1977.

McDargh, John. *Psychoanalytic Object Relations Theory and the Study of Religion: On Faith and the Imaging of God.* Lanham, MD: UP of Amf ica, 1983.

Mahler, Margaret, Fred Pine, and Anni Bergman. *The Psychological Birth of the Human Infant.* New York: Basic, 1975.

Masterson, James. *The Real Self.* New York: Mazel, 1985.

————. *The Search for the Real Self.* New York: Free Press, 1988.

Meissner, William. *Psychoanalysis and Religious Experience.* New Haven: Yale UP, 1984.

Mezei, Kathy. " 'And It Kept Its Secret': Narration, Memory, and Madness in Jean Rhys's *Wide Sargasso Sea.*" *Critique* 28 (1987): 195–209.

Miller, Alice. *The Drama of the Gifted Child: How Narcissistic Parents Form and Deform the Emotional Lives of Their Talented Children.* Trans. Ruth Ward. New York: Basic, 1981.

Miller, Jean Baker. *Towards a New Psychology of Women.* Boston: Beacon, 1976.

Milner, Marion. *The Suppressed Madness of Sane Men: Forty-Four Years of Exploring Psychoanalysis.* London: Tavistock, 1987.

Miner, Madonne M. "Lady No Longer Sings the Blues: Rape, Madness, and Silence in *The Bluest Eye.*" *Conjuring: Black Women, Fiction, and Literary Tradition.* Ed. Marjorie Pryse and Hortense J Spillers. Bloomington: Indiana UP, 1985. 176–91.

Minow-Pinkney, Makiko. *Virginia Woolf and the Problem of the Subject.* New Brunswick, NJ: Rutgers UP, 1987.

Mitchell, Stephen. *Relational Concepts in Psychoanalysis: An Integration.* Cambridge, MA: Harvard UP, 1988.

Modell, Arnold. *Object Love and Reality: An Introduction to a Psychoanalytic Theory of Object Relations.* New York: International UP, 1968.

————. *Psychoanalysis in a New Context.* New York: International UP, 1984.

Moers, Ellen. *Literary Women.* New York: Doubleday, 1976.

Morrison, Andrew. *Shame: The Underside of Narcissism.* New York: Analytic, 1989.

Morrison, Toni. *Beloved.* New York: New American Library, 1987.

————. *The Bluest Eye.* New York: Washington Square Press, 1970.

————. *Playing in the Dark: Whiteness and the Literary Imagination.* Cambridge, MA: Harvard UP, 1992.

————. *Sula.* New York: New American Library, 1973.

Moser, Thomas. "What Is the Matter with Emily Jane? Conflicting Impulses in *Wuthering Heights.*" *Nineteenth-Century Fiction* 17 (1962): 1–19.

Naremore, James. *The World without a Self: Virginia Woolf and the Novel.* New Haven: Yale UP, 1987.

Oates, Joyce Carol. "Updike's American Comedies." *Modern Fiction Studies* 21 (1975): 459–72.

O'Connor, Teresa F. *Jean Rhys: The West Indian Novels.* New York: New York UP, 1986.

Ogden, Thomas. *The Matrix of the Mind: Object Relations and the Psychoanalytic Dialogue.* Northvale, NJ: Aronson, 1986.

Onorato, Richard. *The Character of the Poet: Wordsworth in the Prelude.* Princeton: Princeton UP, 1971.

Ornstein, Paul, ed. *The Search for the Self: Selected Writings of Heinz Kohut, 1950–1978.* 2 vols. New York: International P, 1978.

Panken, Shirley. *Virginia Woolf and the "Lust of Creation": A Psychoanalytic Exploration.* Albany: State U of New York P, 1987.

Poole, Roger. *The Unknown Virginia Woolf.* Cambridge, England: Cambridge UP, 1978.

Rhys, Jean. *The Letters of Jean Rhys.* Ed. Francis Wyndham and Diana Melly. New York: Viking, 1984.

———. *Smile Please: An Unfinished Autobiography* [1979]. New York: Harper & Row, 1980.

———. *Wide Sargasso Sea* [1966]. New York: Norton, 1982.

Rizzuto, Ana-Maria. *The Birth of the Living God: A Psychoanalytic Study.* Chicago: U of Chicago P, 1979.

Rogers, Robert. *Metaphor: A Psychoanalytic View.* Berkeley: U of California P, 1978.

———. *Self and Other: Object Relations in Psychoanalysis and Literature.* New York: New York UP, 1991.

Rose, Gilbert. "The Creativity of Everyday Life." *Between Reality and Fantasy.* 347–62.

———. *Trauma and Mastery in Life and Art.* New Haven: Yale UP, 1987.

Rose, Phyllis. *Woman of Letters: A Life of Virginia Woolf and the Mother-Daughter Relationship.* Baton Rouge: Louisiana State UP, 1986.

Rosenman, Ellen Bayuk. *The Invisible Presence: Virginia Woolf and the Mother-Daughter Relationship.* Baton Rouge: Louisiana State UP, 1986.

Ruderman, Judith. *D. H. Lawrence and the Devouring Mother: The Search for the Patriarchal Ideal of Leadership.* Durham, NC: Duke UP, 1984.

Schapiro, Barbara. *The Romantic Mother: Narcissistic Patterns in Romantic Poetry.* Baltimore: Johns Hopkins UP, 1983.

Schneiderman, Leo. "Modern Fictional Protagonists: Motherless Children, Fatherless Waifs." *American Journal of Psychoanalysis* 50 (1990): 215–29.

Schopen, Bernard. "Faith, Morality, and the Novels of John Updike." *Twentieth-Century Literature* 24 (1978): 523–35.

Schwartz, Murray. "Where Is Literature?" *College English* 36 (1975): 756–65.

Segal, Hanna. *Introduction to the Work of Melanie Klein.* 2d ed. New York: Basic, 1974.

Skerrett, Joseph T. "Recitation to the Griot: Storytelling and Learning in Toni Morrison's *Song of Solomon.*" *Conjuring.* 192–202.

Solomon, Eric. "The Incest Theme in *Wuthering Heights.*" *Nineteenth-Century Fiction* 14 (1959): 80–83.

Spilka, Mark. *Virginia Woolf's Quarrel with Grieving.* Lincoln: U of Nebraska P, 1980.

Sprengnether, Madelon. *The Spectral Mother: Freud, Feminism, and Psychoanalysis.* Ithaca: Cornell UP, 1990.

Stelzig, Eugene. *All Shades of Consciousness: Wordsworth's Poetry and the Self in Time.* Paris: Mouton, 1975.

Stern, Daniel. *The Interpersonal World of the Infant.* New York: Basic, 1985.

Storch, Margaret. *Sons and Adversaries: Women in William Blake and D. H. Lawrence.* Knoxville: U of Tennessee P, 1990.

Sullivan, Harry Stack. *Conceptions of Modern Psychiatry.* New York: Norton, 1940.

Thompson, Wade. "Infanticide and Sadism in *Wuthering Heights.*" *PMLA* 78 (1963): 69–74.

Turner, John. "Wordsworth and Winnicott in the Area of Play." *International Review of Psycho-Analysis* 15.4 (1988): 481–97.

Twitchell, James. "Heathcliff as Vampire." *Southern Humanities Review* 11 (1977): 355–62.

Updike, John. *Assorted Prose.* New York: Knopf, 1965.

———. *The Centaur.* New York: Knopf, 1963.

———. *Hugging the Shore: Essays and Criticism.* New York: Knopf, 1983.

———. Introduction. *Soundings in Satanism.* Ed. F. J. Sheed. New York: Sheed & Ward, 1972.

———. *A Month of Sundays.* New York: Knopf, 1975.

———. *Of the Farm.* New York: Knopf, 1965.

———. *Pigeon Feathers and Other Stories.* New York: Knopf, 1962.

———. *Rabbit at Rest.* New York: Knopf, 1990.

———. *Rabbit Is Rich.* New York: Knopf, 1981.

———. *Rabbit Redux.* New York: Knopf, 1971.

———. *Rabbit, Run.* New York: Knopf, 1960.

———. *Roger's Version.* New York: Knopf, 1986.

———. "A Sandstone Farmhouse." *New Yorker* 11 June 1990: 36–48.

———. *Self-Consciousness: Memoirs.* New York: Knopf, 1989.

———. *The Witches of Eastwick.* New York: Knopf, 1984.

Uphaus, Suzanne. *John Updike.* New York: Ungar, 1980.

Van Ghent, Dorothy. *The English Novel: Form and Function.* New York: Holt, Rinehart, & Winston, 1953.

Verduin, Kathleen. "Sex, Nature, and Dualism in *The Witches of Eastwick.*" *Modern Language Quarterly* 46 (1985): 293–315.

Waugh, Patricia. *Feminine Fictions: Revisiting the Postmodern.* London: Routledge, 1989.

Weiss, Daniel. *Oedipus in Nottingham.* Seattle: U of Washington P, 1962.

Wessling, Joseph. "Narcissism in Toni Morrison's *Sula.*" *College Language Association Journal* 31 (1988): 281–98.

Whitehead, Alfred North. *Nature and Life.* 1934. New York: Greenwood, 1968.

Willis, Susan. *Specifying: Black Women Writing the American Experience.* Madison: U of Wisconsin P, 1987.

Wills, Garry. "Long-Distance Runner." *New York Review of Books* 25 Oct. 1990: 11–14.

Winnicott, D. W. *The Maturational Processes and the Facilitating Environment: Studies in the Theory of Emotional Development.* New York: International UP, 1965.

———. *Playing and Reality.* London: Tavistock, 1971.

———. *Through Paediatrics to Psycho-Analysis.* London: Hogarth, 1958.

Wion, Philip K. "The Absent Mother in Emily Brontë's *Wuthering Heights.*" *American Imago* 42 (1985): 143–64.

Wolf, Ernest, and Ina Wolf. " 'We Perished, Each Alone': A Psychoanalytic Commentary on Virginia Woolf's *To the Lighthouse.*" *Narcissism and the Text.* 255–72.

Woolf, Virginia. *Mrs. Dalloway* [1925]. New York: Harcourt, Brace, & World, 1953.

———. *To the Lighthouse* [1927]. New York: Harcourt, Brace, & World, 1955.

———. *The Waves* [1931]. New York: Harcourt, Brace, & World, 1959.

Wordsworth, William. *The Poetical Works of William Wordsworth.* 5 vols. Ed. Ernest de Selincourt and Helen Darbishire. London: Oxford UP, 1940–1949.

———. *The Prelude* (Text of 1805). Ed. Ernest de Selincourt. 2d ed. revised by Stephen Gill. London: Oxford UP, 1970.

———. *The Prose Works of William Wordsworth.* 3 vols. Ed. W. J. B. Owen and Jane Worthington Smyser. London: Oxford UP, 1974.

Zukov, Gary. *The Dancing Wu Li Masters: An Overview of the New Physics.* New York: Bantam, 1980.

Index

Abel, Elizabeth, 79, 85, 98, 102, 186 n.5
Aberbach, David, 188 n.2
Aldridge, John, 124
Allen, Mary, 108
Analysis of the Self, The (Kohut), 12, 49
Angier, Carole, 86–88, 92
Athill, Diana, 92, 100
Attachment and Loss (Bowlby), 183 n.3
Atwood, George, 24

Barth, Karl, 106–7
Beattie, Ann, 28, 144–60, 163, 181
  Works cited: *Chilly Scenes of Winter,*
  146–54, 156; "Distant Music" *(Secrets
  and Surprises),* 153; "The Lifeguard"
  (Secrets and Surprises), 153; *Falling in
  Place,* 145–150, 152, 155, 159; *Love
  Always,* 147, 154; *Picturing Will,* 157–
  59, 181; "Windy Day at the
  Reservoir" *(What Was Mine),* 155–57;
  "You Know What" *(What Was
  Mine),* 150
Ben-Ephraim, Gavriel, 185 n.3
Benjamin, Jessica, 19, 28, 40–41, 69, 70,
  72–74, 77, 83, 127–29, 133, 136, 141,
  165, 186 n.4, 188 n.(7)1
Bergman, Anni, 11

Berman, Jeffrey, 47, 49, 61, 66, 74, 77–
  78, 185 n.3, 186–187 n.5
Birth of the Living God, The (Rizzuto),
  109
Blake, William, 29
Bloom, Harold, 126
Bollas, Christopher, 22–24, 184 n.8
Bonds of Love, The (Benjamin), 19, 127,
  129, 165
*Borderline Conditions and Pathological
  Narcissism* (Kernberg), 50
Bouson, J. Brooks, 77, 185 n.11, 186–87
  n.5
Bowlby, John, 47, 183 n.3, 185 n.9
Brierly, Marjorie, 44
Brontë, Charlotte, 47, 84
Brontë, Emily, 26, 46–61, 64
  Works cited: *Wuthering Heights,* 26,
  46–61, 100–1, 181
Burgin, Richard, 107

Cat in the Hat, The (Dr. Seuss), 156
Chaos theory, 3
Chase, Richard, 47
Chodorow, Nancy, 14–18, 62–66, 83,
  135, 186 n.5
Clarke, C. C., 29

Clayton, John, 73, 86, 185 n.1
Coleridge, Samuel Taylor, 32
Critical I, The (Holland), 185 n.10
Culture of Narcissism, The (Lasch), 14
Curtis, Jan, 95

Daly, Brenda, 184 n.5
Deri, Susan, 20
de Rougemont, Denis, 106
Dervin, Daniel, 67, 71, 74, 185–86 n.3
DeSalvo, Louise, 186 n.5
Dinnage, Rosemary, 42
Dinnerstein, Dorothy, 16–17, 65
Doll's House, A (Ibsen), 171
Drama of the Gifted Child, The
    (A. Miller), 110, 184 n.4
Dupre, Louis, 44
Dynamics of Literary Response, The
    (Holland), 24

Ellis, David, 36, 40
Erikson, Erik, 11, 18

Fairbairn, W. R. D., 7, 8
Feminine Fictions (Waugh), 64
Fine, Ronald, 54
Flarsheim, Alfred, 35, 184 n.6
Flax, Jane, 14–15, 17, 19, 81, 183 n.1
Freud, Sigmund, 1, 5–7, 9, 83, 87, 107,
    184 n.5
Friedman, Michael, 33
Fromm, Erich, 10
Frosh, Stephen, 15

Gardiner, Judith Kegan, 85–86, 93, 102
Gestures of Healing (Clayton), 185 n.1
Ghent, Emmanuel, 167
Gilbert, Sandra, 46, 48
Gilligan, Carol, 16–17, 26, 63–64, 74, 78,
    83, 135
Gleick, James, 3
Greenberg, Jay, 5–10, 183 n.2
Greiner, Donald, 121
Gross, Terry, 125
Gubar, Susan, 46, 48
Guntrip, Harry, 7–8, 13, 128, 130–31

Hafley, James, 51–52
Harrison, Nancy R., 188 n.1

Hartman, Geoffrey, 29
Heffernan, James, 36
Heisenberg, Werner, 2
Hoffman, Alice, 28, 160–79, 180–81
    Works cited: *Fortune's Daughter*,
    175; *Illumination Night*, 165; *Seventh
    Heaven*, 28, 160–79, 181; *Turtle
    Moon*, 165–66, 175
Holland, Norman, 24, 185 n.10
Horney, Karen, 10
Horvath, Brooke, 105, 111
Howe, Marguerite Beede, 185 n.3
Hulbert, Ann, 145, 158–59

Ibsen, Henrik, 172
Illusion: as creative construction, 21–22,
    28, 35–36, 41, 43, 161–62, 176–78,
    184 n.6. *See also* Object relations: and
    transitional phenomena
In a Different Voice (Gilligan), 17
Internal World and External Reality
    (Kernberg), 50, 61, 145
Interpersonal psychoanalysis, 10
Interpersonal World of the Infant, The
    (Stern), 11–12
Intersubjectivity, 11–12, 19, 21, 31, 40–41,
    69, 72, 74, 129. *See also* Atwood,
    George; Benjamin, Jessica; Stern,
    Daniel; Stolorow, Robert
Introduction to the Work of Melanie Klein
    (Segal), 183 n.2

Jacobson, Edith, 10
Jane Eyre (C. Brontë), 84, 101, 103
Jones, James, 21, 22, 105, 184 n.8
Jordan, Judith, 18

Kernberg, Otto, 10, 38–39, 49–50, 51, 55–
    56, 61, 86, 145
Klein, Melanie, 6, 7, 26, 50, 56, 61, 64,
    81, 91, 121, 132, 183 n.2, 186 n.3
Kloepfer, Deborah Kelly, 188 n.1
Kohut, Heinz, 12–13, 18, 49, 55, 57, 69,
    70, 83, 86, 89, 110, 114, 133, 145,
    148, 185 n.2, 186 n.4
Kuhn, Thomas, 1

Lacan, Jacques, 4, 22–23, 81, 103, 162,
    184 n.5, 185 n.10, 188 n.1
Langer, Suzanne, 21

Lasch, Christopher, 14, 28, 144–45, 154
Lawrence, D. H., 26, 62, 64–77, 80, 83,
  181, 185–86 n.3
  Works cited: "The Blind Man," 73–74;
  The Rainbow, 70; "The Rocking-
  Horse Winner," 66; *Sons and Lovers,*
  65–71, 73, 185 n.3; *Women in Love,*
  65, 68–73
Layton, Lynne, 12–13, 183 n.2, 185 n.12
Lillenfeld, Jane, 186 n.5
Loewald, Hans, 4, 23, 35, 44
Love, Jean O., 186 n.5
Lynch, David, 163

McDargh, John, 21, 44, 109
Mahler, Margaret, 6, 10, 11, 18, 48, 110
Masterson, James, 184 n.4
Meissner, William, 21, 22, 39, 41–42, 110
Mermaid and the Minotaur, The
  (Dinnerstein), 16
Mezei, Kathy, 188 n.1
Miller, Alice, 27, 52, 57, 61, 110–11, 112,
  122, 184 n.4
Miller, Jean Baker, 17–18
Milner, Marion, 13, 43–44, 121
Milton, John, 29
Miner, Madonne, 188 n.(7)1
Minow-Pinkney, Makiko, 186 n.5
Mitchell, Stephen, 1–5, 7–10, 13, 17, 30–
  31, 40, 183 n.2
Modell, Arnold, 13–14, 23, 184 n.7
Moers, Ellen, 46–47
Morrison, Andrew, 89
Morrison, Toni, 27–28, 127–43, 181, 188
  n.3
  Works cited: *Beloved,* 27–28, 127–43, 181,
  188 n.(7)3; *The Bluest Eye,* 130, 188
  n.(7)1; *Playing in the Dark,* 188
  n.(7)3; *Song of Solomon,* 188 n.3;
  Sula, 129, 130, 135–36
Moser, Thomas, 47, 49, 60
(M)other Tongue, The (Garner, Kahane,
  and Sprengnether), 184 n.5
"Mourning and Melancholia" (Freud), 6

Narcissism: and boundaries, 9, 27, 62, 65,
  72, 75, 77, 79, 80, 83, 85–104, 112,
  135–36, 142, 181; and culture, 28, 85,
  103, 126, 144–45, 187 n.9; and

emptiness, 70, 75, 77, 95, 101, 111,
  126, 134, 145–46, 154; and
  fragmentation, 78, 79, 120–21, 138,
  149–50, 155, 187 n.8; and
  grandiosity, 12, 57, 111–12, 115–16,
  122; and idealization, 12, 28, 49, 97,
  147–48; and loss, 24, 53, 100, 130;
  and merging, 38, 49, 62, 65, 69, 71,
  76–77, 81, 89, 100, 135–36, 152, 181;
  and mirroring, 12, 49, 69, 89, 111;
  and mother, 48, 50–52, 62, 65–73,
  90–91, 93–94, 97–98, 101, 112–26,
  154–58, 177, 181, 187 n.9; and
  rage, 24, 26–28, 47–61, 77, 97, 101,
  117, 121, 124, 128–32, 149–57; and
  self-esteem, 12, 49, 70, 79,
  110, 113, 147; and self objects, 12–13,
  49, 57, 59, 89, 111, 114, 115, 148;
  and shame, 56, 70, 88–91, 93, 97–98,
  114–16
Narcissism and the Novel (Berman), 66
Naremore, James, 186 n.5
Narrating Mothers (Daly and Reddy), 184
  n.5
Niebuhr, Reinhold, 109

Oates, Joyce Carol, 124
Object Love and Reality (Modell), 184 n.7
Object relations: and aggression, 7, 32–33,
  50, 61; and ambivalence, 6–7, 32, 50,
  61, 62, 65, 71, 76, 77, 108, 112, 115,
  124, 151–52, 180; and American
  school, 10–14; and British school, 6–
  10; and culture, 13–14, 20–22, 85,
  103, 181; and depressive position, 6–
  7, 61, 64; and gender, 14–17, 26, 62–
  83, 181, 184 n.5; and mirroring, 9,
  49–110, 114, 118–19, 124; and
  mothering, 14–19, 26, 32, 62–83, 148–
  49, 170–72, 176–78; and oedipal
  dynamics, 33, 40, 47, 54–55, 65, 118,
  119; and orality, 57–59, 72–73, 80,
  99, 130–34, 139, 141, 152–53, 187
  n.7; and paranoid-schizoid position,
  6, 26, 50, 57, 64, 91; and splitting, 6,
  26, 47–50, 54–61, 87; and transitional
  phenomena, 10, 20–25, 28, 33–37, 40,
  41, 43–44, 67, 161–62, 166, 178, 180,
  184 n.7; and true and false self, 9, 28,

Object relations *(Continued)*
51–61, 97–98, 102, 111, 123, 162, 164, 168–70, 184 n.4
Object Relations in Psychoanalytic Theory (Greenberg and Mitchell), 5–7, 9–10
O'Connor, Teresa, 85, 90, 91, 96, 98
Oedipus in Nottingham (Weiss), 185 n.3
Ogden, Thomas, 161–62
Onorato, Richard, 33
Ornstein, Paul, 83

Panken, Shirley, 186 n.5, 187 n.6, 187 n.7
Personality Structure and Human Interaction (Guntrip), 8
Pine, Fred, 11
Poole, Roger, 186 n.5
Postmodernism, 4, 81–82, 103, 183 n.1, 185 n.10
Psychoanalysis in a New Context (Modell), 13, 184 n.7

Quantum mechanics, 2

Reader-response criticism, 24
Real Self, The (Masterson), 184 n.4
Reddy, Maureen T., 184 n.5
Relational Concepts in Psychoanalysis (Mitchell), 1–5, 13
Relational model: and conflict, 3–5, 13; and dependency, 8, 14; and drives, 1–3, 6–7, 10; and ego psychology, 10–11; and empathy, 12, 13, 18; and feminist theory, 11, 14–19, 26, 165, 184 n.5; and language, 22–24, 36–37, 125–26; and oedipal complex, 4–5, 14, 40; as paradigm, 1–5, 25; and religion, 21–22, 27, 41–44, 105–10, 122; and sexuality, 3–4, 40; and symbolism, 20–23, 29, 43–44
Reproduction of Mothering, The (Chodorow), 14–15, 62–63
Rhys, Jean, 26–27, 84–104, 181, 188 n.5
Works cited: *Smile Please,* 88; *Wide Sargasso Sea,* 26–27, 84–104, 188 n.1, 188 n.3
Rizzuto, Ana-Maria, 21, 109–10
Rogers, Robert, 23, 24, 32, 184–85 n.9
Romantic Mother, The (Schapiro), 32
Rose, Gilbert, 21, 25, 188 n.2

Rose, Phyllis, 186 n.5
Rosenman, Ellen Bayuk, 186 n.5
Ruderman, Judith, 185 n.3

Schapiro, Barbara, 32, 183 n.2, 185 n.12
Schizoid personality, 8
Schizoid Phemonena (Guntrip), 128, 131
Schneiderman, Leo, 111
Schopen, Bernard, 106
Schwartz, Murray, 23–24
Search for the Real Self, The (Masterson), 184 n.4
Segal Hanna, 50, 183 n.2
Self and Other (Rogers), 24, 184–85 n.9
Self psychology, 12–13, 49. *See also* Kohut, Heinz
Separation-individuation, 11, 18, 20, 47, 48
Shadow of the Object, The (Bollas), 184 n.8
Shame (Morrison), 89
Skerrett, Joseph, 188 n.3
Solomon, Eric, 46
Spectral Mother, The (Sprengnether), 184 n.5
Spilka, Mark, 186 n.5
Sprengnether, Madelon, 15–16, 184 n.5
Stapp, Henry, 2
Stelzig, Eugene, 29
Stephen, Julia, 187 n.6
Stern, Daniel, 11–12, 19, 22, 23, 31, 69, 70, 72, 74, 77, 129, 186 n.4
Stolorow, Robert, 24
Stone Center theorists, 17–19, 21
Storch, Margaret, 67, 71, 73, 74, 185–86 n.3
Suleiman, Susan, 184 n.5
Sullivan, Harry Stack, 10
Surrey, Janet, 18
Surviving Trauma (Aberbach), 188 n.2

Thinking Fragments (Flax), 183 n.1
Thompson, Wade, 47–48
Towards a New Psychology of Women (J. Miller), 18
Trauma and Mastery in Life and Art (Rose), 25, 188 n.2
Turner, John, 30, 35, 37
Twitchell, James, 59

Updike, John, 27, 105–26, 181
  Works cited: *The Centaur*, 107; "A
  Crow in the Woods," 118–19;
  "Flight," 115–17, 120; *Hugging the
  Shore*, 107; *Of the Farm*, 108, 111,
  112–16, 118, 119, 123, 125; *A Month
  of Sundays*, 106; "Pigeon Feathers,"
  106-7, 119–22, 123–24; *Rabbit at
  Rest*, 124, 125, 126; *Rabbit Redux*,
  108, 109; *Rabbit is Rich*, 108–9;
  Rabbit, Run, 108, 123–24; *Roger's
  Version*, 105, 107, 111; "A Sandstone
  Farmhouse," 111, 112–15, 126; *Self-
  Consciousness*, 112; *The Witches of
  Eastwick*, 109
Uphaus, Suzanne, 108

Van Ghent, Dorothy, 53, 54
Verduin, Kathleen, 107, 109

Waugh, Patricia, 64, 81
Weiss, Daniel, 185 n.3
Wells, H.G., 120
Wessling, Joseph, 135
Whitehead, Alfred North, 10
Willis, Susan, 188 n.3
Wills, Garry, 126
Winnicott, D. W., 6, 8, 9, 10, 20–22, 25,
  27, 30, 33, 35, 40, 41, 42, 44, 52, 67,

  72, 83, 85, 87, 103–4, 110, 114, 122,
  124, 161–62, 177, 180, 184 n.6, 188 n.2
  Works cited: *Maturational Processes*, 8,
  9, 52, 162, 188 n.2; *Playing and
  Reality*, 9, 20, 33, 124; *Through
  Paediatrics*, 9, 87, 104
Wion, Philip, 47, 48, 50–51, 53–55, 57–
  59, 61
Wolf, Ernest, 77, 186–87 n.5
Wolf, Ina, 77, 186–87 n.5
Women's Growth in Connection (Jordan et
  al.), 17–19
Woolf, Virginia, 26, 62, 64–65, 75–83,
  186–87n.5–8
  Works cited: *Mrs. Dalloway*, 75, 76–78,
  80–81, 82, 187 n.5; *To the
  Lighthouse*, 65, 75–79, 81–82; *The
  Waves*, 75, 80, 82
Wordsworth, Dorothy, 32
Wordsworth, William, 25–26, 29–45, 64,
  180, 181
  Works cited: "Intimations of
  Immortality," 30, 40; "Preface to the
  Lyrical Ballads," 31; *The Prelude*, 26,
  30–32, 34–37, 39–45; "A Slumber Did
  My Spirit Seal," 37–38; "Tintern
  Abbey," 32, 35, 38

Zukov, Gary, 2